Retooling Development Aid in the 21st Century: The Importance of Budget Support

Retooling Development Aid in the 21st Century

The Importance of Budget Support

Shahrokh Fardoust
Stefan G. Koeberle
Moritz Piatti-Fünfkirchen
Lodewijk Smets
Mark Sundberg

OXFORD
UNIVERSITY PRESS

OXFORD
UNIVERSITY PRESS

Great Clarendon Street, Oxford, OX2 6DP,
United Kingdom

Oxford University Press is a department of the University of Oxford.
It furthers the University's objective of excellence in research, scholarship,
and education by publishing worldwide. Oxford is a registered trade mark of
Oxford University Press in the UK and in certain other countries

Published in the United States of America by Oxford University Press
198 Madison Avenue, New York, NY 10016, United States of America

British Library Cataloguing in Publication Data

Data available

Library of Congress Control Number: 2022946605

ISBN 978–0–19–288219–6

DOI: 10.1093/oso/9780192882196.001.0001

Printed and bound by
CPI Group (UK) Ltd, Croydon, CR0 4YY

Foreword

Despite the growth of private flows to developing countries, aid continues to play a crucial role in financing development needs, both traditional country-level programmes to reduce poverty and the more recent extension towards global public goods. How much assistance, to whom, and through what modalities, have long been debated by the development community. Traditionally, aid was mostly disbursed as support to projects, ringfenced to comply with the priorities and concerns of donors. But starting with the second oil shock in 1979, a modest portion began to be programmed as support to country budgets, helping to close financing gaps and aiming to stimulate growth.

The move to budget support was part of a broader movement to integrate aid into recipient country policies and administrative systems within an overall approach of partnership and mutual accountability. This approach had its heyday in the first decade of this century, with the 2005 Paris Declaration on Aid Effectiveness being the best official articulation of its underlying principles and aspirations. At that time, budget support was widely expected by the donor community to become the major modality for delivering assistance.

That promise has not been fulfilled. Indeed, apart from spurts of lending driven by the need to respond quickly to shocks, the modality is struggling to retain its 10–13 per cent share of aid flows among bilateral donors, though it has averaged more than 20 per cent among Multilateral Development Banks (MDBs)—going beyond the 20 per cent ad hoc limit in some MDBs during crisis periods. Why has this been the case for bilateral donors? Is the retreat based on a negative record of performance? On misperceptions of the record? On competing priorities for donors and a greater desire by them to be associated with specific projects or outcomes? Perhaps the hype around budget support has always outpaced its operational reality. How should the development community view budget support and use it in the future—considering also the new challenges facing the global community?

Retooling Development Aid in the 21st Century: The Importance of Budget Support, by Shahrokh Fardoust, Stefan Koeberle, Moritz Piatti-Fünfkirchen, Lodewijk Smets, and Mark Sundberg—all veteran development practitioners and economists—offers an essential stocktaking of past experience, as well as an in-depth analysis of trends in development thinking. The scope includes applications to global public goods, crowding in private capital through risk-mitigating guarantees, and the implications of a menagerie of new instruments, such as vertical funds and results-based lending. An important conclusion is that the overall performance of budget support in meeting its development objectives has been at least as good as traditional projects, even though—as for other aid modalities—results have varied.

When budget support was initially promoted, its proponents often set out a context wherein the relationship between donors and recipients was a meeting of minds on values, objectives, and the imperative of aid effectiveness. However, as the authors point out, the ideal conditions are rarely found:

> Only a relatively small set of countries ... came close to the ideal model of a reform-oriented recipient country with low-income status, good governance, and a coherent strategy for poverty reduction.

To this one could add that only a relatively small set of donors have come close to living up to the full requirements set out in the Paris, Busan, and Accra Declarations.

A more realistic assessment is that development cooperation is inherently a work in progress, sometimes risky, and requires nuance based on the situation. This requires upfront analysis—conditionality should be based on a realistic assessment and prioritized to focus on fewer, more critical, areas. In many countries, including most democracies, politics and policymaking are messy and it is unrealistic to condition assistance on an unchanging, long-run development strategy – indeed, doing so might create an uncomfortable association between budget support and autocracy. Even in less perfect contexts, budget support has delivered successes, as defined by the development objectives of the operations. But budget support is not for everyone, and fragile and conflict-affected states (FCVs) pose particularly difficult challenges, although the World Bank's recent experience in FCVs has been positive. Nevertheless, with donors feeling pressure to sanction governments in response to unwelcome political developments or to shift funding to more ringfenced approaches; Ethiopia offers a recent example.

Fiduciary concerns have long been cited by donors as a prime reservation on budget support. High-profile cases such as Mozambique's 2012-2016 "Tuna bond" corruption scandal and Malawi's 2013-2014 "Cashgate" heightened concerns of donor governments over the integrity of public financial management systems. However, the study argues, despite some real problem cases, there is no evidence that budget support is more apt to be diverted than supposedly ringfenced project finance. A more recent factor has been the emergence of a multi-polar world, including strategic competition with China, which has implemented a different model of development partnership, oriented towards large, highly visible, infrastructure projects. Largely invisible budget support may not be seen by donors as the best vehicle for influencing "hearts and minds".

Be this as it may, an accurate picture of the past is essential for thinking through the challenges of the future and the potential role of budget support in addressing them. How might the instrument evolve? The study notes many ways in which it has been adapted to increase flexibility—contingent financing against catastrophes, sector budget support, linkage with guarantees to leverage private capital, support for subnational governments. Another interesting development noted in this book has been the growth of results-based operations, such as Output Based Aid and Program-for-Results (PforR), that also provide funding directly to the budget in response to demonstrated results. At present these operations—now quite sizeable—are not considered as budget support by the World Bank, although, as shown by studies at CGD, a considerable part of PforR disbursement is conditional on policy and institutional changes that are not much different from those in budget support operations. Might we be seeing a closer alignment between budget support and the results principle enshrined in the Paris Declaration? Only time will tell.

As the nature of development cooperation continues to evolve, so will the modalities that are used to transfer development finance. This is, therefore, almost certainly not the last study to be written of budget support. It is, however, one that provides an excellent exposition of how the instrument has evolved to date and has many pointers to the challenges and opportunities that lie ahead.

Masood Ahmed
President, Center for Global Development
Washington DC
July 2022

Preface

The idea for this book first arose from the attempt to understand a paradox: why is it that budget support never quite achieved the prominence that was expected as the financing instrument of choice after the 2005 Paris Declaration on Aid Effectiveness? Why did budget support seemingly fall out of favour despite its potential to accelerate development and help achieve the Millennium Development Goals, as promised in a prominent World Bank book?[1] During the subsequent decade, attitudes toward budget support as an instrument to spur economic development, as well as the international aid architecture, changed significantly. The Paris Declaration on Aid Effectiveness and a flourishing literature on aid effectiveness helped to affirm the principles of country ownership, accountability for results, selectivity in favour of well-governed performers, and the harmonization and alignment of aid between donors and developing countries to boost predictability of aid and reduce the compliance burden. But in the ensuing decade support waned, and several influential bilateral donors, such as the United Kingdom, phased out budget support as an aid instrument. Some developing countries also shifted away from demand for budget support, for example in India, where the robust work on subnational budget support operations that had yielded positive results, ground to a halt largely for political reasons.

For the five economists who joined together to write this book, the shift in attitudes was striking. It contrasted with what they had known about the instrument first hand and were learning about programme performance. Each of us has worked on multiple budget support operations and from different perspectives: in preparing background analytic reports to underpin policy work, in development and design of operations, through implementation phases to supervise their execution, and in evaluating budget support performance and research on their effectiveness as an instrument for development. There have been programmes that went sideways and clearly failed to deliver against expectations, often due to political change and failed reforms, at other times due to unanticipated external shocks. But the evidence on performance of budget support, both through validation exercises and deeper evaluation of country experience, did not suggest poor performance and

[1] Koeberle et al. (2006).

failed optimism. In fact, the success rates of budget support operations have often exceeded those of the more traditional project support across multilateral development banks, and which continue to use both instruments. Why were attitudes towards the instrument shifting, and what was the basis for questioning it as an instrument to support critical economic reforms? Were there serious problems with the design and their policy conditionality of programmes that we were failing to see, which warranted greater scepticism?

The main objective of the work presented in this volume is to better understand the role and potential of budget support as a tool for economic development—including the important contribution played by policy conditionality—and to reflect on where budget support should fit in the toolkit of development agencies. The answer to these questions from a lender's perspective depends on the economic circumstances countries face, their capacity to be effective stewards of public funds, and on the credibility of the government counterpart's ownership of a national reform agenda, including perceptions by the private sector, both domestic and international. It is important to distinguish between the very different circumstances countries face which drive their need for budget support. This includes middle-income countries that are generally well integrated in global financial markets but periodically face a sudden shock that constricts access and requires extraordinary financial support. It includes low-income countries struggling to put in place programmatic measures to strengthen economic performance, provide their citizens with sustainable public services, raise household incomes, and to crowd in vitally important private investment. And it includes fragile and conflict-affected states that often lack well-established institutions and capacity to deliver public services, but where financing is critical to help perform the essential government functions and stabilize society. In each of these cases, budget support can be an effective tool for addressing critical development priorities.

The book sets about understanding budget support through a brief review of the history and evolution of the instrument, explores how budget support fits into the broad and evolving landscape of global finance, and looks more deeply into the research and literature on performance of budget support across different dimensions. The background and discussion of performance aim to be useful to policymakers and development practitioners, as well as to students of applied development economics. We also explore the arguments provided by critics of budget support that have led to some disillusionment with this financing instrument. Studying the design and use of conditionality serves to underscore the key function of budget support to foster policy dialogue and build capacity around public policy and institutions in support of efficient service delivery, improve governance, and competitive markets to generate opportunities for inclusive growth. The picture that emerges is a more complex and nuanced role of budget support as a tool that can be effective when it is customized to specific country circumstances, grounded in analytic underpinnings, and cognizant of the political economy, including the willingness of a country's political leaders and intellectual elites to take calculated risks and embrace meaningful policy and institutional reforms. Since the private sector plays a decisive role in economic development, growth, and creating news job, budget support can also be important and effective in improving the business climate and de-risking private investment.

During the course of researching and writing the book, global events also brought into sharp relief the challenges of international development in a time of deep and growing vulnerability that is accentuated by globalization. Interdependencies and risks were exposed by the COVID-19 pandemic, which hit both developed and developing countries very hard, erasing years of progress toward eliminating extreme poverty. Despite this traumatic experience, it is not clear whether developing countries are ready to cope with potential new global public health emergencies. This is occurring alongside increased extreme weather events and incontrovertible evidence that global warming, advancing more rapidly than previously thought, poses an extraordinary risk to the future of humanity. On top of these critical threats, a twentieth-century ground war in Europe brought about by Russia's invasion of Ukraine has added inflation pressures and raised the spectre of global food and fertilizer shortages, particularly for African countries, which are highly dependent on grain and energy imports. These risks do not appear to be short term. Rather, they foretell durable long-term risks that cloud the development horizon and call into question the ability of global systems to even maintain the status quo.

We argue that, against this background of global uncertainty, budget support remains highly relevant to addressing the problems we collectively face in future decades. Facing these multiple threats—global pandemics, climate change, market failure, fragility, and conflict—can only be sustainably advanced through collective action to protect the global commons, to mitigate anthropogenic impacts, and help each nation to adapt. Short-termism remains a scourge that threatens everyone, from Wall Street boardrooms to Kinshasa, where the government of the Congo announced auctioning land rights to petroleum companies in one of the largest old-growth rainforests remaining on Earth. But embracing solutions to twenty-first-century challenges will require facing the reality of enormous disparities in wealth and fungible resources available to speed the adoption of new technologies and protect the global commons. Financial assistance and technology transfer is required to countries that cannot trade off the short-term basic necessities of their people for the long-term protection of future generations. This will also require adequate capitalization of multilateral development banks as the most important providers of budget support to strengthen their role in countercyclical financing, long-term reforms, and institutional strengthening as well as global knowledge. Retooling and reinforcing budget support to flexibly address periodic crises, persist with medium-term development programming, and significantly scale up long-term support to help nations protect the global commons should be, and we argue must be, a vital tool in the global aid architecture.

We hope that this volume will be one small contribution to fostering learning in support of collective problem-solving and the important coordinating role that can be provided by multilateral institutions given their financial, technical, analytical, and convening wherewithal.

Shahrokh Fardoust, Stefan G. Koeberle, Moritz Piatti-Fünfkirchen,
Lodewijk Smets, Mark Sundberg

Acknowledgements

This book is the result of a joint effort by a team of researchers comprising Shahrokh Fardoust, Stefan G. Koeberle, Moritz Piatti-Fünfkirchen, Lodewijk Smets, and Mark Sundberg, with helpful support, at various stages of their research on budget support, from a group of experts, including Shanta Devarajan and Alan Gelb. Zeljko Bogetic, Jeff Chelsky and Aghassi Mkrtchyan provided helpful suggestions at initial stages of this project.

The authors are indebted to Oxford University Press (OUP) for publishing this volume and providing editorial, design, and printing services, under the able direction of Adam Swallow, contributing editor for economics and finance. The team is also grateful for the help and guidance it received from Jade Dixon and her team at OUP, particularly Sandhiya Babu. The authors would like to thank Barbara Karni for her highly professional editorial support in editing the initial manuscript of this volume.

Finally, the authors would like to acknowledge the significant contributions that two former World Bank colleagues, Jan Walliser and Steve Knack, made to the areas of aid effectiveness and policy-based finance. Both were outstanding economists who led work on aid effectiveness and policy-based finance, but sadly passed away at a young age around the time this book began taking shape.

Contents

List of Figures

List of Tables

List of Boxes

Abbreviations and Glossary

AfDB	African Development Bank
AIIB	Asian Infrastructure Investment Bank
Aid activities	Aid activities include projects and programmes, cash transfers, deliveries of goods, training courses, research projects, debt relief operations, and contributions to non-governmental organizations.
ADB	Asian Development Bank
Benchmarks	Implementation progress markers that describe the indicative content and results of a government's programme.
Blended finance	Blended finance is the strategic use of development finance from public or philanthropic sources in order to catalyze private sector investment for economic and social development purposes. It incentivizes private investment and provides returns to investors while enlarging capital flows to developing countries.
Bretton Woods institutions	The Bretton Woods Conference, officially known as the United Nations Monetary and Financial Conference, was a gathering of delegates from forty-four nations that met from 1 to 22 July 1944 in Bretton Woods, New Hampshire, United States, to agree upon a series of new rules for the post–WWII international monetary system, and the creation of the two Bretton Woods intuitions: the International Monetary Fund (IMF) and the International Bank for Reconstruction and Development (IBRD), also known as the World Bank.
CAF	Corporación Andina de Fomento (Development Bank of Latin America).
Capacity building	Capacity building includes activities that enhance the skills of government or non-government stakeholders.
Cat DDO	Catastrophe Deferred Drawdown Option. A CAT DDO is a contingent financing line that provides immediate liquidity following a natural disaster and/or health-related event. Funds become available for disbursement after the drawdown trigger—typically the member country's declaration of a state of emergency—is met.
CDB	Caribbean Development Bank
CDF	Comprehensive Development Framework (World Bank)
Concessionality	A measure of the 'softness' of a credit reflecting the benefit to the borrower compared to a loan at market rate. Technically, it is calculated as the difference between the nominal value of an aid credit and the present value of the debt service as of the date

	of disbursement, calculated at a discount rate applicable to the currency of the transaction and expressed as a percentage of the nominal value.
Conditional aid	Aid that is disbursed conditional upon the materialization of specific events.
Conditionality	The provision of financial transfers made by donors in the form of budget support is typically predicated on agreed reform and institutional measures, budget allocations or policy implementation.
CPIA	Country Policy and Institutional Assessment. The World Bank's allocation of its concessional resources (International Development Association, IDA) is based on the results of the annual CPIA exercise that covers the IDA eligible countries. The CPIA rates countries against a set of 16 criteria grouped in four clusters: (i) economic management; (ii) structural policies; (iii) policies for social inclusion and equity; and (iv) public sector management and institution.
Credit	A financial transfer for which repayment is required on concessional terms.
Criticality	Criticality in policy-based lending involves choosing only actions critical for achieving results as conditions for disbursements.
CRS	Credit reporting system
CSR	Corporate social responsibility
DAC	Development Assistance Committee—of the Organisation for Economic Co-operation and Development (OECD). Also, see OECD-DAC.
Deferred drawdown option (DDO)	A budget support operation with DDO is a contingent credit line that allows the borrower to rapidly meet its financing requirements following a shortfall in resources caused by adverse economic events such as a downturn in economic growth or unfavourable changes in commodity prices or terms of trade. An operation with a DDO provides a formal basis for continuing a policy-based engagement when no immediate need for funding exists.
De-risk	Initiatives or measures used by development agencies, including MDBs, to help attract private investment to development projects.
DPF	Development policy financing (World Bank). DPF provides direct budget support to governments for policy and institutional reforms aimed at achieving a set of specific development results. These operations provide rapid financial assistance to allow countries to deal with actual or anticipated development financing requirements.
EBRD	European Bank for Reconstruction and Development
EC	European Commission
EIB	European Investment Bank
EU MFA	The EU provides macro financial assistance by disbursing directly to treasury with some, but limited, structural reforms.

Ex ante conditionality	With ex ante conditionality, funds are disbursed before conditions are met.
Ex post conditionality	With ex post conditionality, funds are disbursed only after conditions are met.
FCV	Fragility, conflict, and violence
FDI	Foreign direct investment
Fungibility	Aid is considered fungible when it is funding something different than what it was earmarked for.
GAVI	Global Alliance for Vaccines and Immunization
GDP	Gross domestic product
GEF	The Global Environment Facility
General budget support	Unearmarked contributions to the government budget, including funding to support the implementation of policy reforms.
Gleneagles Summit	The 31st G8 summit was held on 6–8 July 2005 at the Gleneagles Hotel in Auchterarder, Scotland and hosted by Prime Minister Tony Blair. Agreement was reached to support Africa's economic development (by agreeing to write off debts of the poorest countries, and to significantly increase aid).
GNI	Gross national income
Guarantees	Financial instruments used by MDBs (and other development financial institutions) to reduce the private sector project cost of funds by reducing risk by providing standby funding where the availability of such funds is contingent on the occurrence of well-defined, low-probability but high-impact adverse events.
HCFCs	Hydrochlorofluorocarbons
HIPC	Heavily Indebted Poor Country Initiative
IBRD	International Bank for Reconstruction and Development
IBSA	India–Brazil–South Africa Facility for Poverty and Hunger Alleviation
ICOR	Incremental capital output ratio
ICSID	International Centre for Settlement of Investment Disputes
IDA	International Development Association
IDB	Inter-American Development Bank
IEG	Independent Evaluation Group, World Bank Group
IMF	International Monetary Fund
Impact investing	Investment by the private sector that seeks to generate socially desirable results in addition to financial returns.
IPCC	International Panel on Climate Change
LICs	Low-income countries
Loan	Transfer for which repayment is required at market terms
MCC	Millennium Challenge Corporation
MDB	Multilateral development banks
MDGs	Millennium Development Goals
MDRI	Multilateral Debt Relief Initiative
MERCOSUR	Caribbean Development Bank and the Southern Common Market

MICs	Middle-income countries
MIGA	Multilateral Investment Guarantee Agency
Monterrey Consensus	The Monterrey Consensus was the outcome of the 2002 United Nations International Conference on Financing for Development, held in Monterrey, Mexico. The Consensus embraces six areas of Financing for Development.
Montreal Protocol	Montreal Protocol on Substances that Deplete the Ozone Layer 1984.
NDCs	Nationally determined contributions embody efforts by each country to reduce national emissions and adapt to the impact of climate change under the Paris Agreement (Article 4, paragraph 2).
Non-concessional funds	Funds provided on non-concessional terms (see concessionality).
ODA	Official Development Assistance
OECD-DAC	Organisation for Economic Co-operation and Development/Development Assistance Committee
OLS	Ordinary least squares
OPEC	Organization of Petroleum-Exporting Countries
Operation	A project, loan, or credit
OPIC	Overseas Private Investment Corporation
Paris Declaration on Aid Effectiveness (2005)	The 2005 Paris Declaration is a practical, action-oriented roadmap to improve the quality of aid and its impact on development. The Paris Declaration—endorsed at the Second High Level Forum on Aid Effectiveness—outlines the five principles for making aid more effective.
Paris Climate Agreement (2015)	The Paris Agreement is a legally binding international treaty on climate change. It was adopted in Paris on 12 December 2015 by 196 parties, and entered into force on 4 November 2016.
Paris Declaration principles	Ownership: developing countries set their own strategies for development; alignment: donors align behind these strategies and use local systems; harmonization: donor countries coordinate aid efforts; results: a shift to focus on development results; and mutual accountability: donors and partners are accountable for development results.
PDIA	Problem Driven Iterative Adaption
PEFA	Public Expenditure and Financial Accountability
PFM	Public financial management
Policy-based finance	The provision of financing to support policy and institutional reforms.
Policy-based guarantees	Policy-based guarantees (PBGs) are a form of budget support that cover private lenders against the risk of debt service default by the sovereign government.

Policy matrix	The policy matrix summarizes all of the policy and institutional actions directly supported by a development policy operation and the results expected from these actions.
PRGF	Poverty Reduction Growth Facility (IMF)
Principal–agent dilemma	Occurs when one person or entity (the 'agent') is able to make decisions and/or take actions on behalf of, or that impact, another person or entity (the 'principal'); agents may be motivated to act in their own best interests, which are contrary to those of their principals.
Prior actions	Policy actions that are deemed critical to achieving the results of the programme supported by a development policy operation. Prior actions are taken by a country before presentation of a development policy operation to the World Bank's (and other MDBs') board of executive directors and are included in the operation's Financing Agreement.
Programmatic DPO	In a programmatic development policy operation, a series of usually single-tranche operations is framed in a medium-term policy programme, with a general but flexible expectation about the timing, policy steps, and financing amount to be involved in each operation of the series.
Program-for-Results (PforR)	Disbursement of funds to treasury that is conditioned on achieving targets of key indicators in a results framework rather than policy reform.
Program lending	The primary instrument through which the ADB has supported policy reforms.
Project finance	Financing in which the disbursement of the financing relies primarily on the expenditures incurred by the specific project. Financing can be on a full recourse, limited recourse, or non-recourse basis. Project assets, project-related company contracts, and project cash flows typically secure the repayment obligations of the client company.
PRSC	Poverty Reduction Support Credit (World Bank)
PRSPs	Poverty Reduction Strategy Papers (IMF/World Bank)
SALs	Structural Adjustment Loans
Samaritan's dilemma	Concept introduced by economist James Buchanan to show that altruism can induce adverse behaviour of potential recipients based on the failure of the donor to act strategically.
SDGs	Sustainable Development Goals
SECALs	Sector Adjustment Loans
Sector budget support	Sector budget support is a financial contribution to a recipient government's budget. In sector budget support, the dialogue between donors and partner governments focuses on sector-specific concerns, rather than on overall policy and budget priorities.
SIDA	Swedish International Development Cooperation Agency

Structural adjustment lending	Early policy-based lending, often focusing on economic stabilization and correction of balance of payments distortions.
Tenor	The time that must elapse before a promissory note becomes due for payment.
Tranche	A tranched operation is a single multi-year operation in which phased disbursement is made.
Triggers	Expected prior actions of the next operation in a programmatic series; they are not legal conditions for disbursement.
UNCTAD	United Nations Conference on Trade and Development
UNFCCC	United Nations Framework Convention on Climate Finance
UNICEF	United Nations International Children's Emergency Fund
UNIDO	United Nations Industrial Development Organization
Utstein Group	Combined representatives from several European development organizations committed to fight corruption and strengthen the effectiveness of their resource flows to developing countries.
Vertical Funds	Global programmes for allocating development assistance that focus specifically on an issue or theme, such as Global Fund to Fight AIDS, Tuberculosis and Malaria, and the Global Alliance for Vaccines and Immunization (GAVI).
Washington Consensus	A set of economic policy recommendations for developing countries, first presented by John Williamson in 1989.
WTO	World Trade Organization

Notes on Authors

Shahrokh Fardoust is a Research Professor at the Global Research Institute and a Visiting Scholar in Economics at the College of William and Mary. From 2008 to 2011, he was Director of Strategy and Operations, Development Economics, the World Bank. His previous positions at the World Bank included Senior Adviser to the Director-General of the Independent Evaluation Group, and Senior Economic Adviser to the Senior Vice President and Chief Economist. Dr Fardoust obtained his PhD in Economics from the University of Pennsylvania. He is a co-editor of and contributor to *Postcrisis Growth and Development: A Development Agenda for the G20* (World Bank, 2011); and *Towards a Better Global Economy: Policy Implications for Global Citizens Worldwide in the 21st Century* (Oxford University Press), 2016. He is a Non-Resident Scholar at the Middle East Institute, Washington, DC; a member of Millennium Challenge Corporation's, Economic Advisory Council; and a Senior Associate at the Economic Research Forum, Cairo, Egypt.

Stefan G. Koeberle is Director, Strategy and Operations in the Middle East and North Africa Regional Vice Presidency at the World Bank. Since joining the World Bank as a Young Professional in 1993, Dr Koeberle has worked in a variety of countries and regions, including postings as Country Economist in Thailand and Country Director in Indonesia. During his assignments in Operations Policy and Country Services, he spearheaded operational policy reforms on development policy finance, procurement and the environmental and social framework. His most recent positions at the World Bank included appointments as Director of Strategy and Operations covering Latin America and the Integrity Vice Presidency of the World Bank Group. Prior to joining the World Bank, Dr Koeberle worked as a postgraduate fellow at the German Development Institute in Berlin. He holds an M.Phil. and a PhD in Economics from Cambridge University. He has published a number of articles and several books on competitiveness, conditionality, and budget support.

Moritz Piatti-Fünfkirchen is a Senior Economist at the World Bank working at the nexus of public finance and health. He is interested in how public financial management reforms can be an enabling force for efficient and equitable service delivery. His work is currently focused on reforms in the Africa region, where he leads various analytical programmes that include how to deploy disruptive technology solutions. During his time at the World Bank's Independent Evaluation Group, Moritz led various evaluations of World Bank support to public financial management reforms and has written extensively on what makes financial management information systems effective. Prior to joining the World Bank, Moritz worked as an advisor in the Ministry of Health in Zanzibar/Tanzania, where he supported the government in budget management and the introduction of health finance reforms. Moritz holds an MSc in Economics for Development from Oxford University and an MA in Economics from the University of Aberdeen.

Mark Sundberg is the Millennium Challenge Corporation's Chief Economist and Deputy Vice President of the Department of Policy and Evaluation. He is responsible for the oversight of economic analysis of growth, beneficiary impact, and project cost–benefit analysis in MCC countries. Prior to MCC, he was Manager for the Economic Management and Country Evaluation work of the World Bank's Independent Evaluation Group responsible for thematic, sector, and project work macro-fiscal management, poverty, governance, and evaluation of country programmes. He was also in the World Bank research department (leading author, 2006 and 2007 Global Monitoring Reports), and economist for several country programmes. From 1996 to 1998 he was regional Chief Economist, Emerging Markets, for Salomon Brothers/Citibank in Hong Kong. Mr Sundberg holds a PhD in economics from Harvard University and BA in Economics and East Asian studies from Yale University.

Lodewijk Smets is a Senior Economist at the World Bank working on Solomon Islands and Vanuatu. In this role, he is responsible for macroeconomic monitoring, policy dialogue on macro-fiscal matters and the provision of budget support. Over the years, Lodewijk developed a deep interest in how donors can support policy reform processes and published several papers on the topic in peer-reviewed journals. Before joining the World Bank, Lodewijk was employed at the Inter-American Development Bank as a Senior Economist, and prior to this, at the World Bank's Independent Evaluation Group, where he led evaluations of budget support for low-income countries. He also provided methodological support to a wide variety of evaluation teams. Lodewijk holds a PhD in Economics from the University of Antwerp, Belgium, and was a Postdoctoral Research Fellow at KU Leuven, Belgium.

Overview and Summary

Developing countries experienced an unprecedented economic crisis after 2020 as a consequence of COVID-19, compounding the potentially existential threats they already faced from global climate change. These challenges have spurred development practitioners and policymakers to take a fresh look at budget support—a form of development financing that has evolved since the late 1940s and was fundamentally redefined in the early 2000s—as a way to provide fast-disbursing financing and incentivize policy reforms that lay the foundation for sustained recovery and growth in developing countries.

Revisiting the rich experience with budget support over the past two decades, this book examines the potential for budget support to live up to its original promise as an efficient instrument to support reform and spur inclusive growth. Its six chapters address its strengths and perceived shortcomings and suggest critical changes that could enhance its effectiveness in the next decade. The book argues for a more prominent role for budget support to tackle the central challenges of the twenty-first century: supporting fiscal needs in the face of economic crises, laying the foundations for sustainable and inclusive growth to eliminate poverty, and providing a conducive investment climate to induce private development finance and to facilitate key measures to protect the global commons.

The Purpose and Promise of Budget Support

Budget support generally refers to a method of financing a recipient country's budget through a transfer of resources from an external financing agency to the recipient government's national treasury. These funds are managed in accordance with the recipient's budgetary procedures and are not earmarked for specific uses. In contrast to traditional project aid—which disburses against specific expenditures associated with a project—budget support is predicated on a policy dialogue between donors and recipients and disburses against compliance with agreed policy and reform measures.

By the early 2000s, a consensus had emerged in the development community about the importance of country ownership, donor coordination, use of country systems, predictability, and alignment with national poverty reduction strategies. In recognizing that the effectiveness of aid fundamentally depends on the appropriate timing and feasibility within a recipient country's own political economy and reform cycle, this new thinking sought to address the shortcoming of earlier assistance efforts.

In contrast with traditional project support, fast-disbursing financing conditioned on reforms brought to the fore the importance of sound macroeconomic policies, good governance, and institutional capacity building. Complementing traditional project lending, budget support emerged over a half century ago as an aid instrument to address macro imbalances conditional on key economic 'reform' supported by the Bretton Woods institutions. It was widely used, and criticized, as an instrument to advance the principles of the Washington Consensus.

As a cornerstone of a new aid architecture, the Paris Declaration and the Monterrey Consensus incorporated a new vision for budget support to be aligned with recipient country development strategies. Budget support was seen as the core instrument for macroeconomic policy dialogue and poverty reduction plans. Through the budget support dialogue, coordinated donor engagement was supposed to bring the donor community and government together around the country's own measures and targets to meet the Millennium Development Goals (MDGs), notably to meet the goal of eradicating extreme poverty.

What made budget support attractive were its specific features that promised to meet key expectations, including greater country ownership, building country capacity and strengthening country systems rather than parallel structures set up to satisfy donor requirements. Expectations also included improved donor coordination rather than aid fragmentation, leveraging results by scaling up funding and influencing overall government expenditure programmes, greater predictability of resource flows, and greater accountability. Budget support was expected to be more efficient and cost-effective per dollar transferred for development purposes due to lower transaction and preparation costs by promoting donor harmonization with uniform reporting requirements and obviating the need for onerous procurement and environmental and social compliance.

The design, use, and content of conditionality are integral features of budget support. To address the mixed track record of previous structural adjustment lending, conditionality under budget support was to focus on a small number of critical country-owned, typically incremental reform measures as part of a medium-term framework, with disbursements of subsequent operations predicated ex post on completion of prior actions rather than ex ante on future (and often unrealistic or overly optimistic) measures.

Global Finance and the Changing Aid Landscape

Over the last decade, the demand for, and contribution of, budget support has been shaped by major trends in global financial architecture, and by a sequence of large adverse shocks to the global economy: food and fuel crisis (2006–7), global financial and capital markets crisis (2008–9), collapse of commodity prices (2014–15), COVID-19 pandemic (2020–22), and the Russian invasion of Ukraine in early 2022. The adverse consequences of recent crises are still unfolding. In the face of these shocks, the procyclical nature of private capital flows (they collapse when most needed) has exacerbated the social and economic impact of the shocks and made developing countries exceptionally reliant on foreign aid and public finances. This has also exposed serious flaws in the global financial architecture, particularly with regard to external debt restructuring in developing countries.

A sharp drop in capital flows to developing countries, or a protracted sudden stop in capital flows, can and does cause widespread solvency problems in developing countries. Understanding complex capital flows, the role of the private sector, public sector, and foreign aid is important for understanding how budget support fits into the current aid architecture, and it can help to mitigate macroeconomic and financial risks. In this context, the global financial landscape has evolved in important ways since the policy-based lending instrument was first introduced more than three decades ago, resulting in a reduced role in some respects, but new and important opportunities in others that are critical to addressing growth opportunities and resilience in the face of daunting global challenges.

External flows to developing economies were insufficient to support sustainable development investments even before the pandemic-induced crisis, which has inflicted a massive adverse shock in many poor countries. While private capital flows to developing countries have been large, they have become highly volatile and pro-cyclical, particularly over the last decade. On the other hand, financial contribution of foreign aid, including budget support to developing countries, has been more stable and countercyclical in character.

In the last two decades, foreign direct investment (FDI) and remittances took on increasing importance. Following the call by the Addis Ababa and Busan High Level Aid Effectiveness forums for greater private financing, a consensus among agencies and development experts emerged that a focus of foreign assistance must be to leverage private sector flows to expand financing for development. Overseas Development Assistance (ODA) flows are far too limited to meet the financing needs of low- and middle-income countries to enhance growth to meet their sustainable development goals. However, this requires a substantial increase in the lending capacities of MDBs, as well as reform of the guarantee instruments to address the existing constraints on both supply and demand side of this potentially highly effective de-risking instrument.

Despite the potential importance for mobilizing private funds for investments, guarantees issued by MDBs have remained a relatively small portion of their portfolios. Except for the International Finance Corporation (IFC) and the Multilateral Investment Guarantee Agency (MIGA), both members of the World Bank Group, the share of guarantees in MDBs' portfolios remained well below 5 per cent in 2010–19. It is important that MDBs undertake the necessary reforms and incentivize greater use of their guarantee instrument, which can be used directly for budget support and policy-based lending and is as an important ingredient in blended finance mechanisms, in helping developing countries address their development challenges as well as global risks, such as climate change and pandemics.

The COVID crisis led to significant financial outflows from developing countries in 2020. Together with developing countries' massive and rising debt, the sharp decline in export revenues, and lost tourism revenues and workers' remittances, the COVID crisis has triggered the most serious economic and financial crisis since the Great Depression.

Although net financial flows associated with budget support (and official lending in general) are small compared with private flows, budget support has been punching well above its weight. It plays a key role in addressing critical economic reforms and supporting structural transformation in debt-stressed and other vulnerable countries. It plays a critical role in facilitating implementation of important reforms that help leverage private capital to finance projects and programmes.

Going forward, budget support could play an even bigger and more central role in: i) supporting low-income and fragile countries: ii) advancing reforms during periods of crisis, including improved fiscal and debt management; and iii) undertaking critical improvements in the investment climate that crowd in private capital to finance green infrastructure, digital technology, and global public goods such as climate-related investments through greater use of policy-based guarantees and insurance.

The Evolution of Budget Support

As new demands and risks emerged over the last two decades, new approaches to budget support were developed, leading to a greater variety in the use of the instrument. From basic support for balance of payments and structural adjustment that characterized its early use to more recent variants, the instrument was adapted to include design options and a broader range of conditionality. Budget support has been deployed across a broad spectrum of countries, and remains an important, albeit not the primary aid vehicle over the last decades. Despite its early promise as an aid modality in support of the Paris Agenda, the share of budget support to lower income countries experienced an overall declining trend, as most bilateral agencies eventually moved away from budget support as a principal aid instrument. Budget support still accounts for a large share of external financing for a number of well-performing, resource-dependent countries.

Multilateral Development Banks have become the most important budget support financiers, financing some 85 per cent of total budget support. Many bilateral agencies have substantially decreased their use of budget support since the mid-2000s. Financing volumes fluctuated significantly on an annual basis, particularly due to one-off balance-of-payments support to middle-income borrowers. Much of the variation in financing volumes is due to short-term countercyclical financing to middle-income countries during times of economic crisis and constrained access to capital markets.

Conditionality became increasingly focused on medium-term institutional reforms, particularly related to public financial management, which was characterized by increasing complexity and incrementalism. Conditionality shifted toward fewer prior actions on average, although in some donor-dependent countries conditions multiplied. Early donor enthusiasm gave way to multiple agendas and fragmentation, with joint financing but disjointed ownership of conditionality.

As low-income countries graduate into middle-income status, budget support becomes increasingly less programmatic. Programmatic approaches, involving a series of operations under a multi-year reform framework, are typically a design feature for lower income countries and not targeted to countercyclical balance of payments financing needs.

New approaches to budget support have emerged over the past decade, leading to a greater variety in the use of the instrument. Among the most notable innovations are deferred drawdown options to provide liquidity during times of crisis, as well as policy-based guarantees to leverage private financing.

Budget support has been deployed across a broad spectrum of countries, across income groups with varying degrees of institutional capacity, governance quality, and political stability. Budget support has also been increasingly used in fragile and conflict-affected country settings.

Budget support operations have been increasingly focused on climate, social sectors, and gender. While institutional reforms in public sector governance continues to make up the greatest share of policy actions, there is a clear shift away from stroke-of-the-pen reforms in private sector development and trade.

Budget support has been frequently deployed in countries with weak public financial management systems. The use of budget support has gradually been extended to least developed countries where poverty remains entrenched and development prospects are uncertain, but also with weak institutional capacity and ability to ensure prudent use of resources. This is a notable departure from a central premise of the effectiveness literature and the Paris Agenda that recommended budget support for well-performing developing countries with a clear poverty-reduction and reform agenda. Under these circumstances, conditionality has been skewed toward measures for improving public financial management and related areas for institutional strengthening.

The Performance of Budget Support

How effective is budget support? Looking at the evidence at the programme level, conventional evaluation metrics indicate that budget support has performed as well as traditional project financing in terms of meeting its development objectives. Econometric analysis shows that factors on both the donor and recipient sides matter for programme success, including programme design, policy dialogue, and the timing of support. Much is still unknown about the factors that make budget support effective at the level of individual operations, however, especially on the recipient side.

A review of empirical evidence and quantitative analysis at the country level indicate that budget support contributes to sustained policy improvements in macroeconomic management, business regulation, social policy, and public sector governance. However, the policy impact depends on the country context, the process of policy dialogue, and the type of support.

Heterogeneity in terms of policy impact indicates that supporting economic policy reform has been more effective than certain areas in public sector governance and social policy. A large evidence base in economic reform and the lack of short-term, tangible benefits in public sector reform may explain these differences.

There is evidence for decreasing returns to policy-based financing, such that over time the ability of budget support to advance reforms and improve governance measurably declines. This may be related to a change to more complex, second-generation policy reforms and a potential trade-off between budget financing and reform feasibility.

Budget support can be effective even in fragile and conflicted-affected states. Despite limited capacity and the need to act carefully in such settings, budget support has been found effective in supporting social policy reform.

Budget support can also be instrumental to support policy reform in times of crisis. Moreover, evidence suggests that the policy impact of budget support may even be higher during an economic crisis.

The analysis shows that in the right context, budget support can be effective in putting the Paris Declaration principles into practice. Budget support has the potential to be an efficient and effective instrument to support a country's own development strategy. In the right context, it can improve development effectiveness by realizing the Paris Declaration principles of ownership, predictability, reliance on country systems, focus on results, and harmonization. One of the key lessons is that if ownership is lacking, however, providing conditional financing generally does not lead to sustained reform.

Promise, Disenchantment, and Sobriety: Learning from Experience with Budget Support

The popularity of budget support as an instrument of development financing fluctuated over the last two decades. The initial promise of budget support for lower income countries eventually turned to a certain disenchantment, particularly as bilateral donors largely disengaged from its use as the instrument of choice to further global development aspirations. Following the initial years after the Paris Declaration's strong support for expanding use of budget support instruments, most European governments rolled back funding for budget support and eliminated it from their foreign assistance programmes—despite the evidence in support of its effectiveness. Use of the instrument across agencies declined during the 2010s, including across most MDBs.

Several factors drove this shift in perception. In the first place, changes in the political environment of donor countries changed to more conservative governments, which were disinclined to continue financing intangible reforms. A stronger results orientation contributed to scepticism towards the effectiveness of budget support and a preference for traditional bricks and mortar projects with tangible, measurable results that are more easily communicated to taxpayers (vaccinations, kilometres of roads built, etc.). Debates were often driven without reference to the evidence base, aid-effectiveness indicators, or end objectives, leading to a disconnect between the demand for and supply of foreign assistance.

High-profile events involving political repression (such as in Ethiopia in 2006) or corruption cases (such as in Uganda in 2012 and Mozambique in 2015) undermined confidence in the viability of supporting the budgets of recipient countries and compelled donor withdrawal. Despite a heavy focus on institutional strengthening and accountability in public finance, fiduciary concerns, and questions over fungibility undermined public trust in budget support and perceptions of greater vulnerability to corrupt practices.

Moreover, expectations of sharply increased aid flows turned out to be unrealistic. Total aid fell well short of pledges made in 2005 at the Gleneagles summit, and budget support bore the brunt of the shortfall. Periods of severe economic distress, such as the financial crisis 2009, saw peaks of fast-disbursing budget support, particularly for middle-income countries cut off from alternative financing sources. Surges in available funds coincided with financial crises, resulting in short-term financing with limited conditionality that were regarded as one-off balance-of-payments financing rather than sustained support for long-term structural reforms.

The role of budget support for low-income countries was further diluted by the erosion of the International Monetary Fund (IMF) and World Bank–driven approach based on Poverty Reduction Strategy Papers (PRSPs). Over time, PRSPs came to be seen as onerous donor requirements that lacked government ownership, were largely prepared by World Bank and IMF staff, and were eventually quietly abandoned.

The participation of multiple donors in popular recipient countries ('donor darlings') contributed to an overloading of budget support programmes with non-critical measures. Instead of streamlining conditionality, donor coordination in some cases became less effective.

Meanwhile, new donors (including China, South Korea, and India) outside the Organisation for Economic Co-operation and Development/Development Assistance Committee (OECD-DAC) emerged, with a different aid framework, incentives, and objectives, which raised new questions about the role of foreign assistance and aid instruments.

The recent resurgence of interest in budget support in response to the economic fallout of the COVID pandemic since 2019 and the 2022 Russian invasion of Ukraine offers an opportunity to address shortcomings. Disenchantment with budget support provides sobering lessons for its future use in addressing the challenges of the coming decade. Drawing on this experience, budget support can be reshaped as an instrument that retains public support and builds on its proven track record of development effectiveness. This will require addressing the key factors that contributed to its falling out of favour, including (i) deeper understanding of political economy and specific development conditions of recipient countries, (ii) addressing fiduciary concerns, (iii) realistic conditionality focused on critical reforms that are recognizably significant and relevant to longer-term development outcomes and public goods, (iv) a clearer division of labour among donors based on their financing and advisory capacity, and (v) a less exuberant, more realistic projection of likely sources of development financing from domestic and international sources, including from the private sector.

How Can Budget Support Meet 21st Century Challenges?

What is the future of budget support, drawing on the lessons from experience and the changing aid landscape? Budget support remains an important tool for policymakers to support reforms in developing countries. But to live up to its full potential it needs to be redesigned, adapted to the priorities of the current international financial architecture, and contextualized to the specific requirements of donors and recipient countries. Compared to the original promise at the turn of the millennium, the experience with budget support over the past two decades has highlighted both its strengths and weaknesses and points toward critical changes to enhance its effectiveness in the coming decades.

Rethinking aid modalities and instruments is also critical given rapid digitalization and the emergence of new technologies; the urgent need to address global climate change; and growing inequality within countries, exacerbated by the economic devastation wrought by the COVID-19 pandemic and the Russian invasion of Ukraine. These have compromised global progress toward resilience in the face of global shocks, notably including the goal eliminating extreme poverty.

Traditional project financing remains dominant, despite several shortcomings (including long preparation time, burdensome compliance requirements, slow disbursement, and the need for costly monitoring). The initial promise of budget support was not realized; too many conditionalities were imposed, without sufficient consideration of country capacity or needs; aid was fragmented; results were underwhelming; and the political winds shifted. As a result, donors lost confidence in budget support. But budget support has a vital role to play in addressing the twenty-first century's signature challenges of eliminating poverty and protecting the global commons. To live up to its potential, it needs to be redesigned, customized to the specific requirements of donors and recipient countries, and adapted to the priorities of the current international financial architecture.

The case for increasing budget support to accelerate development, address resilience to crises, and complement global or regional public goods is strong. The focus of budget support on policy dialogue, country ownership, inclusive and sustainable growth, and the leveraging of private resources makes it well suited to tackling future challenges and rapidly responding to global or regional crises. However, it is not well suited to all situations and it involves taking risks, being selective to country context, design elements, and formulating conditionality in concurrence with authorities to align programmes with country development priorities and with incentive systems that support reform.

Recognition of the limited and declining role of official development assistance points to the need for both better domestic resource mobilization and the mobilization of private capital, through blended financing, using concessional public funds to effectively leverage private development financing toward economic priorities. Coordinated jointly with the private sector arms of multilateral development banks, budget support can help de-risk investments to leverage private investment. While the hopes of 'billions to trillions' in leveraging private finance have not materialized, further efforts to design effective 'de-risking' approaches, alongside use of budget support to address reform for strengthening the investment environment, are promising.

Reshaping budget support to be more effective, drawing on experience since the 2005 Paris Declaration, suggests several directions of change. First, budget support must reflect and respond to country context and not rely on generic 'best practice', with locally adapted design and home-grown conditionality. This book argues that budget support remains a viable instrument for support, not only in well-performing low-income countries, but also to provide countercyclical support during crises (including to middle-income countries with constrained access to financial markets), and provide predictable financing for basic administrative functions in fragile and conflict-affected countries with weak institutions. The design and type of budget support must be tailored to specific country context: well-performing and committed low-income countries need predictable programmatic support. Middle-income countries vulnerable to external shocks can benefit from countercyclical support and actions that restore investor confidence. Fragile post-conflict countries require support that promotes core public services and stronger public financial management and fiduciary oversight.

Second, country ownership is critical for effective reform, but ownership requires a joint understanding between authorities and donors of the analytic underpinning within the local context. Conditions of support should be robust, but also align with the incentives of authorities, ideally also aligning with their constituents to build greater accountability of authorities for effective delivery of public services. Where this is not well established, donors have to judge the risks and be prepared to halt or reassess assistance if agreed measures are not being credibly advanced.

With greater contextualization of policy design based on country realities, country ownership of reforms should be demonstrable. The risk of greater aid dependency needs to be recognized and avoided through efforts to strengthen domestic resource mobilization, fiscal capacity, and efficient public investment management.

Third, making the case to donors and MDBs for greater use of budget support calls for addressing donor concerns that resources are allocated to development priorities, that allocations are being implemented efficiently and with regard to accountability. This requires strong public financial management (PFM) systems that can take decades to build well. At the same time, being less rigid about the strength of domestic PFM systems allows donors to align support for policy reforms and provide fast-disbursing financial resources during times of need. This conflict between the need for confidence in the prudent use of budget support resources on the one hand, and the commitment to providing rapid fiscal support where systems are weak on the other, involves judgement and an understanding of the associated risks.

Fourth, budget support design can be improved by strengthening partnerships, policy dialogue, and collaborative programme design. Effective budget support is developed through deep country knowledge, a strong development dialogue between agencies and partner countries, and contextualized design consistent with country ownership.

Fifth, conditionality emerging from programme design should adhere to the principles of criticality, relevance, efficacy, additionality, and measurability. It should aim to address concerns of both donors and partner countries as to purpose, transparency, and the evidentiary basis, but also recognize that reform cannot be imposed externally and must be shaped by internal forces bridging authorities, businesses, and communities. We propose to shift from a tradition of 'conflictive conditionality' to a vision of 'credible concurrence' between financiers and recipients which requires flexibility in implementing a thoroughly context specific programme with a clear line of sight towards longer term development results.

Sixth, budget support needs to leverage private capital flows for development that can help to augment financing for development finance. Official aid falls far short of needs. New approaches to leveraging private capital for development and addressing market failure are vital. Guarantees to mobilize long-term private investment may prove highly effective.

Seventh, budget support can be a constructive tool to help protect the global commons. This requires recognizing the threat that global climate change, declining biodiversity, and the fragile nature of the institutions in place to protect the Earth's heritage pose to future generations. To contribute, budget support needs to (a) mobilize support for reforms needed to tackle global challenges, including mitigation and adaptation to climate change, and cross-border management of pandemics; (b) support institutional reforms for sustainability of project finance in support of public goods; (c) demonstrate measurable and communicable results; and (d) operate in tandem with traditional project finance to build core national infrastructure. Budget support can and should play a pivotal role in supporting and incentivizing developing countries to advance their nationally determined contributions under the Paris Accord.

Budget support in the new aid architecture should promote division of labour among MDBs and bilateral donors to promote efficiency and coherence. The financial and analytic capacity of multilateral development banks gives them a comparative advantage as the principal sponsors of budget support, particularly in support of public goods, and programmes should accommodate bilateral budget support without fragmenting the design and implementation processes.

Budget support should also preserve flexibility to adapt and adjust as events unfold. New initiatives to promote universal broadband access, support development of carbon credits, or adapt to unforeseen events need attention and agility. The process of adaptation requires iteration, learning new approaches, and unlearning dysfunctional ones.

The quest for supporting good government policies (or avoiding bad ones) has of course been around for a very long time. The fresco paintings reproduced on the cover of this book served as allegoric reminders for the council of the 14th century city state of Siena of the effects of good government (prosperity, a thriving private sector, innovation and cultural life, abundant agriculture and manufacturing). Conversely, the fresco on the back cover depicts the effects of bad government brought about by tyranny, corruption, and greed: fallow fields, conflict and violence, and abandoned businesses.

This volume argues that budget support has a vital role to play in addressing the twenty-first century's signature challenges of eliminating poverty and protecting our global commons. Budget support is designed to accompany traditional project assistance to address core reforms needed to spur shared growth, regulate industry and public services, tackle climate change, and build resilience to manage future shocks. This tool for development assistance has gone in and out of favour for largely political reasons. But the contribution and power of budget support is demonstrated through evaluation evidence and through understanding what will be required to tackle future development challenges: strong analytics and dialogue, fostering country ownership, maintaining a robust learning agenda and agility in responding to changing circumstances and shocks, and building a common framework around private and public sector collaboration.

1

The Purpose and Promise of Budget Support

What is budget support? And what makes it so controversial? In essence, budget support is aid funding that is disbursed directly to a recipient country's national treasury and is allocated to the national budget along the lines of national priorities and processes. Unlike the more traditional project financing that is usually associated with development aid, the provision of budget support is not linked to specific expenditures but to compliance with an agreed set of reforms. It is these characteristics—the untied and fast-disbursing nature of the financing and the inherent conditionality—that make this financing modality different from others (see Box 1.1) and which have historically been at the core of both its promise and its criticism.

At the beginning of the millennium, a fundamental makeover of budget support for development was endorsed by leading aid agencies. It built on and aimed to correct heavy criticism that had been levelled at the experience with 'structural adjustment lending', which had emerged as a complement to traditional project financing since 1980. Designed to create greater ownership and commitment to reform aligned with national development strategies, the new budget support aimed to accelerate growth and poverty reduction through customized development programmes.

Historical Evolution

Budget support has a long tradition. The earliest policy-based financing started soon after the founding of the Bretton Woods institutions. Although the World Bank's Articles of Agreement focused on project financing and guarantees, and merely alluded to the possibility of non-project financing under 'special circumstances', the Bank's first loan, in 1947, already supported a broad programme of expenditures for the post-war reconstruction

Retooling Development Aid in the 21st Century. Shahrokh Fardoust et al., Oxford University Press.
© Shahrokh Fardoust et al., (2023). DOI: 10.1093/oso/9780192882196.003.0001

of France. The $500 million loan went directly to the French Treasury in support of the government's Monet Plan for reconstruction.

The history of budget support reflects the evolution of development economics. As the World Bank shifted toward lending predominantly for development in low-income countries, aid was provided through project support, with funds tied to specified procurements (concrete, steel, machinery) used for project implementation. Policy-based financing was officially introduced in 1980, toward the end of the McNamara presidency. It was established as a financing modality in the context of the second OPEC oil shock in 1979, as the World Bank recognized the need for quick-disbursing funds as balance-of-payments support to address the costs of adjustment for countries facing 'structural' financing imbalances, caused largely by the deterioration in their terms of trade and external debt accumulation. This support to developing countries for managing their balance of payments was termed 'structural adjustment lending'. Initially, it related to the need to recycle petrodollars of the oil-rich countries.

The deployment of budget support linked to policy reform and structural adjustment has evolved through multiple phases, beginning with its early focus on 'filling the gaps', followed by the structural adjustment period of 'getting prices right'. The use of budget support increased steadily after the 1980s but was increasingly volatile, surging during times of crisis. This chapter then describes the phases since the beginning of the millennium when budget support was profoundly redefined, with an increased focus on governance and ownership. Figure 1.1 traces how ODA commitments have followed the evolution of budget support.[1]

Box 1.1   What is budget support and what isn't?

General budget support is disbursed directly through the recipient government's own financial management system and is not earmarked to specific projects or expenditure items. Funds flow against compliance with conditions agreed between the donor and the recipient in support of policy and institutional reform actions.

---

[1] The World Bank's policy-based loans are the main focus of this volume. Three reasons motivate this choice. First, most academic research focuses on World Bank lending and not so much on budget support by other multilateral or bilateral agencies (see Bulman et al. 2017 for a notable exception). Second, the World Bank is by far the main provider of budget support. Third, recent research indicates that results on the success of World Bank lending generalize pretty well across donor agencies (Briggs 2020).

Sectoral budget support is paid directly into the account of a particular ministry and then allocated according to sectoral priorities. Budget support instruments may have different labels depending on the institution (Most MDBs refer to *Policy-Based Financing*; the World Bank refers to *Development Policy Financing*)

Project financing targets funds to implement a specific and predefined set of development activities over a specified period of time. Funds are disbursed as expenditures are incurred. Project aid may involve the use of government systems or parallel systems.

Sector-Wide approaches (SWAps) are not financing instruments but coordination mechanisms for mobilizing and allocating resources to sectoral priorities. Using a Joint Financing Arrangement to pool government and donor resources, SWAps serve to plan, budget and monitor progress towards achievement of sectoral objectives in an integrated fashion.

Results-Based financing (RBF) or performance-based financing is an umbrella term that refers to a range of financing mechanisms where a programme or intervention provides payments to individuals or institutions after taking measurable actions towards agreed-upon results are achieved and verified. Disbursements are linked directly to the achievement of specific programme results.

- *Output-based aid (OBA)* is a form of RBF designed to deliver access to infrastructure and social services for the poor. Service delivery is outsourced to a third party-public or private that receives a subsidy to complement or replace the required user contributions. The service provider is responsible for pre-financing the project, and is reimbursed after the services have been identified and independently verified.
- In 2012, the World Bank introduced the *Programme for Results (PforR)* as a new lending instrument where disbursements to client country governments are linked to the achievement of particular milestones or disbursement-linked indicators that are tangible, transparent and verifiable and uses a country's own institutions and processes.
- *Conditional Cash Transfers (CCT)* provide cash payments to programme beneficiaries, typically poor households, which meet certain desired behaviour, generally related to the use of services such as children's health care or school enrolment.

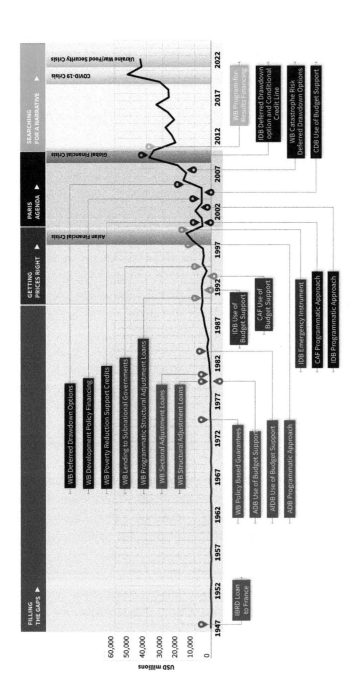

Figure 1.1 Evolution of budget support and financing commitments, 1947–2022

Source: Multilateral Development Banks' evaluation reports and annual reports; OECD Development Assistance Committee (DAC) Creditor Reporting System (CRS); and World Bank Business Intelligence.

Note: Commitment data are in current prices and in US dollars. All World Bank commitment data are actuals. For other agencies, data for 2021-22 are projections based on historic trends.

Phase 1: Filling the Gaps (1980–1990)

The antecedents of budget support lie with the structural adjustment programmes of the 1980s, which evolved in response to the developing country debt crisis following the second oil shock (1979). During this time, it became clear that traditional project lending could not fill the financing gaps of countries in economic distress, nor could it address the underlying structural distortions that had given rise to unsustainable economic performance.

The justification for budget support during this period focused on addressing macroeconomic imbalances. It grew from the prevailing view in development economics, embodied in the two-financing-gap model developed for closed economies by Harrod (1939), Domar (1947), and later for open economies by Chenery and Strout (1966), which viewed growth as fundamentally determined by the *savings gap* (inadequate domestic savings to finance investment requirements for growth) and the *foreign exchange gap* (inadequate export revenues to finance imported capital goods or materials for development). The two-gap model stipulated that the aggregate investment rate required to achieve a given growth rate is proportional to the growth rate by a constant known as the incremental capital output ratio (ICOR); aid and foreign borrowing requirements are determined by the investment requirements to reach a target growth rate, as determined by the ICOR, to fill the two financing gaps. For many countries, rising foreign debt repayment obligations outgrew debt service capacity, and foreign aid was viewed as the critical constraint to boosting growth.

For foreign exchange–constrained economies, adjustment financing was usually seen as complementary to balance-of-payments support through International Monetary Fund (IMF) programmes. Programmes typically supported first-generation fundamental reforms (e.g., privatization of state-owned enterprises, and trade tariff reforms) to address economic distortions in return for alleviating short-term balance-of-payments needs in conjunction with IMF-supported programmes. These programmes often caused severe austerity through required cuts in government expenditures and led to economic disruption (World Bank 2000). The size of the financing was primarily determined based on a calculated external financing gap. To justify budget support, however, efforts were also made to estimate the domestic cost of reforms (e.g., for social programmes and civil servant compensation packages).

Structural adjustment lending was often designed to address macroeconomic crises. Complementing traditional project-based financing, Structural Adjustment Loans (SALs) were introduced in the early 1980s to address pressing macroeconomic imbalances through quick-disbursing financing in middle-income and lower-income countries. Middle-income countries (such as Colombia, Indonesia, Mexico, and Turkey) were able to draw on structural adjustment financing to address acute balance-of-payments needs. Where the focus of reforms was more narrowly focused on a specific sector such as agriculture, Sector Adjustment Loans (SECALs) provided a similar function.

During the 1980s, many African countries received adjustment loans to help them meet debt obligations, which were coming due to the IMF, particularly in the wake of the OPEC oil-price shock and low commodity prices, which had devastating effects on many African countries. Africa's debt amortization costs rose from $2.3 billion in 1980–82 to $8 billion in 1985–87 as many short-term loans fell due, including to the IMF. The expansion of SALs to Africa in the 1980s was significantly influenced by the 1981 Berg Report of the World Bank, which argued that persistent balance-of-payment problems arose primarily because of poor export performance and lack of economic liberalization, which reflected not only external factors (deteriorating terms of trade) but also policy biases against agriculture, increasing consumption, and policies that led to market rigidities (World Bank 1981).

Structural adjustment lending was increasingly conditioned on policy measures to address economic distortions, including exchange rate devaluations, to improve export incentives; lower domestic industry protection; and civil service reform to downsize the public sector. Most policy programmes supported by budget support at that time were based on core first-order reforms aimed at reducing distortions such as overvalued exchange rates, excessive tariffs and non-tariff barriers, populist price controls over basic commodities, and persistent deficits brought about by a bloated public sector.

During this period, 'conditionality' took the form of fundamental reform measures to allow real price flexibility and signaling through markets aimed at equilibrating external accounts and bringing supply and demand into alignment. The objective of budget support was typically to provide self-standing, one-off adjustment programmes to correct imbalances and return to traditional project financing once economic distortions had been addressed. Financing volumes were based on some notion of the perceived strength of a programme. They were typically disbursed in two tranches tied to compliance with the stipulated adjustment lending conditions.

Phase 2: Getting Prices Right (1990s–early 2000s)

Fiscal gap financing emerged as the focus during the 1990s. In the early 1990s, the emphasis of budget support shifted increasingly to relaxing fiscal constraints in low-income countries through the provision of longer-term financing in support of public expenditure programmes. Budget support financing supported a broader range of medium-term structural and institutional reforms, reflecting the prevailing views among economists summarized by the term 'Washington Consensus', coined in 1989 to summarize ten policies that were thought to be critical for Latin America (Williamson 2009).

Subsequently pejoratively labelled 'market fundamentalism', the Washington Consensus focused on structural reforms related to market failure and pricing, to address constraints to growth and stabilize economies. This standard package of advice included a set of policies designed to create economic stability by controlling inflation and reducing government budget deficits. Government spending would be reduced and interest rates would be raised to reduce the money supply. A subsequent stage was the reform of trade and exchange rate policies to integrate the reforming country into the global economy. That involved the lifting of state restrictions on imports and exports and often included the devaluation of the currency. A final stage consisted of allowing market forces to operate freely by removing subsidies and state controls and engaging in a programme of privatization. While the prescriptions of the Washington Consensus have been refined over time in response to increasing criticism, including by focusing on social protection, poverty reduction, and civil society involvement, many of the prescriptive reforms remain relevant to development thinking today (Irvin 2020).

The design of budget support reflected the support of medium-term structural policy reforms. Frequent balance-of-payments crises meant that borrowers returned to repeated adjustment financing. It was recognized that budget support funding flows were disbursed based on promised future structural reforms, before the policy reform had impact (which typically occurred only over the medium term, as first-generation fundamental measures addressed at economic distortions gave way to second-generation medium-term structural reforms). Sequential adjustment loans for low-income countries were designed to phase in market reforms, often linked to competitiveness through tariff and exchange rate reform.

Toward the end of the decade, programmatic lending was introduced, consisting of a series of subsequent operations in support of a medium-term reform programme. Spreading disbursements over time was intended to better incentivize and track reform implementation, but it also led later to criticism that this practice was heavy-handed, undermined fiscal management, and reinforced aid dependence.

Over time, it became clear that market reforms often had profound adverse social impacts, which led to increasing calls for 'adjustment with a human face' (Cornia, Jolly, and Stewart 1987). This need was underscored by the collapse of the socialist command economies, which faced the grim reality of massive budget shortfalls and severe social dislocation. Multilateral development banks and the IMF came under increasing pressure to address the social costs of adjustment.

Phase 3: Governance and Ownership (2000s–2010)

Over the years, policy-based lending stirred substantial controversy. Criticism of adjustment lending grew louder in the late 1990s, with critics arguing that conditionality undermined government sovereignty and ownership of programmes; bound parliaments and budgets to the disbursement practices of the multilateral development banks; and had grown unwieldy, creating high compliance costs, driven by fragmented donor practices that were onerous for countries with limited technocratic capacity.

The mixed performance of adjustment lending has been well documented (Mosley et al. 1991). Adjustment lending by the World Bank has been the subject of extensive research and numerous internal reviews (World Bank 1988, 1990, 1992, 1994; Thomas and Nash 1991). A 2001 evaluation of developments in adjustment lending examined its appropriate use and the design of conditionality within the Bank's menu of lending instruments (World Bank 2001b). Based on several country studies, the Structural Adjustment Participatory Review Initiative drew broader conclusions about specific areas of policy reform, including privatization, agriculture, and the public sector (SAPRIN 2002; World Bank 2001a). Easterley (2003) finds no effect of IMF and World Bank adjustment lending on growth but a lowered growth elasticity of poverty, meaning that economic expansions benefit the poor less under structural adjustment, but at the same time economic contractions hurt the poor less. The World Bank regularly considered its experience with policy-based lending and conditionality as part of its periodic reviews of operational policies and lending instruments in support of country strategies and programmes (World Bank 1988, 1990, 1992, 1994, 1999, 2001a, 2001b, 2000a, 2005b, 2015, 2022). Changes in incentive structures and relative price changes brought about by structural adjustment programmes were also recognized to have an impact on the environment as growth and structural shifts affect the extraction of natural resources and the level of pollution emissions (Gueorguieva and Bolt 2003; Seymour and Dubash 2000).

The Washington Consensus and Structural Reforms

Conditionality tended to reflect the specific policy recommendations at the core of the Washington Consensus, ranging from fiscal discipline to tax reform, trade liberalization, and deregulation. Confidence in the universality of this policy consensus eroded in the late 1990s and early 2000s, with the backlash against market fundamentalism and 'one-size fits all' prescriptions (Stiglitz 2008). Adjustment programmes were criticized as paying insufficient attention to specific economic structures within developing countries and for recommending a much more circumscribed role for the state than the successful East Asian economies had embraced. Reviewing the collapse in output in the post-Soviet economies and the lack of sustained growth in reforming Sub-Saharan African countries, the World Bank (2005) concluded that there was no universal set of rules or best practices. Instead, it advocated selective and more graduated, context relevant reforms and policy diversity. Criticism of trade liberalization by the anti-globalization movement and vocal socialist governments in Latin America, neo-Keynesian criticism of financial orthodoxy, and the success of China's growth model undermined confidence in the universality of the Washington Consensus.

Aid Effectiveness and the Quality of Aid

The mid-1990s saw a lively debate about the effectiveness of aid. Talk of donor fatigue was accompanied by well-founded critiques that aid did not work (OECD 2011). The early quantitative aid-growth literature arrived at widely different conclusions. Researchers such as Easterly (2003) questioned whether aid had been effective in reducing poverty. Boone (1996) and Rajan and Subramanian (2008) found no significant effects of development assistance on growth. Examining the vast literature on aid effectiveness, Doucouliagos and Paldam (2009) concluded that after 40 years of development aid, the preponderance of the evidence indicated that aid had not been effective.

These doubts over the effectiveness of aid were counterbalanced by several influential studies. Burnside and Dollar (2000) found the impact of development aid on economic growth to be conditional on a sound policy environment. This line of research supported the broader message that aid will be used more productively in countries with sound economic management, fewer policy distortions, less rent-seeking, and competent government bureaucracies (Dollar and Kraay, 2002, Dollar and Levin 2005). Research also suggested that both the predictability and the timing of resource flows were critical to the effectiveness of aid and particularly helpful to well-performing countries at a turn-around point in the reform process (World Bank 1998). A third line of research found that aid increases the growth rate, and this result is not conditional on 'good' policy (see, e.g., Hansen and Tarp 2001).

A further line of research focused on the multiple types of aid and differences in short—and long-term impacts. Differentiating aid into short-term vs. long term impacts, Clemens et al. (2012) find that there is a large, positive, and causal relationship between short impact aid and economic growth. More recently, Easterly (2019) identifies the long-term impact of core Washington Consensus reforms in the 1980s and 1990s and concludes that there is a robust correlation over the long-term between the reforms supported through structural adjustment lending and IMF programmes, and positive growth outcomes in Africa and Latin America. If disappointing growth accompanying reforms led to doubts about economic reforms in the 1980s and 1990s, improved policy outcomes since then should lead to 'some positive updating of such beliefs' (Easterly 2019).

The main reasons for diverging findings on aid effectiveness were methodological, particularly the way in which the causal effect between aid and growth is identified.[2] Many confounding variables may simultaneously affect development assistance and economic growth. For example, the 2020 COVID-19 crisis caused large economic downturns as well as massive inflows of official development assistance. Simply correlating economic growth with aid would thus lead to a negative, but potentially spurious, relationship between aid and growth. To correct for confounding variables, researchers relied on instrumental variable techniques that, in retrospect, turned out to be invalid.

A more recent strand of literature aims to address these methodological problems. It finds positive impacts of aid on growth (see Arndt, Jones, and Tarp 2016 for a review). For instance, Clemens et al. (2012) use ordinary least squares (OLS) regression with fixed effects and lag aid by a period. They find that a 1 percentage point increase in the aid to gross domestic product (GDP) ratio causes the economy to grow by 0.2 percentage points. Galiani et al. (2017) exploit quasi-random variation in passing the International Development Association (IDA)[3] threshold. They find that a 1 percentage point increase in the aid to gross national income (GNI) ratio raises annual real per capita growth by about 0.35 percentage points. Temple and Van de Sijpe (2017) construct a synthetic measure of aid. Their results show that aid increases net imports and total consumption.

---

[2] Other methodological problems include measurement error and the timing of development assistance. See Clemens et al. (2012), Bazzi and Clemens (2013), and Galiani et al. (2017).

[3] The World Bank Group consists of the International Bank for Reconstruction and Development (IBRD), the International Development Association (IDA), the International Finance Corporation (IFC), the Multilateral Investment Guarantee Agency (MIGA), and the International Centre for Settlement of Investment Disputes (ICSID). IBRD provides loans on market terms to middle-income countries. IDA provides credits and grants on concessional terms to low-income countries. MIGA guarantees investments against non-commercial risk, and ICSID is devoted to international investment dispute settlement.

Underlying the debate on aid effectiveness is a classic political economy problem that can be framed within a principal–agent framework: the possible divergence of interests and asymmetric information between the principals that commission certain tasks (donors supporting a reform agenda) and the agents that perform the tasks (recipient countries). Donors regard themselves as committed to public good objectives such as poverty reduction and economic development and rely on the assumption of an alignment of interests with benevolent recipient governments to implement a policy programme supporting these objectives (Box 1.2). To deal with the agency problem of development aid, donors traditionally relied on ring-fenced projects and political and technical conditions for the provision of aid (Booth 2011). Most aid has been delivered through specific investment projects that disburse as expenditures are incurred. The track record of this aid modality is uneven. Investment lending requires not only the close involvement of donors in the design and planning of projects but also intrusive micromanagement to monitor implementation. Observing the agent creates high transactions costs and requires significant administrative capacity in recipient countries (Chauvet et al. 2015). These costs are higher the larger the divergence between donors' expectations and recipient country realities in terms of fiduciary, procurement, environmental, and social standards.

Aid effectiveness depends not only on aligning the incentive structure between principals and agents but also on the ability of donors to send coherent messages to recipient countries. In practice, the heterogeneity of donor preferences regarding policies, strategic perspectives, and aid modalities leads to aid fragmentation. By increasing direct and indirect transactions costs, the proliferation and fragmentation of aid donors, systems, and channels significantly reduces the value of aid. In fact, the donors that are most likely to insist on their own aid delivery systems are especially likely to be suppliers of aid to recipients suffering most from fragmentation (Acharya et al. 2006).

Acknowledging the problem of collective action among donors highlights the political economy dimension of the aid system. Applying theoretical insights of the new institutional economics, Gibson et al. (2005) argues that the failure of aid is related to the institutions that deliver it, which often create perverse incentives (like the Samaritan's dilemma) that promote inefficient and of the design, resource mobilization, learning, and evaluation of development assistance programmes.

At the same time, experience with policy-based lending suggested that compliance with externally imposed conditionality as an attempt to address misalignment between donor and recipient preferences was generally ineffective and unsustainable (Mosley et al. 1991; Killick et al. 1998; Dollar and Svensson 2000; Koeberle 2003).

Box 1.2 Budget support as a principal–agent problem

The provision of budget support can be modelled as a principal–agent problem. Azam and Laffont (2003) provide a benchmark study that analyses foreign aid as a contract where the North gives a transfer to the South conditional on poverty reduction. They approach this issue from a principal–agent relationship between a donor and a recipient who have conflicting views about the desirability of poverty alleviation and redistribution. The recipient country cares partly for the general welfare of the country, and partly for the welfare of a restricted elite. The donor is assumed to only care about the former.

The authors investigate how an aid contract between donor and recipient can affect a (developing) country's redistribution policy in case of asymmetric information. Moral hazard is raised by the fact that the recipient government controls the consumption of the poor. The authors come to the conclusion that conditional aid can indeed help in supporting policy reform (and poverty reduction), provided the right type of contracts are devised.

However, there are some inherent difficulties in using contracts for policy change. Historically, contract theory originated when studying labour relations between employer and employee. Applying these methods to sovereign nations fundamentally limits the use of verifiable variables. In other words, when contracting for policy reform, an independent arbitrator, such as an international court of law is lacking to punish any player who breaks contract stipulations. In case a recipient government cannot commit to contract conditions, the incentives provided in the contract will no longer guarantee effective policy reform. As Azam and Laffont (2003, p. 52) note, a possible way to get around post-contractual opportunism is for the donor to commit aid ex-ante and design a credible contract such that aid is disbursed only after observing reform. However, Svensson (2003) argues that donors often lack a credible commitment technology due to the problem of time inconsistency. Consequently, without commitment the moral hazard problem persists and the relationship is characterized by a Samaritan's Dilemma (Buchanan, 1975).

Realizing the limitations of ex-ante, donor-driven lending, the development community implemented a shift in its approach of development assistance, based on the principles of the 2005 Paris Declaration. Most importantly, donors aim to base their support on the country's own vision for development, looking for policies and programmes for which evidence of domestic ownership exists. In other words, the principles of the Paris Declaration try to resolve the principal–agent problem by aligning the objectives of the donor and the recipient and moving from donor-driven conditionality to consensual conditionality. Chapter 5 discusses the difficulty of implementing this aspiration in practice.

The Millennium Consensus on Aid Effectiveness

The dawn of the new millennium brought new attention to development. One reason was the high-profile Jubilee campaign, which focused attention on the unsustainable debt burden of developing countries. A perhaps more important reason were the attacks on the United States on September 11, 2001. As the Organisation for Economic Co-operation and Development (OECD) pointed out, 'the events of 11 September have strengthened the conviction that a world without violence, terrorism and conflict also means a world freed from exclusion, vulnerability and inequality, a world where opportunities exist for all' (OECD 2011).

Scaling up Aid and Reliance on Country Systems

A series of high-level forums in the early 2000s enshrined what would become a new consensus on aid effectiveness. The Monterrey Consensus (2002) committed donors to scaling up aid in support of the Millennium Development Goals (MDGs).[4] Signed by more than 100 countries, the Rome Declaration on Harmonization (2003) and the Paris Declaration on Aid Effectiveness (OECD 2005) brought implementation issues to the fore of the aid effectiveness debate and called for increased use of recipient systems in managing aid. Donors committed to coordinate their efforts and to seek greater alignment with country ownership of development strategies. The Third High Level Forum in Accra (2008) took stock of the Paris commitments and set the agenda for accelerated advancement toward the Paris targets. The Busan Partnership Agreement (2011) provided a framework that explicitly included emerging economies, South–South cooperation, civil society, and the private sector alongside traditional donors.

Underpinning the emerging consensus were the notions of increasing aid flows and emphasizing the quality and value of aid. The commitment to

---

[4] The eight Millennium Development Goals (MDGs)—which ranged from halving extreme poverty rates to halting the spread of HIV/AIDS and providing universal primary education, all by the target date of 2015—formed a blueprint agreed to by all countries and all leading development institutions.

base overall support on partner countries' national development strategies, institutions, and procedures saw the emergence of a new consensus on aid effectiveness aimed at improving donor coordination through harmonization and alignment with country-driven medium-term poverty reduction plans. These ideas of aid effectiveness formed a pillar of a seminal publication by the OECD's Development Assistance Committee (DAC) entitled *Shaping the 21st Century: The Contribution of Development Co-operation* (OECD 1996). It laid the foundation for the MDGs and gained momentum with the 2005 Paris Declaration on Aid Effectiveness.

Achieving this broad consensus was encouraged and facilitated by an influential like-minded group of bilateral ministers with social democratic backgrounds who emphasized the importance of policy coherence. Formed in 1999 during a meeting at Utstein Abbey on the west coast of Norway, the Utstein Group combined representatives from several European development organizations committed to fight corruption and strengthen the effectiveness of their resource flows to developing countries.[5] These ministers pushed hard for the adoption of the MDGs as the dominant framework for marking what had been achieved and what still needed to be done in world development. Most strikingly, it set an ambitious target for reducing by half the proportion of people living in absolute poverty by 2015. The Organisation for Economic Co-operation and Development (OECD), the United Nations, the World Bank. and the IMF supported the MDGs by developing strategies and indicators for monitoring progress toward them. Their efforts widened the perspective on development from how much aid is being spent to how well it is being allocated and how much is being achieved.

A New Aid Architecture Emerges

Building on the themes that had been discussed in development circles since the beginning of the 2000s, the 2005 Paris Declaration implicitly recognized that neither traditional project aid nor policy conditionality addressed transactions costs, because of the underlying principal–agent tensions in

---

[5] The Utstein Group included the Norwegian Agency for Development Cooperation (Norad), the United Kingdom's Department for International Development (DFID), the German Corporation for International Cooperation (GTZ), the Ministry of Foreign Affairs of the Netherlands, and the Swedish International Development Cooperation Agency (SIDA). The four original members of the group included Ms Eveline Herfkens, Minister for Development Co-Operation, the Netherlands; Ms Clare Short, Minister for International Development, the United Kingdom; Ms Heidemarie Wieczorek-Zeul, Minister of Economic Co-operation and Development, Germany; and Ms Hilde F. Johnson, Minister of International Development, Norway.

the donor–recipient relationship or the collective action problem of aid fragmentation brought about by divergent donor preferences.

The Paris Declaration Principles

The Paris Declaration produced a set of five principles to guide aid effectiveness, backed by concrete indicators that could be monitored:

- *Country ownership*: Developing countries set their own strategies for reducing poverty, improving their institutions, and tackling corruption.
- *Alignment*: Donor countries align behind these objectives and use local systems.
- *Harmonization*: Donor countries coordinate, simplify procedures, and share information to avoid duplication.
- *Results*: Developing countries and donors shift focus to development results, and results get measured.
- *Mutual accountability*: Donors and partners are accountable for development results.

Shifts in the aid architecture underpinned the emergence of budget support. Promising increased resource envelopes and more predictable resource flows, key features of the emerging architecture included the following:

- The Heavily Indebted Poor Country Initiative (HIPC) and the Multilateral Debt Relief Initiatives (MDRI) sought to take the debt burden off countries and use the additional fiscal space for development purposes.
- The focus was sharpened on country-driven poverty reduction strategies that set out medium-term priorities for public policies and expenditures for each low-income country. The driving idea was that such strategies should not be imposed, that developing countries should come up with their own plans on how they want to develop and the specific steps to get there. There was overlap between this notion and World Bank President Wolfensohn's concept of the Comprehensive Development Framework, which was eventually superseded by the Poverty Reduction Strategy Paper (PRSP).
- The International Monetary Fund (IMF) and the World Bank introduced PRSPs in September 1999, in order to help aid-recipient countries meet the MDGs. PRSPs must be submitted before a country can be considered for debt relief under the Heavily Indebted Poor Countries

(HIPC) initiative. They should be country-driven, result-oriented, comprehensive, partnership-oriented, and based on a long-term perspective.

The Promise of Budget Support

Against the background of a shifting aid architecture and dissatisfaction with earlier aid instruments, 'general budget support' or 'partner budget support' emerged in the late 1990s and early 2000s. Budget support involves the disbursement of unearmarked funds in support of a developing country's programme of development policies and reforms. Post-millennium budget support was explicitly anchored in the partnership aspect of the post-millennium aid architecture, to draw a contrast with what was perceived as externally imposed conditionality of the structural adjustment era of the 1990s. Development partners and developing countries welcomed the 'new' budget support, because its features promised to meet key expectations of the Millennium Consensus on Aid Effectiveness (Koeberle, Stavreski, and Walliser 2006), including the following:

- *Country ownership*: Greater country ownership, achieved by aligning the financing instrument with a country's own poverty reduction strategy, drawing on the countries' own development plans, avoiding parallel structures, and allowing greater flexibility in the choice of paths to achieve defined development goals.
- *Donor coordination*: Improved donor coordination through reference to a country-owned strategy.
- *Country systems*: Increased effectiveness of overall public expenditures and strengthening of recipient countries' planning and implementation capacity, by channelling funds through national systems.
- *Results*: Leveraging of results, by scaling up funding and influencing overall government expenditure programmes.
- *Predictability*: Enhancement of state functions, through predictable and reliable payment of salaries for public officials.
- *Disbursement*: Reduced transaction costs, more manageable resource flows, and more meaningful aid commitments, by limiting parallel reporting requirements and entanglement in donor-driven projects with gold-plated procurement and safeguard policies.
- *Accountability*: Greater accountability, by relying on country's own budget, reporting and audit system.

Common Design Features

Budget support focuses on implementing an agreed upon underlying strategy in support of a development objective rather than monitoring the specific use of funds, as traditional project financing does. Funds are disbursed as reforms are implemented, rather than as expenditures are incurred. Budget support also typically involves a degree of conditionality that donors attach to the disbursement of funds.

Building on different traditions, legal concepts, and governance structures, a new millennium approach to budget support among development partners emerged, with several key common features (Koeberle 2003):

- Recognition of the importance of *predictable aid flows* to secure public expenditure, moving away from disruptive fiscal swings.
- Support for recipient countries' budget processes and overall government expenditure programmes and *country systems* rather than discrete projects that are small relative to the size of government programmes.
- A *common framework of the MDGs and greater results orientation*, to provide a framework for development programmes. Conditionality was supposed to focus more on programme results in support of the ultimate objective of poverty reduction and less on the micro-management of the specific steps taken to get there.
- A shift from ex ante conditionality based on promises to *ex post conditionality based on performance.*
- A shift from stroke-of-the-pen reforms to reduce economic distortions to *incremental longer-term complex reforms* of a more institutional and political nature, often focused on public financial management.
- Budget support was expected to be *more efficient and cost-effective* per dollar transferred for development purposes, thanks to lower transactions and preparation costs, achieved by promoting *donor harmonization* with uniform reporting requirements and obviating the need for onerous procurement and environmental and social compliance.

Conditionality

The design, use, and content of conditionality are integral features of budget support. A key aspect of the redesigned instrument in the new millennium was the break with precedent by reconsidering the traditional approach to conditionality, which remained controversial and which many considered intrusive, ineffective, or even harmful (Mosley et al. 1991). Although use and design varied considerably across countries and donors, a handful of principles emerged as good practice design features for budget support conditionality, including on when and how to use it.

Drawing on the insights of the aid effectiveness literature and mixed experience with policy-based financing during the 1980s and 1990s, an emerging consensus among development practitioners circumscribed when budget support would be most effective:

- Budget support was seen as the *core instrument for macroeconomic policy dialogue and poverty reduction strategies*. Through budget support dialogue, coordinated donor engagement was supposed to bring the donor community and government together around a country-led poverty reduction strategy. Although the rhetorical emphasis on alignment of donor and recipient objectives around a single development agenda served to paper over the reality of divergent interests between principals and agents, conditionality remained an integral feature of post–Paris Agenda budget support, whether explicitly included ex ante or implicitly recognized ex post.
- When used with judicious selectivity and tailored to country circumstances, conditionality could be a useful *commitment device*—but not a substitute for country ownership. Because economic policies are driven primarily by domestic political processes, conditionality was considered appropriate only if there was commitment and capacity to reform.
- Research on aid effectiveness emphasizes the importance of focusing policy-based financial support on *countries with good policies and institutions*.
- Although *country ownership* of reforms is critical, it is difficult to assess. A country's track record was considered among the most robust indicators of its readiness and capacity to reform. The history of policy-based financing was littered with inaccurately assessed windows of opportunity for reform, however.
- Building capacity and providing advice based on *analytical work* were considered better ways of nurturing reforms in their early stages and helping countries reach critical reform consensus rather than undermining the reform incentives with premature financing.

Enhancing the development effectiveness of policy-based lending requires making judicious use of different design options, so that conditionality reflects specific country circumstances, including the number and nature of conditions and the phasing and tranching:

- Disillusionment with traditional ex ante conditionality led to an effort to consider a more results-orientated approach focused on *ownership, selectivity, and partnerships.*
- In practice, this meant a move toward a more *programmatic approach* to policy-based financing, with ex post conditionality based on actual performance rather than promises of future reform. Programmatic approaches to conditionality recognize the importance of country ownership through increased flexibility, reflecting countries' track records, and supporting sustained engagement for complex medium-term institutional and policy reforms.
- Programmatic budget support called for a prudent mix of government policies, intermediate benchmarks, and ultimate outcomes embedded in a medium-term policy framework and involving a series of operations linked by specific but flexible triggers. Most attempts to address performance deficiencies and capacity limitations through a larger number of more complex conditions were ineffective. Conditionality should therefore focus on priorities grounded in country ownership and capacity and be *limited to policy and institutional actions under the control of the executive branch.*
- Although research on aid effectiveness encourages *phasing and tranching based on performance rather than promises,* a pure outcome focus is fraught with practical difficulties and is no substitute for conditionality.
- Good practice also suggests the need for a *clear medium-term framework* for policy-based lending linking policy actions, progress indicators, and expected outcomes.
- *Conditionality customized to country circumstances* implies strengthening countries' capacity to monitor and evaluate progress toward development objectives.
- Effective conditionality involves more than just financing; it also serves as a *vehicle for policy dialogue.* Ideally, it is underpinned by a deep understanding of economic and political constraints to development gained through analytic work.

Donor Approaches to Budget Support

The design of budget support operations varied significantly across donors in terms of definitions, tranching, the scope of conditionality, and the scale of budget support relative to other aid modalities. Budget support covered a spectrum of options, from general budget support to more narrowly defined sector-specific budget support instruments. There was also significant variation in the degree to which budget support was underpinned by analytic work and accompanied by technical advice, capacity building, or other inputs, such as procedures for dialogue or donor efforts to harmonize their aid and align it with national policies and procedures (Lister and Carter 2006).

By the early 2000s, most OECD Development Assistance Committee (DAC) donors followed the lead of the World Bank and other multilateral finance institutions and embraced general budget support as the principal instrument to implement the principles of the Paris Declaration.[6] The European Union and its member states supported the use of general budget support as a means to improve the effectiveness of aid, each with a somewhat different emphasis:

- Viewing budget support as an effective instrument for implementing the Paris Declaration principles, the **European Commission** emphasized joint programming, implementation, and pooling of resources as main guiding principles for EU development policy in its 'New European Consensus on Development' (EC 2005). It states that 'coordinated work by the EU and its Member States on budget support will help to promote SDG implementation efforts in partner countries, improve macroeconomic and public financial management, and improve the business environment. Budget support, when applicable and with those willing to participate, will be used to strengthen partnership, political dialogue, country ownership and mutual accountability with developing countries, based on shared principles, objectives and interests and in response to partner countries' political, economic and social contexts.' In an effort to reduce the intrusiveness of conditionality, the European Commission also became a champion of results-based conditions.
- The **United Kingdom's Department of International Development** (DFID) emerged as one of the strongest bilateral champions of budget support, which it considered 'the instrument most likely to support improvements in the accountability and capability of the state' (DFID 2004).
- The **Netherlands** started providing budget support as early as 1998, linking it to specific requirements such as the PRSP process, effective policy dialogue on good governance, and poverty reduction and measurable results (Netherlands Ministry of Foreign Affairs 2012).

---

[6] The Development Assistance Committee (DAC) of the Organisation for Economic Co-operation and Development (OECD) is a forum for the discussion of aid, development, and poverty reduction in developing countries. It describes itself as the 'venue and voice' of the world's major donor countries.

- In its support for the aid effectiveness agenda, **France** declared budget support as its instrument of choice (CICID 2007).
- Other prominent supporters for budget support included **Denmark, Finland, Germany,** and **Sweden**, albeit with greater selectivity and stricter eligibility criteria.

To support government-led poverty reduction programmes in low-income countries, the **World Bank** introduced Poverty Reduction Support Credits (PRSC), which consisted of policy and institutional actions to accelerate growth and human development. Typically implemented through a series of programmatic operations linked to medium-term PRSPs, these credits were intended to provide predictable financing in support of poverty reduction by strengthening public financial management, improving the investment climate, addressing bottlenecks for service delivery, and encouraging economic diversification (World Bank 2005b; IEG 2010). PRSCs were intended to be the World Bank's institutional counterpart to the IMF's Poverty Reduction Growth Facility (PRGF). Drawing lessons from the experience with policy-based financing, the World Bank introduced development policy financing in 2002. In response to the criticisms of structural adjustment lending, it created Development Policy Financing (DPF), designed to embrace government ownership (World Bank 2002).

Structural adjustment lending had already begun shifting away from its focus on market fundamentalism, paying greater attention to governance and the investment climate. The introduction of DPF marked a shift away from the short-term macroeconomic stabilization and trade liberalization reforms of the 1980s and 1990s toward more medium-term institutional reforms. DPF was intended to systematically map to the development strategies of the government and include measures to improve public financial management, strengthen voice and accountability, and address constraints to private investment. The focus on government ownership and donor responsibility to support the local development strategy directly reflected the narrative enshrined in the Paris Declaration.

Reflecting some of the earlier lessons of experience, the World Bank's introduction of DPF emerged as a promising way to reconcile the debate between the traditional ex ante approach and the aspirations of the results-based approach to conditionality (Koeberle 2003). With increasing reliance on selective ex post conditions, the Bank aimed to make conditionality more systematic and transparent by spelling out how the policies and institutional reforms they support would contribute to the achievement of country objectives (World Bank 2002).

Phase 4: Searching for a Narrative (since 2011)

In response to the 2008/09 financial crisis, budget support increased markedly. International financial institutions responded strongly to the crisis, providing the largest volume of budget support disbursements to date. The World Bank was in a strong position to provide financial support because low demand from the International Bank for Reconstruction and Development (IBRD) before the crisis left headroom to nearly triple lending in FY2009/10 and increase its equity-to loan-ratio to 38 per cent, well above its target of 23–27 per cent. The International Development Association (IDA) funding envelope, which was determined before the crisis, was significantly more constrained. It allowed for an increase of about 25 per cent.

The following decade since 2011 saw continued volatility against a declining trend in the use of budget support. It could be described as a period in search of a clearly defining narrative, with heterogeneous design options and a more heterogenous approach to conditionality. This included the deployment of budget support to a broader set of sectors through multiple approaches, including to countries with limited institutional capacity, and in response to the COVID-19 pandemic.

It was not until the end of the decade when total budget support again increased to support economic recovery from the COVID-19 pandemic. However, the rate of increase and the volume of lending were markedly lower than they were during the 2008/09 financial crisis. The ratio of quick-disbursing budget support to investment lending decreased marginally (Duggan et al. 2020).

The last decade of budget support was accompanied by profound changes in the international financial architecture which are examined in chapter 2. Chapter 3 provides a detailed analysis of shifts in the design and use of budget support and the content of conditionality. Chapter 4 discusses to what extent budget support lived up to its promises.

Conclusion

Budget support emerged more than half a century ago as an instrument for addressing macro imbalances conditional on key economic reforms supported by the Bretton-Woods institutions. It was widely used as an instrument for advancing the principles of the Washington Consensus.

In the early 2000s, a new aid architecture rose to prominence through the 2005 Paris Declaration and the Monterrey Consensus. Budget support was redesigned to align with recipient countries' own development strategies and to impose lighter conditionality. Budget support was intended to be used as a key instrument for achieving the MDGs. Most donors followed the lead of the World Bank and other multilateral finance institutions and embraced general budget support as the principal instrument for implementing the principles of the Paris Declaration.

Budget support was expected to become a key instrument of the new aid architecture. What made it attractive were its greater country ownership, its emphasis on building country capacity and strengthening country systems rather than creating parallel structures set up to satisfy donor requirements. Key objectives of budget support included improved donor coordination, leveraging results by scaling up funding and influencing overall government expenditure programmes, increasing the predictability of resource flows, and improving accountability. Moreover, budget support was also supposed to be more cost-efficient and cost-effective than traditional financing, thanks to less onerous procurement and environmental and social compliance.

Budget support was seen as the core instrument for macroeconomic policy dialogue and growth strategies. Coordinated donor engagement was supposed to bring the donor community and government together around a country-led development strategy.

The design, use, and content of conditionality are integral features of budget support. To address the mixed track record of previous adjustment lending, conditionality under budget support was to focus on a small number of critical, country-owned, typically incremental reform measures as part of a medium-term framework, with disbursements of subsequent operations predicated ex post on completion of prior actions rather than ex ante on future (and often unrealistic or overly optimistic) measures.

Since the turn of the millennium, budget support has become a well-established and widely used instrument for providing financing and support for reforms in developing countries. But its use and popularity have fluctuated widely, reflecting significant changes in the international financial architecture, lessons of experience, and broader trends in development thinking. What was conceived as an aid modality to provide predictable financing to well-performing developing countries in support of the MDGs was used in a wide variety of circumstances that were very different from the original plan. Economic crises such as the global financial crisis of 2008/09 highlighted the significant role of budget support in providing large volumes of countercyclical financing for middle-income countries. The donor community recognized that fragile, conflict, and violence-affected countries could benefit from budget support despite the weakness of their institutional and governance situations. The devastating economic impact of climate change, conflict and violence and the COVID-19 pandemic highlight the potential of budget support to transcend the boundary of national reform agenda by addressing global public goods.

2
Global Finance and the Changing Aid Landscape

Over the last decade, the demand for, and contribution of, budget support has been shaped by major trends in global financial architecture, and by a sequence of large adverse shocks to the global economy: food and fuel crisis (2006–7), global financial and capital markets crisis (2008–9), collapse of commodity prices (2014–15), COVID-19 pandemic (2020–22), and the Russian invasion of Ukraine in early 2022. The adverse consequences of recent crises are still unfolding. In the face of these shocks the procyclical nature of private capital flows (which collapse when most needed) has exacerbated the social and economic impact of the shocks and made developing countries exceptionally reliant on foreign aid and public finances. This has also exposed serious flaws in the global financial architecture, particularly with regard to external debt relief and restructuring in developing countries.

A sharp drop in capital flows to developing countries, or a protracted sudden stop in capital flows, can and does cause widespread solvency problems in developing countries. Understanding complex capital flows, the role of the private sector, public sector, and foreign aid is important for understanding how budget support fits into the current aid architecture, and it can help to mitigate serious macroeconomic and financial risks.[1] In this context, the global financial landscape has evolved in important ways since the policy-based lending instrument was first introduced more than three decades ago, resulting in a reduced role in some respects, but new and important opportunities in others that are critical to addressing growth opportunities and needed resilience in the face of daunting global challenges.

This chapter analyses the evolving global financial and foreign aid architecture, which provides the international context in which budget support has played an important role in financing development, particularly since the early 2000s, as described in Chapter 1. After a brief review of the longer-term trends in aid and other capital flows to developing countries before 2008, it

---

[1] Obstfeld (2022).

Retooling Development Aid in the 21st Century. Shahrokh Fardoust et al., Oxford University Press.
© Shahrokh Fardoust et al., (2023). DOI: 10.1093/oso/9780192882196.003.0002

briefly examines the impact of the global financial and economic crisis on official and private financial flows to developing countries. It then discusses opportunities and challenges concerning the mobilization of private capital using budget support and guarantees for financing much-needed investments in sustainable infrastructure and human development in developing countries.

In this context, some of the main challenges in the way guarantees by multilateral development banks (MDBs) are used is discussed and attention is drawn to some of the limitations of, and risks associated with, the highly ambitious investment targets set by the Sustainable Development Goals (SDGs), given the mounting external debt facing many developing countries and the formidable economic and financial challenges caused by the pandemic, the subsequent food and fuel crisis, and climate change. Also discussed is how the changing landscape of aid—including the emergence of new donors, such as China; vertical funds, such as the Global Fund to Fight AIDS, Tuberculosis and Malaria; and 'impact investing'[2]—have increased the complexity, as well as the fragmentation, of the aid architecture over the last decade.

The last decade also saw the increasing indebtedness of developing countries, particularly to the private sector, which highlights the importance of economic reform and support for structural transformation in countries vulnerable to shocks. Financial flows to developing countries, particularly to low-income countries, were sharply affected by the global financial crisis of 2008–9 and the COVID-19 pandemic since 2020. These adverse shocks exacerbated imbalances in the demand for and supply of financing of SDG-related investments and other balance-of-payments challenges across different groups of developing countries.

In sum, this chapter provides an overview of the changing international aid architecture and patterns of capital flow as the context for the evolving role of budget support by MDBs and bilateral donors helping developing countries address development challenges and seize opportunities. The focus is on the increasingly important (and interlinked) areas in which budget support and closely related financial instruments, such as policy-based guarantees, are likely to play a critical role over the coming decade—namely, the mobilization of private capital for promoting inclusive and sustainable growth, fighting poverty, and mitigating the effects of climate change.

---

[2] Impact investing, which is discussed in more detail later in this chapter, refers to investments made in firms, institutions, and funds with the overarching objective of generating a measurable, socially and environmentally beneficial impact, together with a positive financial return.

Chapters 3 analyses the evolving role of budget support, particularly its role during global crisis. In Chapter 4, we show that budget support has been effective in supporting private sector reform and improving the business environment.[3]

Official Aid and Development Goals

In 2015, the Millennium Development Goals (MDGs) were replaced by the more ambitious Sustainable Development Goals (SDGs).[4] These seventeen goals provide a more comprehensive vision as well as a framework for ramping up financial support and global action.

In 2014, the United Nations Conference on Trade and Development (UNCTAD) estimated the total financing gap in key SDG sectors at $2.5 trillion a year between 2015 and 2030.[5] The highly ambitious magnitude of the investments needed made it clear that official development assistance (ODA) alone at less than $200 billion per year could not finance the SDGs and that such assistance must therefore be provided by raising domestic resources and leveraging private sector flows to expand the pool of financial resources available to developing countries. However, starting in 2020, the adverse impact of the pandemic in developing countries is estimated to have substantially increased the costs of achieving the SDGs while lowering their available domestic resources and reducing their access to private capital markets.[6]

Over the last decade, on aggregate, private financial, equity and debt flows to developing countries exceeded foreign aid and official lending by a substantial margin, and foreign direct investment (FDI) and workers' remittances took on increasing importance in many developing countries. However, unlike private flows, official flows, particularly budget support, not

---

[3] It is important to note that policy-based lending/budget support has not been unambiguously successful in addressing corruption and other key public sector governance constraints, which have often been cited as key bottlenecks in increasing private investment in an economy.

[4] United Nations (2022).

[5] UNCTAD (2014).

[6] The pre-COVID-19 $2.5 trillion annual SDG financing gap corresponded to about $500 billion for low-income countries and $2 trillion for other developing countries (15% and 4% of GDP, respectively, of additional spending per year). According to new estimates, the gap to finance the SDGs is expected to increase during the post-pandemic period from $2.5 trillion per year to $3.9 trillion due to expected shortfalls in private finance (FDI, portfolio flows, etc.), in export revenues (including from international tourism), and in domestic tax revenues, as well as an emergency public spending response to the pandemic. See OECD (2021b) and OECD (2022).

only were countercyclical in nature but also provided an opportunity for policy dialogue on reforms in the recipient countries, complementing the provision of financing and technical assistance, for implementing the needed economic and institutional reforms.

Over the last three decades, the number of donors rose from fewer than twenty bilateral donors reporting to the Development Assistance Committee of the Organisation for Economic Co-operation and Development (OECD/DAC) to more than fifty in 2020.[7] Moreover, there was explosive growth in the number of agencies and other entities under these countries and institutions that provided official finance, from 191 to 502 during the same period.[8]

In addition, South–South cooperation initiatives grew (they tend to be less transparent and do not report on their activities regularly). Rather than increasing aid flows, however, this growth in the number of donors increased fragmentation, reduced coordination, and placed a heavier compliance burden on beneficiaries—in direct contravention of the pledge made by over one hundred countries in the Paris Declaration on Aid Effectiveness in 2005 to increase aid harmonization and alignment to reduce fragmentation and the compliance burden.

In this context, budget support by MDBs emerged with strong potential to play a greater role in addressing the multiple constraints facing developing economies, particularly lower-income countries. These countries had limited access to global financial markets, and the risk of a new debt crisis loomed, particularly in sub-Saharan Africa, before the pandemic and the food and fuel shocks. (Chapter 4 presents new results on the effectiveness of budget support in low-income countries.)

Setbacks in Financing and Development

The pandemic-led crisis of 2020–22 erased decades of development gains in a matter of months. Recent estimates by the World Bank indicate a sharp increase in global poverty, with nearly 90 million more people living on less than $2.15 (at 2017 purchasing parity prices, PPP) a day in 2022, raising the global extreme poverty rate by about 1 percentage point to 8.4 per cent.[9] As

---

[7] OECD (2021).
[8] Nishio and Tata (2021).
[9] World Bank (2022d).

a result of rising inflation worldwide, the pandemic, and the food and fuel crisis that resulted from the Russian invasion of Ukraine, have put the goal of reducing global extreme poverty to 3 percent by 2030 nearly out of reach.[10]

Both the development and financing setbacks in 2020 have been unprecedented in terms of magnitude and speed. In 2020, aggregate net external financial inflows, debt, and equity in low- and middle-income countries (excluding China) are estimated to have fallen by about $130 billion below their 2019 level and about $470 billion below their level in 2012. Total official and private net flows from the OECD (DAC members) to developing countries fell by $210 billion (entirely because of the collapse of net private flows at market terms) in 2020 compared with their levels in 2019,[11] although these flows are estimated to have recovered in 2021. Preliminary estimates indicate that net equity inflows to developing countries in 2021 rose by more than 30 per cent. However, much of this increase was concentrated in Asia and the other developing regions continued to experience net outflows of equity (portfolio) investments.

In this challenging context, actions by both private and public sector actors, including MDBs, are needed to better align investment decisions and their financing with what developing countries need to sustain growth, make their economies more resilient, and avoid the huge human costs that characterized the pandemic. Action must be taken by donors and MDBs to avoid a development finance collapse that would send millions of people back into poverty and further destabilize the development process, especially in low-income countries.

Agenda 2030—the international blueprint for achieving the SDGs—faced strong headwinds even before the pandemic. The slower than expected pace of progress for many goals mainly reflected excessive ambition, inadequate domestic and foreign resource mobilization, inadequate policies, and tightening of external financing conditions. Critical investments in sustainable infrastructure will not be made without heavy reliance on private capital. In the evolving global financial and aid architecture, private flows, particularly FDI, constitute the bulk of global resource flows to developing countries. Although private flows to developing countries, at the aggregate level, have remained stagnant since the Great Recession in 2008–09 (because of their procyclical nature and the multiple crisis that have griped the global economy), they continue to exceed official flows by a large margin. Nevertheless,

---

[10] According to the World Bank's revised projections, the global extreme poverty is likely to reach 7 percent (of the world population) by 2030, which is more than twice the pre—2020 estimate (3 percent). See World Bank (2022d).

[11] OECD (DAC) statistics on resource flows to developing countries, Table 2.3 Total Net Flows by DAC Country. https://www.oecd.org/dac/financing-sustainable-development/development-finance-data/statisticsonresourceflowstodevelopingcountries.htm

official aid and lending by multilateral institutions continue to play important roles in financing development projects and programmes, particularly in low-income countries.

Official Development Assistance in 2020–21

In 2020, foreign aid by DAC countries to the eligible developing countries[12] amounted to $162.6 billion, equivalent to 0.33 per cent of their combined gross national income (GNI) of the DAC donors.[13]

Based on preliminary data for 2021, ODA increased by 4.4 per cent in real terms over 2020 to an all-time high of $178.9 billon, equivalent to 0.33 per cent of the donor countries' GNI, the same as 2020 but well short of the 0.7 per cent of GNI target.[14,15] (Figure 2.1). Only a few donors met or exceeded the 0.7 per cent of GNI target, and only a few major donor countries have been using the budget support instrument actively.[16] (See Chapter 3 for more detailed analysis).

The increase in ODA in 2021 largely reflected donors' support for COVID-19 vaccines to developing countries, which amounted to $6.3 billion (3.5 per cent of total ODA).[17] Overall, DAC countries spent $18.7 billion in 2021, 10.5 per cent of their combined net ODA, on COVID-19-related activities.[18]

---

[12] DAC list of eligible countries to receive ODA in 2020: https://www.oecd.org/dac/financing-sustainable-development/development-finance-standards/DAC-List-of-ODA-Recipients-for-reporting-2020-flows.pdf

[13] This total included $158 billion in grants, loans to sovereign entities, debt relief, and contributions to multilateral institutions (calculated on a grant-equivalent basis); $1.3 billion in development-oriented private sector instruments; and $1.9 billion in net loans and equities to private companies operating in ODA-eligible countries. Total ODA in 2020 rose by 3.5 per cent in real terms over 2019.

[14] OECD-DAC (2022).

[15] In 1969, the Pearson Commission proposed a target of 0.7 per cent of donor GNP. This suggestion was taken up in a UN resolution in 1970. DAC members other than the United States accepted the 0.7 per cent target for ODA as a long-term objective. For official definition and coverage see https://www.oecd.org/dac/financing-sustainable-development/development-finance-standards/officialdevelopmentassistancedefinitionandcoverage.htm

[16] Germany, France, Japan, and South Korea, as well as the European Union, have been using the budget support instrument actively. The United States ($42.3 billion) and the United Kingdom ($15.8 billion), the largest and fourth-largest DAC donors, do not provide budget support in their aid-recipient countries.

[17] Some in the international donor community have criticized DAC's decision to include aid for vaccines in their aid budget. 'Donors have thrown out the rule book by counting vaccine donations in aid budgets', according to Oxfam (2022).

[18] OECD-DAC (2022).

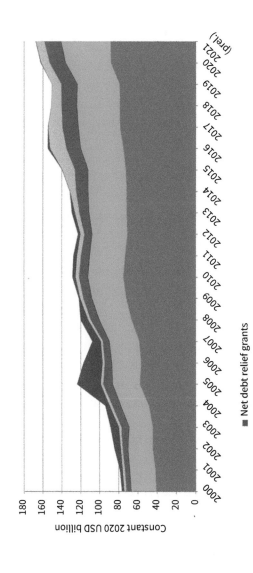

Figure 2.1 Official Development Assistance by DAC member countries, 2000–21 (constant 2020 US dollars, billions)

Source: OECD-DAC (2022). ODA Levels in 2021. Detailed Summary Note—Preliminary data for 2021. https://www. oecd.org/dac/financing-sustainable-development/development-finance-standards/ODA-2021-summary.pdf.

Financial Implications of the COVID-19 Pandemic

Although donors as a group have failed to meet their ODA commitments,[19] the continued increase in the aggregate level of ODA clearly demonstrates its role as a countercyclical source of development finance, particularly for poorer economies.[20] However, multilateral aid in 2021 rose significantly faster than bilateral aid and provided the bulk of the much-needed counter-cyclical financing to developing countries, including many middle-income countries. Nevertheless, critical SDG investments, such as sustainable infras-tructure (power, transport, telecommunication/digital, water and sanitation etc.), will not be made without heavy reliance on private capital.

In the evolving global financial and aid architecture, private investment constitutes the bulk of global resource flows to developing countries. As of 2019, cross-border greenfield investments[21] in SDG-related sectors in devel-oping countries is estimated to have reached about $134 billion a year,[22] and international project finance had risen to more than $178 billion a year. By comparison, total ODA by DAC countries averaged about $150 billion in 2018–19, with only a third of it devoted to investment projects. Combin-ing these public and private flows still falls far short of the SDG's ambitious investment requirements, underscoring the need for strengthening domestic resource mobilization, augmenting official flows, and incentivizing greater private investment.

While both cross-border greenfield investments and international project finance fell sharply in 2020 (by 30 per cent), they recovered in 2021. However, the recovery in both categories of the SDG-related investments were very uneven across sectors, with much of the recovery in the overall investment levels being heavily concentrated in renewable energy in emerging market economies.

Developing countries faced a large shortfall in financing of their balance of payments in 2020, because of the adverse impact of the pandemic shock on their own revenues, trade, and capital flows. At the same time, they needed to raise their investments by at least $1 trillion (to $3.9 trillion per year) over and above the existing target if they chose to stay on track for reaching their development goals, according to estimates (OECD 2020b; OECD 2022).

---

[19] Donors as a group have not been able to meet their commitments (0.7 per cent of GNI), including to least developed countries, for example, the distribution of COVID-19 vaccines to the poorest countries has been inadequate. Ibid.

[20] United Nations (2022).

[21] Greenfield investment refers to a form of foreign direct investment where a parent company starts a new venture in a foreign country by constructing new operational facilities.

[22] UNCTAD (2022a, 2022b).

The net non-debt creating private inflow to developing countries (excluding China) fell by about $126 billion in 2020 compared to its level in 2019. The drop in net FDI inflows (excluding China) to these countries is estimated to have been about 26 per cent in 2020. The decline in net private inflows, both FDI and portfolio investments, to low-income counties was similarly large. Preliminary estimates of FDI inflows to developing countries indicate a strong recovery of about 38 per cent in 2021.

However, the global environment for international business and cross-border investment changed dramatically in 2022 with the Russian invasion of Ukraine. The war impacted the global economy, causing a food, fuel, and financial crisis, with rising inflation and worsening of debt problems in many developing countries. The increased uncertainty, which is in part resulting from global supply chain disruptions due to the flare-up of the pandemic in China, as well as tightening of monetary conditions in advanced economies, put significant downward pressures on FDI inflows to developing countries in 2022.[23] The continuing relative importance of private financial flows, the high volatility of such flows, and their procyclical nature have exposed a major weakness in the aid architecture: During global recessions, private inflows to developing countries typically collapse exactly when they are needed most. The pandemic is also putting downward pressures on concessional development aid from advanced economies to low-income countries, as a result of tightening of financial conditions and a possible recession in a number of advanced economies in 2023.

The Debt Problem

In 2020, global debt rose by 28 percentage points of GDP, the largest increase since the Second World War, increasing the global public debt ratio to just below 100 per cent of GDP. Although the sharp increase reflected the fiscal policy responses of governments around the world to the COVID-19 pandemic, there had been a sustained increase in government and private debt over last 10 years, in response to series of shocks, facilitated by abnormally low interest rates as a result of highly accommodative monetary policies in the United States, the European Union, and Japan (Figure 2.2).[24]

The composition of debt in developing countries has changed significantly, which, according to a recent assessment by the International Monetary Fund (IMF) and the World Bank, has made these countries more vulnerable to

---

[23] UNCTAD (2022b).
[24] IMF and World Bank (2022).

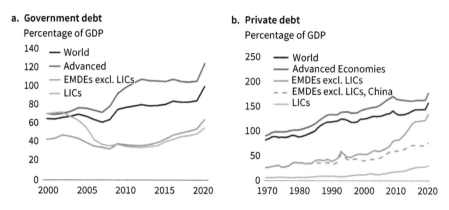

a. **Government debt**

Percentage of GDP

— World
— Advanced
— EMDEs excl. LICs
— LICs

b. **Private debt**

Percentage of GDP

— World
— Advanced Economies
— EMDEs excl. LICs
- - EMDEs excl. LICs, China
— LICs

Figure 2.2   Government and private debt, 2000–20

Source: IMF and World Bank (2022).
Note: EMDEs = Emerging Market and Developing Economies; LICs = Low-Income Countries.

financial market volatility.[25] The composition of public sector debt has shifted away from multilateral and Paris Club bilateral creditors toward bondholders, commercial banks, and non–Paris Club bilateral creditors, particularly China. In an increasing number of low-income countries, government debt is non-concessional.

According to the World Bank (2022b), the share of short-term debt in the total external debt of developing countries reached 38 per cent in 2021, and the share of long-term non-guaranteed private debt rose from less than 30 per cent during the global financial crisis to 44 per cent in 2021. Although much of this increase has been concentrated in higher-income countries, low- and middle-income countries also experienced sharp increases in private indebtedness.

The rise in private sector debt represents a potentially large contingent liability on the balance sheets of public sectors in these countries, with the extent of vulnerability varying across countries. Given the massive global and regional development challenges, global development finance is in need of serious reforms to ensure its resilience in the face of the high volatility of private flows during global cyclical downturns.

The COVID-19 shock has exacerbated debt trends aground the world. Global debt across all sectors reached $255 trillion in early 2020, 40 per cent higher than at the start of the 2008–9 financial crisis. Debt growth was fuelled mainly by private sector debt in developed economies; developing countries experienced an increase in both public and private borrowing (UN 2022).

[25] Ibid.

Lending from private creditors was the fastest-growing component of the external debt of developing countries, resulting in the stock of long-term external private debt (including non-guaranteed private debt) to increase by more than 110 per cent between 2010 and 2021. By comparison developing countries' stock of long-term external official debt rose by 50 per cent during the same period (World Bank 2022b). Before the onset of the pandemic, thirty-six of seventy low-income countries and some middle-income countries were already at high risk of—or already in—debt distress. The pandemic put pressure on public finances, as a result of both additional spending needs and dwindling revenues. As of early 2021, many countries had announced unprecedented discretionary fiscal support measures. Debt-financed discretionary fiscal policy measures helped advanced economies address the health crisis and contain the adverse economic consequences of the pandemic in 2020–21. Many developing countries, however, faced tight financing constraints that inhibited necessary fiscal responses in the absence of external financial support.

The Role of Multilateral Development Banks in Financing Investments

MDBs have been playing an increasingly important role in developing countries, particularly since the global financial crisis of 2008–9. They have supported low-income countries partly by front-loading concessional resources, particularly in response to the COVID-19 shock, with a significant portion of lending routed through fast-disbursing budget support. The non-concessional lending windows of MDBs have also been providing an important financing alternative for middle-income countries, by enabling them to access long-term finance at below market interest rates.

However, financial capacity constraints are limiting MDB support for middle-income countries, as recent capital increases have proved inadequate in the face of large adverse shocks at the global level.[26] Strengthening MDBs' financial capacity is critical for providing predictable countercyclical support at highly concessional terms in times of crisis, as well as for supporting developing countries in mitigating global risks, such as climate change, infectious diseases, and financial crisis.

One way that some MDBs have tried to expand their financial support to developing countries to help them meet their investment needs is through the

---

[26] The US Secretary of Treasury Janet Yellen has urged MDBs to bolster their lending to help deliver the needed financing to tackle multiple global crisis. Doing so, however, may require that they relax their capital requirements to boost their lending; see Yellen (2022).

use of guarantees.[27] Guarantees by MDBs have helped mobilize private capital to finance the investments developing countries need to meet their development goals. Despite some success, however, efforts have fallen short of ambitious targets, and a substantial portion of the private financing mobilized by MDBs has gone to middle- and upper-middle-income countries. Low-income countries have seen very few infrastructure transactions supported by private finance. Moreover, investment in infrastructure projects with private participation in developing countries has been volatile. In sub-Saharan Africa, for example, both the number of infrastructure projects and the value invested fell in recent years, declining from a peak of $15 billion in 2012 to about $6.4 billion in 2019, before recovering to $9.4 billion in 2020.[28] However, preliminary data indicate a significant decline in 2021 and in the first half of 2022 (World Bank 2022e).

Financial Policy Response to the Pandemic

Global financial conditions, which had eased in 2021, became increasingly volatile in early 2022, following the Russian invasion of Ukraine. By then, only about half of emerging market economies and developing countries were experiencing economic recovery from their deep recession caused by the pandemic. Many developing countries were still experiencing capital outflows, which forced them to increase their borrowing. To help the most vulnerable countries, international financial institutions responded with emergency measures.

During 2020–21, accommodative monetary policy support in advanced economies helped provide additional liquidity to developing countries. It was supplemented with continued fund flows and bond purchases by middle-income countries and some low-income countries. Official lending, including lending by MDBs and financial support by the IMF—including its Rapid Financing Instrument (RFIs) and Rapid Credit Facility (RCFs) loans,[29] the

---

[27] In this chapter, guarantees are defined as financial instruments used by MDBs (and other development financial institutions) to reduce the private sector project cost of funds by reducing risk by providing standby funding where the availability of such funds is contingent on well-defined low-probability but high-impact adverse events occurring. Every MDB defines its guaranteed instruments, their coverage, pricing, and use differently. The World Bank defines a guarantee as an instrument that helps member countries mobilize commercial financing for projects and policies with a clear and defined development impact. This definition follows that of the OECD, which identifies mobilization of private funds for investment purposes as the critical goal of all blended finance, defined as the strategic use of development finance, particularly guarantees by MDBs.

[28] Lee and Gonzalez (2022).

[29] For information on the IMF's rapid financing instruments, see https://www.imf.org/en/About/Factsheets/Sheets/2016/08/02/21/08/Rapid-Credit-Facility

Debt Service Suspension Initiative (DSSI), and the more recent IMF allocation of Special Drawing Rights (SDRs)—helped provide liquidity support to developing countries, including many low-income countries.

Both low- and middle-income countries benefited from MDB countercyclical support during the pandemic. Concessional loans by MDBs (net disbursements basis) rose sharply in 2020 and 2021 from their 2019 level of $16.6 billion, to $30.9 billion and $21.9 billion, respectively. For example, net disbursements by the World Bank Group's International Development Association (IDA) in 2020 amounted to $15.4 billion, a 21 per cent increase compared to the previous year, with about 24 per cent as fast-disbursing budget support operations,[30] and the IMF's Poverty Reduction and Growth Trust provided SDR 12.4 billion in new PRGT lending during 2020–21, which was substantially higher than its SDR 2.4 lending in 2019.[31]

The IDA, the concessional lending arm of the World Bank, accounted for 55 per cent of all MDB concessional lending in 2020–21. Non-concessional loan disbursements by MDBs rose by more than 33 per cent to about $85 billion in 2020, which accounted for much of their support for developing countries. MDB lending increased significantly in the public sector—particularly health and social protection—and the financial sector. MDB non-concessional lending provided a critical financing window to many middle-income countries that were unable to access private capital markets in the aftermath of the pandemic.

In general, there was greater uptake of MDBs' 'unconditional' loans and credits than of loans with conditions. World Bank budget support, which initially was disbursed mostly through supplemental lending associated with ongoing operations, contained conditionality later on.[32] In contrast, the Asian Development Bank provided unrestricted budget support through its COVID-19 pandemic response window.[33] Despite a slow start, however, the World Bank Group delivered more than $200 billion in financial support (gross disbursement) to public and private sector clients during 2020–21 in response to the pandemic. Of this amount, about $135 billion was disbursed by the World Bank, including IDA $60 billion by the International Finance Corporation (IFC), and $9 billion by Multilateral Investment Guarantee Agency (MIGA).

---

[30] IDA FY21 (2021).
[31] IMF (2022).
[32] UN (2022); and Landers and Rakan Aboneaaj (2021). In Chapter 4, it is shown that budget support can be used to support economic reform in times of crisis, and that budget support may be more successful in times of crisis.
[33] ADB (2021).

From the start of the pandemic to the end of 2021, the IMF approved approximately US$170 billion in new financing, of which about 70 per cent were flexible credit/precautionary and liquidity lines, covering 90 countries. IMF assistance to low-income countries totalled approximately $23.9 billion, covering fifty-five countries.[34,35]

Increasing Lending by MDBs by Optimizing Their Balance Sheets

The non-concessional lending windows of MDBs have been providing an important financing alternative for middle-income countries by enabling them to access long-term finance at below market interest rates. This financing is critical to building back better and stimulating growth and development. However, the financial capacity constraints of MDBs are limiting support for middle-income countries. Strengthening MDB financial capacity is critical for providing predictable countercyclical support at concessional terms needed in times of global or regional crises, particularly through budget support that provides quick-disbursing fiscal support and can help advance policy reform (see Chapter 4) and meeting future development challenges due to global risks (see Chapter 6).

The need for MDB intervention is greater than ever, because the COVID-19 pandemic (and more recently the Russian invasion of Ukraine) substantially reduced the volume of private financial flows to developing countries. MDB guarantees and associated vehicles could play a growing role in mobilizing private capital by de-risking well-targeted sustainable investments in developing countries. Guarantees by MDBs have proven to be a more powerful leveraging instrument than other instruments, such as co-financing, syndicated loans, shares in Collective Investment Vehicles (CIVs),[36] and credit lines in mobilizing private capital. Their wider use, however, has been hampered by both supply and demand constraints.

Given the potential high demand for MDB lending, the G20 agreed to an action plan on 'balance sheet optimization' in 2015 to increase MDB lending.[37] Adopting more flexible criteria—such as lower equity-to-loan ratios, including the callable capital of shareholders in capital adequacy calculations or possibly managing diversification across the entire balance sheet as called

---

[34] IMF (2021).
[35] IMF (2022).
[36] Pooled investments offered to private, institutional, and individual investors. https://en.wikipedia.org/wiki/Investment_fund
[37] G20 (2015).

for in the Addis Ababa Agenda (2015)—could more than double MDBs' lending volumes. In this context, the G20 commissioned an independent review of the capital adequacy frameworks of MDBs, which is scheduled to be completed in 2022. The recommendations of the review could become the basis for game-changing reforms of the MDB business model, by allowing a significant scaling up of their lending capacities without causing a significant increase in their borrowing costs.

For its part, the IMF extended debt service relief to the twenty-nine poorest countries and supported the G20's efforts to provide debt relief through the Debt Service Suspension Initiative (DSSI),[38] which allows seventy-three low-income developing countries to temporarily suspend payments of debt service to their bilateral official creditors. As of early 2022, forty-eight of seventy-three eligible countries had participated in the initiative. This programme delivered an estimated $13 billion in debt-service suspension from May 2020 to December 2021.[39] A fiscal assessment showed that the DSSI helped countries respond to the pandemic, as it was complemented by additional financing provided by the World Bank Group, the IMF, and other MDBs.[40]

China's Emergence as a Global Lender and Investor

According to a recent comprehensive study,[41] China has emerged as one of the largest official creditors to developing countries, with more than $350 billion in official finance committed to developing countries between 2000 and 2014. Although China's investment and lending activities cover virtually all sectors in all developing regions, its most visible—and the largest—set of investment and lending activities have been through its Belt and Road Initiative (BRI), amounting to more than $1 trillion cumulatively.

By the end of 2020, total outstanding public external debt of developing countries owed to China (as an official bilateral creditor) in countries eligible under the debt service suspension initiative (DSSI) increased by $5 billion from $105 billion in 2019 to $110 billion in 2020. The largest increases in outstanding public external debt to MDBs, from 2019 to 2020 were with the IMF ($18.3 billion), the World Bank ($17.1 billion), the Asian Development Bank (US$6.1 billion).

Moreover, China was the biggest single creditor in seventeen of the DSSI countries, and about 26 per cent of the total debt service paid by the DSSI

---

[38] See https://www.worldbank.org/en/topic/debt/brief/debt-service-suspension-initiative-qas
[39] Paris Club creditors accounted for less than $5 billion of the total amount suspended. See https://www.worldbank.org/en/topic/debt/brief/debt-service-suspension-initiative-qas
[40] IMF and World Bank (2021); IMF and World Bank (2022).
[41] Dreher, Fuchs, Parks, Strange, and Tierney (2022)

countries in 2022 would go to China as compared to 17 per cent to bond-holders, and 9 per cent to the World Bank-IDA.[42] China, as the largest bilateral creditor, had deferred payments that amounted to about 37 per cent of the total deferred payments of US$5.7 billion under the DSSI. China has promised to redistribute $10 billion (or 23 per cent of its allocation) of the IMF SDRs, mainly to African countries.[43]

New SDR Allocations

As of mid-2021, the IMF had made its largest allocation of SDRs since their inception, in 1969, amounting to about $650 billion. This financing injected additional liquidity into the global financial system, supplementing countries' foreign reserves and reducing their reliance on more expensive domestic or external debt. The SDR allocations will help step up international financial institutions' response to the pandemic and the Ukraine war. To magnify its impact, policymakers in the international developing community have been advocating voluntary transfers of a portion of the SDRs from countries with strong external buffers, such as a strong international reserve position, to countries in need.

Budget support combined with guarantees, in the form of policy-based guarantees,[44] can play an important role, because it transfers resources more efficiently than other types of support, addresses institutional dimensions of sustainable development, supports global public goods, and helps mobilize private funds (Box 2.1). (Chapter 4 discusses the evidence indicating that budget support can be successful in supporting policy reforms; Chapter 6 discusses this topic in the context of longer-term development challenges).

Box 2.1   New allocations of Special Drawing Rights and their potential use

---

SDRs are an international type of monetary reserve currency created by the IMF in 1969 that operate as a supplement to the international foreign exchange reserves of the Fund's member countries. The value of an SDR is based on a basket of the world's five leading currencies—the US dollar, the euro, the Chinese yuan, the

---

[42] Green Finance and Development Center (2022).
[43] Ibid.
[44] Independent Evaluation Group (2016).

Japanese yen, and the British pound. The SDR is an accounting unit for IMF transactions with member countries and a stable asset in countries' international reserves. It is a way of supplementing Fund member countries' foreign exchange reserves, allowing members to reduce their reliance on more expensive domestic or external debt for building reserves. SDRs provide liquidity support to many developing and low-income countries that are financially struggling,

SDR allocations are distributed in proportion to countries' participation in the IMF's capital, which is closely related to the size of their economies. There have been three general allocations. The most recent was in 2009, during the global financial crisis, when the IMF allocated the equivalent of $250 billion in new SDRs to its members. This allocation is widely seen as having contributed to stabilizing financial conditions around the world.

Of a possible $650 billion SDR, the latest allocation, an estimated $274 billion would be allocated to developing countries, a 10 per cent boost to their international reserves. Low-income countries would receive about $21 billion. An SDR allocation is cost-free. Allocating SDRs does not require contributions from donor countries' budgets. SDRs are a reserve asset, not foreign aid. An SDR allocation does not add to a country's public debt burden. From the start of the pandemic in early 2020 to the end of 2021, the IMF has mobilized some $20 billion in SDRs which were voluntarily pledged by some members. These funds were lent to low-income countries at zero interest rate.

On 13 April 2022, the Executive Board of the IMF approved the establishment of the Resilience and Sustainability Trust (RST), with effect from 1 May 2022. The RST will complement the IMF's existing lending toolkit by focusing on longer-term structural challenges—including climate change and pandemic preparedness—that entail significant macroeconomic risks and where policy solutions have a strong global public good nature. It will channel SDRs contributed by countries with strong external positions to countries in which the needs are greatest, providing policy support and affordable longer-term financing to strengthen members' resilience and sustainability and thereby contributing to prospective balance-of-payments stability.

The RST will be a loan-based trust, with resources mobilized on a voluntary basis. About 75 per cent of the Fund's membership will be eligible for longer-term affordable financing from the RST. This funding will likely compete with policy-based lending/budget support by MDBs. Access will be based on countries' reforms and debt sustainability considerations and capped at the lower of 150 per cent of quota or SDR 1 billion. The loans will have a twenty-year maturity and a ten-and-a-half-year grace period, with borrowers paying an interest rate with a small margin over the three-month SDR rate, with the most concessional financing terms provided to the poorest countries. The RST is likely to commence lending operations in 2022 Fundraising toward the estimated total resource needs of about SDR 33 billion (equivalent to US$45 billion) will be initiated before the end of 2022. Countries with an excess of SDRs that lend to developing countries through the trust will end up with the holdings again when the loan is repaid.

Source: IMF (2022). 'Proposal to Establish a Resilience and Sustainability Trust'. IMF Policy Paper, April. Washington, DC.

The Role of Private Investment in Financing Development

Capital raised from the private sector has been critical in financing a significant portion of developing countries' investments, according to the United Nations.[45] MDBs' mobilization efforts received a boost in 2015 from the Paris Agreement, in which MDBs pledged to support the mobilization of $100 billion a year by advanced countries by 2020 to counter climate change (African Development Bank et al. 2015).

In 2017, MDBs issued a joint statement following the G20 meetings in Hamburg in which they committed to increase private sector mobilization by 25–30 per cent in order to boost infrastructure investment in developing countries by 2020 (G20 2017). In 2018, the G20 Eminent Persons Group endorsed the Hamburg Principles (G20 2018).[46] A key proposal was 're-orienting MDBs' business models to focus on risk mitigation', through instruments such as 'first-loss guarantees, and co-investments to catalyze private investment'.[47]

Financing by MDBs and national development finance institutions, which together averaged about $200 billion a year since 2015, is not nearly sufficient to meet the investment needs of all low- and middle-income developing countries, where the financing gap in infrastructure, health, and education is massive.[48] These investments cannot occur unless their effectiveness and

---

[45] United Nations (2022).

[46] The Principles of MDBs Strategy for Crowding-in Private Sector Finance for Growth and Sustainable Development (henceforth the Hamburg Principles) provide a common framework for MDBs to increase levels of private investment in support of development. Based on their experience to date in working with the private sector, the MDBs agreed to focus their efforts on three main areas: 1) strengthening investment capacity and policy frameworks at national and subnational levels; 2) enhancing private sector involvement and prioritizing commercial sources of financing; and 3) enhancing the catalytic role of MDBs themselves.

[47] G20 Eminent Persons Group (2018).

[48] Infrastructure spending alone would need to more than double in developing countries, from its recent level of less than $1 trillion to more than $2 trillion a year (UNCTAD 2014). A more recent estimate of the required infrastructure investment in developing countries puts the figure at $1.6 trillion per year by 2030, with about 70 per cent by the private sector (OECD, 2022).

efficiency improve, through structural reforms and improvements in the business climate, where policy-based lending by MDBs and other official donors can play a critical role.

Governments have used some of the concessional resources at their disposal to mobilize private funds directly, by blending instruments with either guarantees or subsidies. However, this approach has been available mainly to middle-income countries.[49] A report by the OECD (2018b) concludes that guarantees have proved to be the most powerful instrument in mobilizing (leveraging in) private finance, followed by syndicated loans and direct investment in companies (OECD DAC 2020).

Private sector investment in infrastructure has grown in a number of developing countries since the early 1990s. Continued private sector–led growth, however, is likely to be constrained by a number of factors, particularly the increased risk aversion of domestic and international investors and financiers in the aftermath of the global financial crisis and the worldwide recession as a result of the COVID-19 pandemic.

Since 2015, MDBs have played an important role in a number of cases, not only by providing financing for infrastructure directly but also by creating and providing financing instruments that 'de-risk' or better allocate risks between creditors and borrowers. Over time, MDBs can also help mitigate informational deficiencies facing the private sector, by providing screening, evaluation, monitoring, and, where needed, their own capital, partnering with private investors in co-financing. MDBs can also help better address the development needs of low-income as well as middle-income countries, by providing them with concessional resources.

The MDBs and the OECD are developing new methodologies for measuring and assessing the leveraging effects of de-risking instruments (through alternative and possibly more accurate measurement of both the direct and the indirect effects of mobilizing private funds) and related financing vehicles. Discussions are ongoing in the international development community concerning the mobilization of resources. The MDBs have developed their own approach. They have been following a coordinated reporting on their mobilization efforts through the International Finance Corporation (IFC 2019).[50]

In 2016, the G20 asked the MDGs to find ways to optimize their balance sheets in a coordinated manner, in order to enable them to substantially

---

[49] This definition follows that of the OECD, which identifies mobilization of private funds for investment purposes as the critical goal of all blended finance, defined as the strategic use of development finance, particularly guarantees by MDBs (and/or other development finance institutions) for the mobilization of additional (commercial) finance toward sustainable development in developing countries.

[50] In 2021, the World Bank Group's Independent Evaluation Group (IEG) conducted its first systematic assessment of the institution's approaches to mobilizing private capital to achieve development outcomes by engaging with investors and project sponsors. The evaluation found that private capital mobilization approaches have been relevant to both country and corporate clients, albeit only partially meeting

enhance their ability to leverage additional private sector funding without adversely affecting their credit ratings.[51] Their response was the 'billions to trillions agenda' (Box 2.2).

Box 2.2   From billions to trillions: Mobilizing private capital to support the SDGs

In 2015, six MDBs (the African Development Bank, the Asian Development Bank, the European Bank for Reconstruction and Development, the European Investment Bank, the Inter-American Development Bank, and the World Bank Group) and the IMF issued a report entitled *From Billions to Trillions: Transforming Development Finance*. In it, they committed 'to promote and catalyze private investment, addressing risk and uncertainty, helping to mobilize and scale up resources and co-investment from traditional, institutional and other public and private investors'.

A 2017 report for the Development Committee of the World Bank Group and the IMF presented the concept of 'maximizing finance for development', echoing the shift set out in *Forward Look: A Vision for the World Bank Group for 2030*. It introduced the "cascade" approach, which emphasizes the use of private finance for infrastructure investments whenever possible, and argues for focusing on the quality—and ultimately impact—of development finance rather than only its quantity. It also proposed making better use of the interactions of the various actors and sources of finance for sustainable development—by, for example, creating incentives for channelling remittances toward productive investment rather than final consumption, thereby creating opportunities for new economic linkages between local firms and broadening the tax base in the receiving countries. Actions by different players, from

---

investors' expectations. It also found the mobilization approaches are most effective in mobilizing private capital and points to the untapped mobilization potential that still exists even in low-income and lower-middle income countries. The evaluation also highlights gaps in the Bank's mobilization targets, which 'have not cascaded to' all regional units and global practices within the institution. The report's key recommendations include the need to expand private capital mobilization platforms, guarantees, and disaster risk management products commensurate with project pipeline development, develop new guarantee products, and improve their alignment with the risk appetite and needs of new investor groups and partners. See IEG (2021).

[51] Participants at the Third International Conference on Financing for Development, held in Addis Ababa in July 2015, recognized that the financial resources needed to achieve the SDGs far exceeded current financial flows. In adopting the Hamburg Principles, in 2016, the G20 countries welcomed the role of the MDBs in mobilizing and catalysing private capital and endorsed a target of increasing mobilization by 25–35 per cent by 2020. The mobilization report, coordinated by the IFC, documents the private investment mobilized through direct and indirect channels. As defined by the G20 International Financial Architecture Working Group in the 'Principles of MDBs' Strategy for Crowding-In Private Sector Finance for Growth and Sustainable Development' (April 2017), 'private investment catalyzed' is private sector financing that results from an activity or activities of an MDB that have a development impact. It includes investments made as a result of an operation up to three years after completion.

finance providers to regulators, are required to facilitate the mobilization of private financing for domestic investments.

Upscaling from billions of dollars of support to trillions is challenging, particularly given the current economic and financial difficulties in developing countries and globally. A study by the Overseas Development Institute (2019) argues that doing so is unrealistic, that the goal should instead be billions to a few more billions. Inadequate macroeconomic policies and poor business climates in many recipient countries present additional challenges for the private funding of the needed investments.

Shifting from billions to more billions is a far more realistic goal, particularly given the post-pandemic global recession. The global economy has the financing needed to support sustainable development; it needs to be better targeted to sustainable and inclusive growth. For example, governments spend some $450 billion a year on fossil fuel subsidies. These subsidies contribute to environmental damage that far exceeds the value of this subsidy. Shifting the fuel subsidy to more sustainable uses would have a huge positive effect on sustainable development.

Source: African Development Bank et al. (2015); IFC (2019); World Bank (2018).

In a typical year, global savings/investible funds exceed estimated SDG financing requirements by a substantial margin. By end-2021, global financial assets amounted to $486 trillion, 7.7 per cent higher than a year earlier. Financial intermediaries such as banks, asset managers, and institutional investors own and manage a rising share of these assets (Financial Stability Board 2022). Investments in the SDGs constitute a very small portion of investments by long-term institutional investors (OECD 2020a).

According to OECD-DAC, less than 20 per cent of global financial assets are held by institutions in countries eligible for ODA, and only about 7.5–8.0 per cent of total global assets (about $36 trillion) include some 'sustainability measurement' in their investment decisions—an SDG-related criteria that requires sustainability of investment impact.[52] Only about 10 per cent of these assets also seek to measure impact (OECD 2020a). Total global assets amount to 220 times the amount needed to bridge the investment gap facing developing countries; less than 1 per cent qualifies as investments in SDGs.

Demand for financing the SDGs competes with demand for other types of financing. Investments in global supplies of fossil fuels (about $800 billion a year, including about $100 billion a year investments in coal, mainly by China

[52] For a definition of sustainability measurement, see OECD (2017).

and India), for example, was about twice the level of investments in renewable power in 2019–2020 (International Energy Agency 2022). The case for financing SDG-related needs and its expected rising share in total investable funds must be established in a clear and transparent manner.

A global investment-related financing gap exists partly because of the perceived high risks of investments, including SDG-related investments, in developing countries, because of weak institutions, poor policies, and relatively high cost of doing business. These financing challenges must be met by improving investment climate in developing countries, mobilizing more domestic and international financial resources, increasing the supply of funds, and remedying market failures by redirecting resources toward unsatisfied demand.

Doing so may require better structuring of the financing market, by increasing transparency and efficiency to avoid asymmetry of information and other market failures and providing policy incentives to guide savings toward financing investments in developing countries.

Recognizing this need, international donors have increasingly focused on new and innovative financial instruments to support private sector investments in developing countries. Impact investing appears both as a market-led trend on international financial markets and as a channel to stimulate international donors' efforts.

The Changing Aid Landscape

The funding landscape of multilateral organizations evolved over the last two decades, as the sources of funding available to them and their relative importance changed. ODA financing from DAC countries still accounts for a large portion of funding for most multilateral development organizations, but other sources are emerging or growing in importance. The most important among them are China and other large emerging economies, the private sector, philanthropy, and new multilateral organizations.

The evolution of these new sources of funding will have important implications for the funding of the development agencies of the UN system; MDBs, including the World Bank; and vertical funds, such as the Global Fund to Fight AIDS, Tuberculosis and Malaria and the Global Alliance for Vaccines and Immunization (GAVI).[53] These institutions receive 50–60 per cent of

---

[53] https://en.wikipedia.org/wiki/The_Global_Fund_to_Fight_AIDS,_Tuberculosis_and_Malaria

the ODA resources that are channelled through the multilateral development system (Gartner and Kharas 2013).

Multilateral development financing has changed in the following ways in recent years (OECD 2018; Kharas and Dooley 2021):

- ODA by DAC countries has been growing slowly; at 0.33 per cent, it remains substantially below the target of 0.7 per cent of donor countries' GNI, although it remains the largest source of funding for international development. As of 2017–18, ODA accounted for more than 60 per cent of total funding for the United Nations' development programmes, about 30 per cent of contributions to the International Development Association (IDA) (the part of the World Bank that serves low-income countries), and more than 80 per cent of funding for the Global Fund.
- Contributions by nontraditional donors, such as China, South Korea, Brazil, India, and some oil-exporting countries, such as Saudi Arabia and the United Arab Emirates have reduced IDA's dependence on a few top donors.
- The vertical funds, which have been increasing their contributions to the concessional windows in MDBs, to about $6.5 billion a year, remain heavily focused on the health sector and dependent on a few top donors (such as the Bill & Melinda Gates Foundation).
- China has emerged as a leading donor. Starting with the 18th Replenishment of IDA (IDA18), in 2016–17, it has become one of IDA's top funders. It has increased engagement with and its influence on some MDBs, including the Asian Development Bank and the World Bank, and played a key role in establishing initiatives such as the G20 Global Infrastructure Connectivity Alliance and the G20 Initiative in Supporting Industrialization in Africa and LDCs. It has substantially increased its contributions to the UN development system. China's foreign aid (on grant basis), including its contributions to the UN system, is estimated to have averaged between $5.5 to $6.5 billion a year in 2014–19.
- Financing innovations through new lending instruments and financial vehicles, including guarantees (discussed later in this chapter and in Chapter 3), have allowed private finance to play a more active role in raising funds in support of the multilateral development system. Some of these innovations are incentivizing private funding to expand the lending capacity of MDBs, such as IDA, and to increase earmarking for the UN development system.

- The private sector; philanthropies, including vertical funds; and non-governmental organizations remain a small part of the funding of the UN development system (contributing less than 10 per cent in 2019).[54] Unmanaged funding, especially from corporations, can lead to fragmentation and misalignment of resources. According to recent estimates based on a survey (OECD 2021), private philanthropy for development from more than two hundred foundations, amounted to $42.5 billion between 2016 and 2019, or about $10.5 billion a year.
- Multilateral organizations, including the European Union, have become increasingly important funders to the multilateral development system. However, the growing number of agencies providing ODA has led to fragmentation, higher compliance costs, and greater differentiation among actors. This is particularly true for vertical funds and large global trust funds.
- South-led development funds—such as the China South–South Cooperation Assistance Fund, the India–Brazil–South Africa Facility for Poverty and Hunger Alleviation (IBSA), and the India–United Nations Development Partnership Fund—have been active in combatting COVID-19. South-led regional and subregional development banks are also playing an important role. The Central American Bank for Economic Integration allocated nearly $2 billion for emergency aid and regional purchases of medicines and medical equipment. The Andean Development Bank provided emergency credit lines of up to $2.5 billion. The Caribbean Development Bank and the Southern Common Market (MERCOSUR) scaled up finances and opened credit lines. The AIIB made $5–$10 billion available under its COVID-19 Crisis Recovery Facility.
- Since the 1990s, special purpose funds have proliferated. The Global Environment Facility (GEF) was created in 1991 (see Chapter 6). It was followed in the 2000s by the establishment of GAVI and the Global Fund. The Green Climate Fund (GCF) was launched in 2010. It is intended to be the primary vehicle for channelling the $100 billion pledged to developing countries under the United Nations Framework Convention on Climate Finance (UNFCCC). Following its first pledging conference, in 2014, it became one of the largest vertical funds. In 2016, it received $1.7 billion in ODA financing. As of end-2021, the

---

[54] Dag Hammarskjöld Foundation and UN Multi-Partner Trust Fund Office (2021).

GCF had disbursed $2.3 billion to projects during the year and $6.7 billion in projects under implementation across the world (GCF 2022).

- As a result of the rising economic power of China and other emerging economies, new multilateral organizations have been established that are not dependent on traditional donors. They include the Corporación Andina de Fomento (CAF); the Asian Infrastructure Investment Bank (AIIB), created in 2015 under China's leadership, with members from both developed and developing economies; and the New Development Bank, established in 2015 by the BRICs (Brazil, Russia, India, China, and South Africa).

- Non-DAC[55] countries are increasing their contributions to the multilateral system, although their share remains relatively small. Their combined contributions account for about 5 per cent of the total funding of the UN development system and about 2 per cent for IDA. They account for about 1 per cent of contributions to the Global Fund.

Some new (or growing) sources of funding represent new forms of designated funding (earmarking) that could challenge the ability of the multilateral development system to deliver a unified development agenda. The practice of earmarking contributions through the multilateral development system has gained considerable traction since the 1990s through the multilateral development system of the UN. Many DAC members employ a mix of funding approaches, including earmarking their support the multilateral system. As of 2021, earmarked funds by DAC members, mainly supporting humanitarian programmes, reached $24.9 billion, which was less than its level in 2017 ($25.1 billion), despite escalating levels of need, particularly in 2020–21 due to the pandemic and the massive increase in the number of refugees as a result of the Russian invasion of Ukraine in 2022.

In the context of stagnating donor resources and substantial financing needs to overcome the development challenges and to help developing countries make progress towards their ambitious development agenda, development finance institutions need to broaden their funding base and try to access alternative sources of financing. However, additional funding resources should align with the mandates of the multilateral organizations and developing countries' needs. Moreover, safeguards may be needed, especially for private sources of funding.

---

[55] Non-DAC donors includes several oil and gas exporters, as well as Brazil, China, Hungary, India Israel, Latvia, etc.

Impact Investing

Impact investing—investment by the private sector that seeks to generate socially desirable results in addition to financial returns—increased substantially over the last decade. These investments are now being viewed as contributing to the investments needed to meet the new development challenges facing low- and middle-income countries the Together, official and private sources of funding investments in developing countries—through risk-sharing instruments, such as guarantees by MDBs or bilateral aid agencies—could blend external inflows with their own domestically mobilized resources to finance the SDG-related investments. Impact investing has emerged as a potential bridge between the financing requirements of the SDGs and ODA in low-income countries.

Impact investing has proven to be fairly resilient to adverse shocks, particularly compared with FDI and portfolio investment inflows into developing countries (OECD 2021; Kharas and Rivard 2022). The OECD estimates that about 4 to 4.5 per cent of total global finance assets (of about $486 trillion as of end-2021) meets environment, social, and governance (ESG) criteria. Of these assets, only about $500 billion are from impact investing funds (OECD 2020a).[56] Although impact investing in developing countries is increasing, a substantial portion of these investments have been flowing to advanced and emerging market economies. Impact investing in developing countries is estimated to represent less than 5 per cent of total net flows (or between $20 to $25 billion a year) to developing countries in 2019–20.[57]

Private Foundations

Private philanthropy is another dynamic player taking part in reshaping the development landscape. Private foundations are playing an increasingly prominent role by providing targeted resources and support to many communities worldwide.[58] Their support for developing countries increased from about $6 billion in 2013 to $8.2 billion in 2019. Over 205 foundations participated in the OECD-DAC survey of Private Philanthropy for Development, which resulted in an up-to-date database on contributors, with grants and

---

[56] An alternative methodology, used by the Global Impact Investing Network (GIIN) based on its survey of about 1,700 impact investors, indicates a significantly larger impact investing market, of about $715 billion in 2020.

[57] Kharas and Dooley (2021).

[58] The second edition of Private Philanthropy for Development by the OECD was prepared using a fairly comprehensive database on philanthropic giving. See https://www.oecd-ilibrary.org/development/private-philanthropy-for-development-second-edition_cdf37f1e-en

projects representing more than $42.5 billion of funding between 2016 and 2019, an annual average of $10.6 billion.

Much of this funding is cross-border flows, with more than half coming from the United States ($24.3 billion). Health and reproductive health account for more than two-thirds of project and programme allocations; contributions from the Bill & Melinda Gates Foundation provided $16.1 billion, or 38 per cent of total philanthropic funding. A total of 116 (out of 205) foundations in the sample are based in emerging markets, which together provided about $8 billion, or 19 per cent, of philanthropic flows for development in 2016–19. The largest domestic philanthropy in the sample was the Tata Trusts, which allocated about $900 million in India. The top ten cross-border foundations provided about $26 billion, or about three-quarters of all cross-border financing.

The philanthropic funds are expected to continue to grow in the coming decade. A finding of the OECD survey is that foundations have been using 'responsible investing to achieve their goals' and exploring ways, through advocacy, to mobilize additional resources to promote sustainable development.

Remittances

Worker remittances soared over the past decade. In 2020, they represented the largest source of external finance for many developing countries, exceeding both ODA and FDI to low- and middle-income countries. In some countries, remittance inflows account for 20–30 per cent of national income. As non-debt-creating inflows, they are also an important contributor to resilience in the face of economic or humanitarian crises caused by adverse shocks and conflict.

Remittance flows to developing countries remained resilient in 2020, declining marginally despite the COVID-19 shock. Officially recorded remittance flows to low- and middle-income countries were about $542 billion in 2020, down by less than 1 per cent over 2019 (Figure 2.3). The resilience of remittance flows is even more impressive when compared with the sharp decline in FDI flows to developing countries in 2020. Remittance flows to low- and middle-income countries (excluding China) in 2020, at $482 billion, was more than double the sum of net FDI and portfolio investment inflows and net ODA inflows ($163 billion) (Figure 2.3 and Table 2.1). The main drivers for the steady flow of remittances included the massive fiscal stimulus in advanced economies, which resulted in better-than-expected

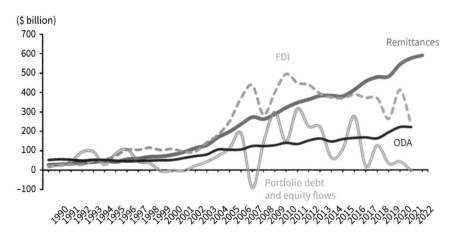

Figure 2.3 Inflows of foreign direct investment, portfolio debt and equity, official development assistance, and workers' remittances to low- and middle-income countries (excluding China), 1990–2022 (US$ billions)

Source: Dilip Ratha, Eung Ju Kim, Sonia Plaza, Elliott J Riordan, and Vandana Chandra. 2022. Migration and Development Brief 37: Remittances Brave Global Headwinds. Special Focus: Climate Migration" KNOMAD-World Bank, Washington, DC. License: Creative Commons Attribution CC BY 3.0 IGO.
Note: Figures for 2022 are forecasts.

economic conditions in host countries. In 2021, remittance inflows in developing countries (excluding China) rose by more than 12.5 per cent to $543 billion. Remittance flows to poorer countries, which remained resilient during the pandemic, are expected to grow modestly in 2022–23.

Capital Flows to Developing Countries and Global Economic Conditions

To understand whether private flows exhibit regular patterns in response to changes in the global environment, it is necessary to examine how net capital flows to developing countries, which finance their balance-of-payments requirements, behave over time and during periods of macroeconomic and financial turbulence—situations in which budget support/policy-based lending can play a uniquely important role. To answer this question, one needs first to examine how net capital flows to emerging market and developing economies behaved as global conditions changed (IMF 2011, 2021). Net capital flows, which were volatile between 2008 and 2011, became even more volatile in the more recent period.

Table 2.1 Net financial inflows, debt and equity in Low- and Middle-income countries, 2008–2021 (billions of US dollars)

	2008	2009	2011	2012	2013	2014	2015	2016	2017	2018	2019	2020	2021
Net financial inflows, debt and equity	633	636	1323	1244	1462	1122	296	894	1275	1109	910	904	1191
Percent of Gross National Income (%)	4	4	6	5	6	4	1	3	4	4	3	3	3
Net debt inflows, long-term	184	156	414	494	477	406	269	426	425	326	319	323	280
Use of IMF Credit	10	17	–1	–6	–11	–2	7	6	4	31	21	45	1
Official creditors	18	52	33	42	44	53	47	51	54	53	43	76	55
Multilateral	20	43	21	26	21	30	34	34	31	32	37	65	49
o/w: World Bank/IDA	7	17	6	12	13	15	18	15	13	15	19	27	20
Bilateral	–2	9	11	17	24	24	13	17	22	20	6	11	7
Private creditors	193	50	381	452	433	353	119	217	371	273	276	247	225
Bondholders	–14	47	148	221	168	157	74	120	281	197	234	228	142
Banks and other private	207	3	233	232	265	186	46	97	90	75	42	19	83
Short-term	–26	4	304	120	363	142	–489	–36	322	231	32	11	278
Net equity inflows													
Foreign direct investment	503	358	602	539	564	493	488	453	457	483	490	464	640
Portfolio equity	0	124	4	97	69	83	21	45	67	38	48	61	47
Change in reserves (– = increase)	–451	–621	–467	–294	–527	101	615	286	–314	64	–194	–303	–99
Memo Items:													
ODA by DAC members (grants, US$ bil)	120	122	135	127	135	138	132	145	147	150	148	163	185
Workers remittances (US$ bil.)	281	270	382	404	422	444	446	440	477	524	546	541	597
Multilateral share in total offical net inflows %	111	83	64	62	47	56	72	67	57	60	86	85	89
Debt ratios:													
External debt stocks to exports (%)	64	85	77	82	90	95	99	109	105	102	107	123	103
External debt stocks to GNI (%)	21	22	21	23	24	25	25	26	26	25	27	29	26
Multilateral to external debt stocks (%)	11	12	11	9	8	8	8	9	9	8	8	9	9
Reserves to external debt stocks (%)	114	125	113	107	102	94	91	83	79	73	72	73	68

Source: Authors' calculations based on World Bank (2022). *International Debt Statistics* (http://datatopics.worldbank.org/debt/ids/) and World Bank (2022). *World Development Indicators* (https://data.worldbank.org/products/wdi).

Emerging market and developing economies have experienced greater capital flow volatility than advanced economies. Bank and other private flows across economies were the most volatile and portfolio debt the least persistent. Historically, changes in global financing conditions have been associated with temporary tides of net flows to developing counties, which rise during periods of low global interest rates and risk aversion and fall afterward. For this reason, private inflows in developing countries tend to be procyclical. Moreover, analysis by the IMF indicates that economies that have direct foreign financial exposure to the United States experience an additional decline in their net capital flows in response to US monetary tightening over and above what is experienced by economies with less or no exposure.

How should these findings inform policymakers' expectations? Given the direct financial exposure of most economies to the US economy, it is reasonable to expect that monetary tightening in the United States, which began in the first half of 2022, will have a significant negative impact on net capital inflows to developing countries, especially in an environment of low global interest rates and risk aversion. The extent of a country's financial exposure to the United States will determine the size of the impact. The variability of capital flows is likely to continue in a climate of increasing financial globalization.

Financial globalization creates many risks (Kose et al. 2008). It also highlights the importance of deep and liquid domestic financial markets, greater exchange rate flexibility and prudential regulation, and fiscal prudence to reduce these risks. In the face of highly variable capital net flows (see Table 2.1), key policy response in the post-2011 period should have been to follow sound macroeconomic policies, avoid the build-up of short-term and expensive private debt, and encourage exports while maintaining adequate levels of foreign exchange reserve.

Prospects for a continued economic recovery in the aftermath of the pandemic shock in 2022–23 (IMF 2021), albeit highly uneven since advanced economies were recovering more quickly than most developing economies, is poor. Ramifications of the pandemic, combined with the adverse global macroeconomic shock resulting from the Russian invasion of Ukraine, raise serious concerns about the prospects of for a rebound in capital inflows in emerging market and developing economies and their economic recovery. These concerns were amplified by the huge fiscal packages in the United States and other advanced economies rising inflation, and the tightening of monetary policy in most advanced and emerging market economies.

Increases in interest rates in the United States and other advanced economies have important ramifications for financial conditions in emerging market and developing economies. Policymakers in developing countries will need to take these factors into account as they consider increasing their reliance on private funds to finance their high priority investments to support inclusive growth and increase resilience over the medium to long term. Their investment strategies need to be supported by meaningful economic and structural reforms and improvements in their business climate to reduce risks and improve risk-adjusted returns on their investments. Budget support, along with policy-based guarantees, can play a critical role in supporting the needed reforms while ensuring a stable macroeconomic framework and providing at least part of the needed financing.

The global economy performed relatively poorly in the aftermath of the global financial crisis of 2008–9. By 2020, the average annual growth rate of the world economy over the decade since the global financial crisis had slowed to 3 per cent, about 1.5 percentage points lower than over the preceding decade. Much of this decline reflected the sharp slowdown in the average economic growth of developing countries, which as a group experienced a significant slowdown in the pace of growth of their exports as well as a marked deterioration in their terms of trade, largely as a result of declines in the prices of the commodities they exported. Growth in advanced economies also slowed.

In this context, net capital flows to developing countries have been volatile around a moderately declining trend since 2011–13. These flows are characterized by the following:

- In low- and middle-income countries, net FDI inflows declined substantially between 2011 and 2020 (see Table 2.1). Excluding China, there was a further decline of more than 20 per cent in 2020. Portfolio investments in developing countries have been even more volatile.
- Dependence on net private inflows—particularly *bond financing* and short-term borrowing—increased, although there has been a sharp secular decline in borrowing from private banks and other private financial institutions.
- Net official inflows have been more or less stagnant, net inflows from multilaterals have been rising moderately, and net inflows from bilaterals have been declining, even though ODA (grants) by DAC members has been rising at a modest pace.
- Remittances grew rapidly until 2020, when the pace of growth slowed considerably in many recipient countries as a result of the pandemic.

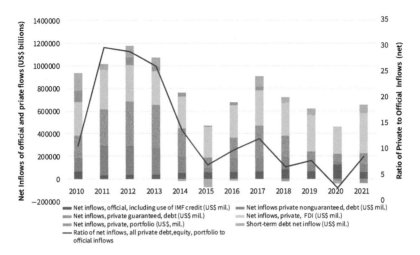

Figure 2.4 Net financial flows to low- and middle-income countries, 2008–2021 (US$ billions)

Source: Authors' calculations based on World Bank Debt Tables 2022.

In 2020, remittances were larger than either net official inflows or net equity inflows. Since 2020, as a result of a sharp declines in FDI and portfolio inflows, personal remittances have become the largest inflows into developing countries.

- Since 2013, the ratio of private to official inflows has declined sharply, although net private flows continue to be significantly larger than net official flows (see Table 2.1 and Figure 2.4).
- For low-income countries, the most important inflows have been ODA, FDI, and remittances.
- In all developing countries, the ratios of equity to debt inflows and private to official inflows have been either stagnant or declining since 2013 (Figures 2.4 and 2.5).

Debt Finance

Most debt finance from MDBs and bilateral donors takes the form of loans, on concessional or non-concessional terms. Standard loans constitute a small portion of concessional flows; loans make up the majority of non-concessional flows, which constitute about 95 per cent of loans by DAC and 100 per cent of loans by non-DAC providers. Multilateral providers tend to have larger shares of non-concessional finance in their portfolios and are

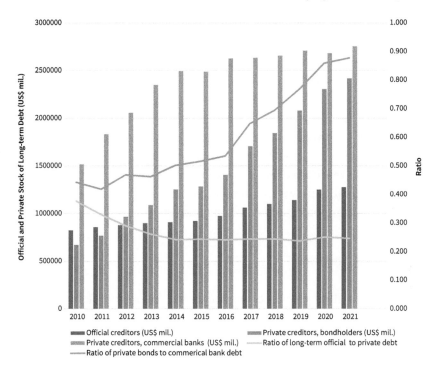

Figure 2.5 External debt of low- and middle-income countries by type of creditor, 2012–2021 (US$ millions)

Source: Authors, based on World Bank (2022). World Debt Tables (online): https://datatopics. worldbank.org/debt/ids/regionanalytical/LMY#.

leading providers of loans. In 2018, loans represented nearly 95 per cent of their non-concessional commitments and 82–94 per cent of their total commitments; equity and guarantees constituted the rest.

Most privately extended debt in developing countries takes the form of loans. However, in line with a global shift toward more capital market and bond financing, the ratio of bonds to total debt levels of developing countries has risen steadily since 2015. Governments and companies in lower-middle- and even low-income countries have been increasingly accessing capital markets, though this trend may have slowdown as a result of the pandemic and slowdown in the global economy.

This increasing use of debt capital markets has led to a change in the composition of the providers of financing. Unlike providers of non-tradeable loans, investors in debt capital markets can easily sell their debt to new creditors. This can have negative consequences for any required debt restructuring, as it can become more difficult to ensure the creditor coordination needed to produce comprehensive agreements acceptable to all major creditors.

In low- and middle-income countries, private debt flows and the ratio of debt to bondholders relative to debt to commercial banks have risen. Long-term debt rose by $1.8 trillion between 2015 and 2021. Of this amount, about half was due to publicly guaranteed private bonds and a third to private non-guaranteed debt holders, including about $340 billion lent by private bondholders. Private bondholders accounted for nearly two-thirds of the increase in long-term debt of developing countries between 2015 and 2021. The pandemic shock during 2020–21 and the subsequent tightening of monetary policy in the United States and other advanced economies in 2022 resulted in capital outflows and depreciation of currencies and rising bond yields in many developing and emerging market economies.

Equity Investments

Equity, traditionally a private sector instrument, has a more stabilizing effect than debt on recipients of finance, because its providers share some of the risks. Because equity investments are riskier than debt, providers generally earn higher returns but face more volatility. Equity instruments are used mainly for private sector investments, with more than 80 per cent of net FDI holdings taking the form of equity. Equity also constitutes a substantial part of portfolio investments, making up more than half of such holdings.

Recent years have seen a shift away from equity toward more debt financing in developing countries, with possible repercussions on debt sustainability and vulnerability to macroeconomic shocks. This shift corresponds to a global pattern driven by a multitude of factors, including demographic changes and financial regulatory reforms, that make debt more attractive than equity.

At the same time, equity investments are receiving increasing attention from the public sector. Overall, the equity portion of the financing provided by MDBs is still low (5–6 per cent in 2018). It varies across institutions, however. In 2019, equity investments made up more than 32 per cent of the portfolio of the IFC, for example. Around 15 per cent of the portfolio of the European Bank for Reconstruction and Development (EBRD) is in equity. However, growth in the equity portfolio of official providers brings new risks. Most development finance institutions that use equity instruments enjoyed double-digit returns before the 2008–9 financial crisis but then suffered major losses during and in the immediate aftermath of the crisis.

Guarantees by Multilateral Development Banks

A guarantee provides protection, partial or full, against the political and/or commercial risks of an investment. It obliges the provider to pay to the investor an agreed-upon amount if the guaranteed party is not able to pay back a claim. Both private and public entities provide guarantees. Private entities are profit motivated in the pricing of the premium; official providers take other objectives, such as social returns, into consideration and may offer subsidized pricing.

Guarantee activity is still relatively small compared with other forms of development finance, but guarantees are receiving increasing attention from official providers and international financial community. They can be part of blended finance, an approach that uses concessional development finance to mobilize other sources of financing. As guarantees involve the risk of disbursement in the future rather than the immediate disbursement of donor funds to developing countries, some donors allocate a smaller proportion of capital to guarantees than they would to an equivalent loan, as guarantees currently do not count as a form of ODA, which acts as strong disincentive for bilateral donors to provide loan or credit guarantees to eligible developing countries.[59]

Depending on the donor's risk management policies, guarantees can be very efficient mobilizers of private finance. A survey by the OECD found that twenty of the thirty-five respondents issued guarantees in order to leverage private resources (Benn, Sangaré, and Hos 2017).

For institutions that do not benefit from this budget leverage, guarantees and equivalent products offer the opportunity to increase the leverage of their operational and staffing resources by allowing them to shift much of the transaction structuring, arranging, and ongoing investment monitoring responsibilities to their private sector partners. For multilateral donors, for example, obtaining maximum leverage for each dollar of resources is of crucial importance. The ability to leverage public resources to mobilize complementary private funding is important to meeting universal public needs. It is in this context that guarantee and insurance products in particular enjoy advantages over direct funding solutions.[60]

---

[59] Approving a $50 million guarantee that is not called therefore gives the donor country less credit than giving a $1 million grant. Providers of ODA are therefore incentivized to engage in simple transfers rather than use blended finance. To circumvent this problem, advanced economies could set up a third-party vehicle (such as an SDG guarantee fund) to receive grants from donors, thereby allowing them to get the 0.7 per cent foreign aid credit, and then aggregate the capital to provide guarantees or equity to financial institutions to enhance their assets.

[60] Lee, Betru, and Harrocks (2018).

The scope of a guarantee can change over time in ways that reduces tax-payer exposure through official aid and allow the private sector to shoulder an increasing amount of risk. This is akin to increasing the participation of private capital, thereby fulfilling the ultimate development goal.[61]

In 2018, the OECD conducted a survey to quantify the mobilization effect of blended finance instruments. The results showed that that over a four-year period (2012–15), official development finance interventions mobilized more than $85 billion from the private sector. Guarantees and equivalent products mobilized the largest share, at $37 billion (43.5 per cent of the total).

The results of a 2021 survey (OECD, 2021d) indicate that similar trends continued during 2016–20, when the private sector mobilized $221 billion, indicating guarantees have continued to be important in mobilizing private capital for development, accounting for about 30 per cent of the total. Moreover, the survey indicated that in 2012–20 about $300 billion was cumulatively mobilized from the private sector through interventions by MDBs and bilateral development agencies. However, the upward trend in mobilization of private capital was briefly reversed in 2019, when mobilized funds were 4 per cent below the level mobilized in 2018. The upward trend in mobilization of private capital re-emerged in 2020 as the total level of mobilized private capital increased by more than 10 per cent above the level mobilized in 2019. Guarantees were the second largest contributor to mobilization of the private sector between 2012 and 2020, accounting for about a third of the mobilized private capital. However, their contribution fell to 26 per cent, the second largest, in 2018–20 (Figure 2.6).

MDBs remained crucial institutions in mobilizing private capital; they mobilized close to 70 per cent of the funds in 2018–20. More than three-quarters of these guarantees went to middle-income countries; only about 23 per cent went to low-income countries. However, guarantees remain important in mobilizing private capital in low-income countries. During 2018–20, they were the largest leveraging instrument in sub-Saharan Africa, accounting for 36 per cent of the $16.5 billion in private finance mobilized.

---

[61] For examples of how the scope of guarantees could change and the implications of such a change, see Zhengrong, Chao, and Sheppard (2019).

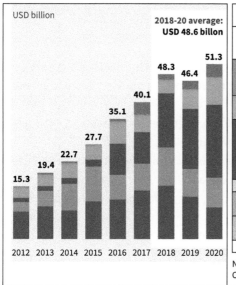

	2018–20 average	2018–20 average
Instrument Utilized	**Amounts mobilized, US$ billion**	**Share in total**
Simple Co-financing	2.6	5.0%
Credit Lines	5.9	12.0%
Direct investment in companies and SPVs	18.3	38.0%
Shares in CIVs	4.0	8.0%
Syndicated Loans	5.3	11.0%
Guarantees	12.4	26.0%
Total	48.6	100%

Notes: SPVs=Special Purpose Vehicle funds; CIVs=Collective Investment Vehicle.

Figure 2.6 Private funds mobilized by multilateral development banks and bilateral donors, by instrument, 2012–20 (US$ billion)

Source: OECD (2021). Amounts mobilized by Official Development Finance Interventions, 2018–2020: Highlights.
Notes: SPV = special purpose vehicle. CIV = collective investment vehicle. Figures in right-hand panel are 2018–20 averages.

Combining Budget Support and Guarantees: Policy-Based Guarantees

Policy-based guarantees (PBGs) are used mainly by the World Bank Group. They are designed to support access to international financial markets for well-performing middle-income countries when markets are temporarily constrained or blocked (Box 2.3). Policy-based guarantees support policy objectives similar to budget support operations with ex ante reforms undertaken and monitoring against a set of reform indicators.

Box 2.3 How effective were policy-based guarantees in Ghana?

In 2015, the World Bank and the government of Ghana initiated a macroeconomic reform policy-based guarantee operation. The operation—the First Macroeconomic Stability for Competitiveness and Growth—included a $400 million guarantee that enabled Ghana to raise up to $1 billion in the international bond market. The operation was noteworthy in many ways:

- It was the first policy-based guarantee-supported bond issuance in the market (in fourteen years) that supported the Bank's (and the Fund) macroeconomic support programme.
- It was the longest Eurobond vertical fund (fifteen years) achieved by a sub-Saharan Africa sovereign other than South Africa.
- The yield was 150–200 basis points lower than a theoretical uncovered fifteen-year Eurobond (theoretical because Ghana did not have stand-alone access).
- It was oversubscribed by 100 per cent, with a more diversified investor base than stand-alone bonds.
- About 15 per cent of the final order book went to new investors, which helped expand the investor base.

Ghana used the proceeds of the issue to refinance short-term domestic debt (ninety days to two years), coming up for refinancing at a nominal interest rate of 25 per cent at a time when there was no market access.

Investors first assessed Ghana's stand-alone creditworthiness, which they considered the key investment driver. But being convinced by the creditworthiness assessment was a necessary but not sufficient condition for investment; the policy-based guarantee was instrumental in institutional investors' decision to invest. Investors benefited from the World Bank's independent assessment of Ghana and relied on a set of prior actions as part of the reform programme of the World Bank and IMF, helping lay a foundation for positive medium- and long-term prospects.

Due to Ghana's weak macroeconomic situation a prerequisite for the PBG was a solid IMF macroeconomic program which was agreed to in 2015. Following this the World Bank introduced the PBG to support the issuance of Eurobonds in 2015 which were earmarked for refinancing and buying back high-interest debt. It also resumed policy-based lending to help contain the public wage bill, eliminate petroleum subsidies, and strengthen debt management. In 2019, Ghana successfully completed an IMF program. However, the momentum behind these reforms started to weaken and additional fiscal pressures arose from a costly financial sector restructuring and financial liabilities of the energy sector in 2018–20. Since then multiple shocks (COVID, war in Ukraine, sharp currency devaluation) leave Ghana again facing serious macroeconomic challenges.

Independent World Bank evaluations of PBGs conclude that the requirement of an adequate macroeconomic framework for policy-based loans is especially important in the context of large budget support operations supported by PBGs (IEG, 2016). Under a comprehensive and robust macroeconomic framework, PBGs can both facilitate and serve as important leverage for policy reforms in support of fiscal sustainability.

Sources: Authors; Independent Evaluation Group (2021, p. 33); Independent Evaluation Group (2016). 'Lessons from Policy-based Guarantees.' The World Bank, Washington, DC. https://ieg.worldbankgroup.org/evaluations/lessons-policy-based-guarantees

Policy-based guarantees are partial credit guarantees that the World Bank began using in the late 1990s (Box 2.4).[62] They cover a portion of debt service on a loan or bond issued by private foreign creditors in support of agreed upon structural, institutional, and social policies and reform. World Bank guarantees are used only to support debt investments.[63] In 2019, guarantees represented approximately 3.7 per cent of the total exposure outstanding of the World Bank. (Chapter 3 discusses PBGs, along with DDOs and CAT DDOs)

Box 2.4 A brief history of guarantees

The creators of the World Bank initially envisioned its primary mission as facilitating private capital flows to developing countries through the use of guarantees. Guarantees were to be supplemented with direct loans only when necessary.

This approach was deemed unrealistic, as guaranteeing loans to countries with weak financial sectors and risky business climates would undermine the Bank's financial reputation and thus complicate its efforts to issue its own bonds in global financial markets, which were critical to its business model. In addition, for many developing countries, borrowing from private commercial banks with MDB guarantees would end up being more costly than borrowing directly from the MDB itself. As a result, the World Bank and other MDBs moved directly into lending, with guarantees issued only during the 1980s debt crisis. The issues of reputational risk and the cost-effectiveness of guarantees versus loans remain as relevant today as they were seventy-five years ago, but in much larger and more complex economic and financial settings.

The urgency to start using guarantees in the 1980s and early 1990s was driven mainly by relatively low FDI flows to developing countries and the aftershocks of the debt crises. The MDBs believed that new instruments were necessary to stimulate private capital flows to developing countries.

---

[62] The first PBG was extended to Argentina in 1998. It sought to help Argentina improve future access to private foreign capital and broaden the group of investors for Argentine public debt (See World Bank (1999).

[63] The World Bank Group provides political risk cover (insurance) for equity investments through the Multilateral Investment Guarantee Agency (MIGA), its insurance arm.

All major MDBs now issue guarantees. The World Bank Group created a specialized guarantee division (the Multilateral Investment Guarantee Agency [MIGA]) in 1988. Since then, guarantees have become increasingly relevant in development, as many emerging economies seek assistance in accessing private sources of finance rather than relying entirely on traditional development loans. The scale of many projects is beyond the ability of individual MDBs to finance directly. Instruments like guarantees can leverage external resources. Over 2012–20, MDBs were responsible for more than two-thirds of all private sector finance mobilized. The leading MDBs providing these products were IFC, MIGA, the Asian Development Bank, the African Development Bank, the European Investment Bank, and the World Bank. The European Bank for Reconstruction and Development and the Inter-American Development Bank made only limited use of guarantees during this period. MIGA is the stand-out user of guarantees and the leader in terms of mobilization. Its insurance products include political risk cover and sovereign non-honouring cover in the form of partial or comprehensive risk insurance cover. Leading bilaterals offering partial or comprehensive guarantees were the United States (the Overseas Private Investment Corporation [OPIC] and the US Agency for International Development [USAID]); France (l'Agence Française de Développement); and Sweden (the Swedish International Development Cooperation Agency [SIDA]).

A consensus emerged over the last decade, which was ultimately reflected in the Hamburg Principles (see footnote 45, above) that there is potential to expand the use of guarantees, particularly as they have been effective across sectors (they were the primary mobilizers of private capital in the banking, energy generation, and industrial sectors). They often represent a cost-effective way of mobilizing capital.

Sources: Humphrey and Prizzon (2014); Ahluwalia et al. (2016).

Guarantees were also the most effective instrument for mobilizing funds from multiple sources (foreign and domestic) and across key economic sectors. This attribute is particularly important for local capital market development, as stipulated in the OECD-DAC blended finance principles (OECD 2020). About a quarter of the funds mobilized during the review period were mobilized at the beneficiary country level, where guarantees helped mobilize the second highest amount of local finance after credit lines.

Private sector development has become a central pillar of the global development agenda; aspirations for a major sustainable infrastructure push by the MDBs will depend on their ability to crowd in the private sector. The MDB approach to private sector engagement has not done enough to demonstrate that they are truly catalytic when it comes to private investment (that is, that they are crowding in and not crowding out private finance).

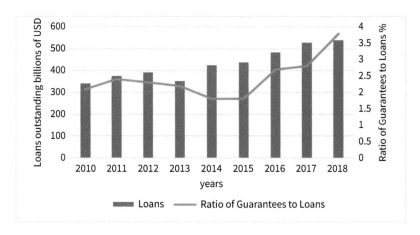

Figure 2.7 Loans by and ratio of guarantees to loans at multilateral development banks, 2010–18

Source: Authors, based on data from Tables 2.1 and 2.2.

Direct lending to governments and firms continues to dominate MDB portfolios (see Figure 2.7), even with growing recognition that the MDB insurance function is better matched to supporting the development of private markets and the flow of private funds to developing countries.

MDB use of guarantees remained limited even after 2015 and joint declarations by MDBs on their importance. The major MDBs (including MIGA but excluding the European Investment Bank's activities within the European Union) issued a combined total of about $38 billion in project (nontrade) guarantees as of end-2018 (Table 2.2). Of this total, about $18 billion was issued since 2015, with the World Bank Group (the International Bank for Reconstruction and Development, IFC, and MIGA) accounting for 69 per cent of the increase. The $38 billion in project-related stock of guarantees (as of end-2018) represented only 3.3 per cent of the $540 billion in development related stock of loans by the same institutions.

Although the share of guarantees in the portfolios of several MDBs has risen since 2015, it remained well below 5 per cent, except for IFC, which has always had a much higher guarantees to loans ratio than other MDBs (private sector lending and guarantees account for more than 70 per cent of IFC's overall business). Including MIGA, which is dedicated solely to insurance and does not undertake development lending, the ratio of guarantees (including political insurance) to loans rose to 6.9 per cent in 2018.

In 2016, a high-level panel of experts called on MDB shareholders to set clear targets for the use of guarantee instruments, as a concrete way to shift the MDBs toward a catalytic role for private sector investment. They also recommended a target of 20 per cent of portfolios for nontrade finance

Table 2.2 Volume of non-trade guarantees by selected multilateral development banks, 2010–18 (US$ millions)

Institution	2010	2011	2012	2013	2014	2015	2016	2017	2018	*Annual percentage change*	
										2010–15	2015–18
Asian Development Bank	1,969.1	1,995.2	1,904.9	1,780.0	1,740.0	1,407.0	2,105.0	2,173.0	2,631.0	–6.5	23.1
African Development Bank	2.8	14.1	20.12	104.03	231.4	626.6	565.5	552.9	1,239.5	195.1	25.5
European Bank for Reconstruction and Development	525.5	624.9	708.5	708.5	709.6	650.9	638.4	898.3	1,003.4	4.3	15.5
European Investment Bank (excluding the European Union)	340.8	416.2	410.6	571.5	617.5	624.9	766.0	1,786.7	2,087.6	12.8	49.5
Inter-American Development Bank	814.0	980.0	761.0	871.0	251.0	207.0	230.0	353.0	454.0	–23.9	29.9
International Bank for Reconstruction and Development	1,726.0	1,969.0	1,753.0	1,744.0	1,713.0	1,367.0	5,198.0	5,658.0	6,325.0	–4.6	66.6
International Finance Corporation	1,889.0	2,932.0	3,420.0	2,070.0	2,474.0	3,168.0	3,478.0	3,528.0	4,096.0	10.9	8.9
Total	7,267.1	8,931.4	8,978.1	7,849.0	7,736.5	8,051.4	12,980.9	14,949.8	17,836.5	2.1	30.3
MIGA gross exposure	7,723.0	9,122.0	10,346.0	10,758.0	12,409.0	12,538.0	14,187.0	17,778.0	21,216.0	10.2	19.2

Source: Authors, based on G20 (2020) background technical documents and annual financial statements of multilateral development banks.

guarantees (Ahluwalia et al. 2016). As of end-2018, the gap between the actual and recommended levels of guarantees remained wide.

A key issue that has made more widespread use of guarantees by MDBs difficult is the fact that MDBs' balance sheets are conservatively structured in order to maintain their high credit ratings, which reduces their cost of funds and maintains their competitiveness compared with private lenders (Humphrey and Prizzon 2014).[64]

Comparing MDBs' experience with guarantees before and after 2015 reveals the following:

- During 2010–18, guarantees by MDBs represented a relatively small portion of their portfolios. Except for IFC and MIGA, the share of guarantees in MDBs' portfolios remained well below 5 per cent throughout this period.
- There was a significant increase in the amounts of guarantees issued by all major MDBs between 2015 and 2018. The increase appears to have been in response to the new 'from billions to trillions' strategy for financing the massive SDG-related investments in developing countries (Figure 2.8).
- Lending by MDBs in 2015–18 continued to grow rapidly; outstanding loans rose by about $100 billion while the stock of guarantees issued

Figure 2.8 Loan guarantees by multilateral development banks: guarantees and ratio of guarantees to loans by selected multilateral development institutions, 2018 (US$ billions, and percent)

Source: Authors' calculations, based on data from annual reports of multilateral development banks.

Note: Institutions include ADB, AfDB, EBRD, EIB (non-EU), IDB, IBRD, and IFC.

[64] Independent evaluations of several MDBs reveal that staff performance appears to be based primarily on lending and advisory activities, which typically exclude guarantees. For their part, borrowers prefer traditional lending to guarantees, because of their familiarity with traditional tools. See EBRD (2020).

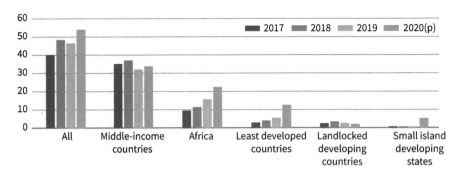

Figure 2.9 Mobilization of financing from the private sector by official development finance interventions, 2017–20 (US$ billions)

Source: United Nations (2022). 'Financing for Sustainable Development Report 2022', Inter-agency Task Force on Financing Development. April, New York (https://developmentfinance.un.org/fsdr2022), based on OECD data.
Note: Figures for 2020 are preliminary.

rose by only about $10 billion (excluding MIGA). Continuation of these trends would make realization of 'billions to trillions' increasingly unlikely.

- MDBs did not substitute guarantees for their regular lending; they used guarantees more intensively to mobilize additional private finance.
- The use of guarantees in mobilization of private capital has been heavily skewed toward middle-income countries (Figure 2.9).

Coming Financial Turbulence: Budget Support to Rescue?

A sharp drop in capital flows to developing countries, or a protracted sudden-stop in capital flows, could cause widespread solvency problem in developing countries, particularly if the pandemic and the Russian invasion of Ukraine have long-lasting consequences. The current international architecture, particularly when it comes to external debt restructuring in developing countries, is inadequate and could result in a serious financial crisis. The experience of the last two years has made it clear that the closing of existing development financing gaps is challenging, particularly because of the pandemic and the Russian war shocks to the world economy. One important implication of the current situation is that development finance needs to be scaled up.

After the 2008–9 financial crisis, enhanced regulations helped reduce global financial instability. However, these regulations also disincentivize investment in the developing and emerging markets that are most in need of capital to stabilize and finance their development goals. Although guarantees and equivalent products provided by development institutions have shown great promise in overcoming this disincentive, they are not realizing their full potential for mobilizing private capital to help developing countries achieve their sustainable development goals. Budget support, including policy-based guarantees, is likely to continue to play an important role, both in supporting the needed reforms and in helping developing countries follow countercyclical policies during periods of financial turmoil.

An analysis by the Milken Institute and the OECD of products from institutions representing more than 80 per cent of the development guarantee market reveals considerable misalignments with respect to financial regulatory policies, FDI incentives, and financial institutions' business practices.[65] It finds that nearly half of guarantees are not written for maximum efficiency, leverage, and impact (Box 2.5). Their analysis documents a misalignment between development guarantees and banking sector regulations. The report recommends that more research be conducted. Additional regulations, such as Solvency II for insurance companies, also tend to slow the flow of capital. Exploring the compatibility of guarantees with these regulations is important to maximizing private capital participation in development.

More research is needed about MDBs' policies that create many of the challenges in guaranteed contracts, to ensure that modifications are pursued in a holistic manner that is aligned with their private sector users. The independent review of the capital adequacy frameworks of MDBs commissioned by the G20, which is due to be completed in 2022, could be the basis for reform that would allow a significant scaling up of lending by MDBs.

Box 2.5 How much capital have multilateral development banks mobilized?

MDBs can mobilize private resources by reducing political and credit risks. Multilateral guarantees and the extension of MDBs' preferred creditor status implies that their loans, which can be excluded from debt rescheduling, can reduce credit risk. Projects with MDB participation have had catalytic effects in various settings. The 2008 expansion of the Panama Canal, for example, mobilized almost $10 billion in private investment, about 1.8 times the project's cost. European Investment Bank (EIB), Inter-American Development Bank (IDB), and IFC participated in the project.

---

[65] See World Bank (2018c).

Beyond anecdotal evidence, however, there is limited evidence on whether MDBs can mobilize significant additional resources from the private sector. Estimating the effect of MDBs on private capital flows requires taking into account the fact that an MDB's decision to invest in a country is not exogenous and may indicate market failure and high risk.

Broccolini et al. (2019) address this issue by using loan-level data from the syndicated loan market to test whether MDB lending in a given country–sector pair is associated with a subsequent increase in private lending. Bringing the analysis to a more disaggregated level has the advantage of controlling for all time-varying factors that are specific to a given country or sector and that could drive MDB and private sector lending. In particular, it allows them to control not only for country and year fixed effects but also for country–sector, country–year, and sector–year fixed effects, greatly diminishing the possibility of omitted variable bias and increasing the accuracy of the estimates.

Their results indicate that the volume of syndicated lending, the average number of lending banks per loan, and the average loan maturity increase in the years following a syndicated loan with MDB participation in a given country–sector pair. They find that for every $1 an MDB invests through syndicated loans, about $7 is mobilized in syndicated lending by private banks over a three-year period. They find no evidence that MDB mobilization effects crowd out development finance flows. They also find that MDB lending is less effective in mobilizing private bank flows to low-income countries (where the multiplier effect is substantially lower than seven).

Another study (Attridge and Engen 2019), by the Overseas Development Institute (ODI), finds that on average, every $1 of MDB and development finance institutions (DFIs) invested mobilizes $0.75 of private capital for developing countries. This ratio falls to only $0.37 for low-income countries. The ODI study concludes that expectations that blended finance can bridge the massive gap in the SDG financing are unrealistic based on current practices and business models.

Sources: Authors; Broccolini, et al. (2019); and Attridge and Engen (2019).

Conclusion

External financial flows to developing economies were insufficient to support sustainable development investments even before the pandemic-induced crisis, which has inflicted a massive adverse shock in many poor countries. While private capital flows to developing countries have been large relative to official flows, they have become highly volatile and pro-cyclical, particularly over the last decade. On the other hand, financial contribution of foreign aid, including budget support to developing economies, has been more stable and countercyclical in character during the same period.

In the last two decades, FDI and remittances took on increasing importance. Following the call by the Addis Ababa and Busan High Level Aid Effectiveness forums for greater private financing, a consensus among agencies and development experts emerged that a focus of foreign assistance must be on leveraging private sector flows to expand financing for development. ODA flows are far too limited to meet the financing needs of low- and middle-income countries to enhance growth to meet their sustainable development goals. However, this requires a substantial increase in the lending capacities of MDBs, as well as reforms of their guarantee instrument to address the existing constraints on both supply and demand side of this potentially highly effective de-risking instrument.

ODA has continued to play a core function in the emerging global aid architecture. A significant portion of it is delivered through budget support in addressing the needed policy and institutional reforms, and it continues to play a critical role in financing investments for achieving country-specific development goals. It is increasingly being used to help poorer countries address challenges posed by global risks, such as climate change, pandemics, and cross-border financial instability. At the current aggregate level of only 0.33 per cent of GNI of DAC member countries, however, it is inadequate, as the financing needs of developing countries have grown more rapidly than the ODA, which has hardly grown in real terms. As a result of inadequate levels of official concessional aid and grants, the last decade saw increasing indebtedness of low-income countries and the increased risk of a serious developing country debt crisis, particularly in Africa.

The emergence of vertical funds, new donors, and private foundations outside the traditional ODA framework has changed the international aid architecture, making it more complicated and fragmented. Philanthropic funds, which provide an average of about $10 billion a year, could play an increasingly important role in financing innovative projects, however, particularly in low-income countries.

Despite the potential importance for mobilizing private funds for investments, guarantees issued by MDBs have remained a relatively small portion of their portfolios. Except for IFC and MIGA, the share of guarantees in MDBs' portfolios remained well below 5 per cent in 2010–19. It is important that MDBs undertake the necessary reforms and incentivize greater use of their guarantee instrument, which can be used directly for budget support and policy-based lending (i.e. policy-based guarantees) and as an important ingredient in blended finance mechanisms, in helping developing countries with sound macroeconomic policies and satisfactory debt management systems address their development challenges as well as global risks, such as climate change and pandemics.

The COVID crisis led to significant financial outflows and declines in FDI inflows in many developing countries in 2020. Together with developing countries' massive debt, which has been rising rapidly as a result of their fiscal interventions in response to the pandemic, as well as a sharp drop in export revenues, tourism revenues, and tax revenues, it has triggered the most serious economic and financial crisis since the Great Recession.

Although net official financial flows associated with budget support (and official lending in general) are small compared with private flows, budget support has been punching well above its weight. It plays a key role in addressing critical economic reforms and supporting structural transformation in debt-stressed and other vulnerable countries. It plays a critical role in facilitating implementation of important reforms that help leverage private capital to finance projects and programmes.

Going forward, budget support could play an even bigger and more central role in the following areas:

- supporting low-income and fragile countries;
- advancing reforms during periods of crisis, including improved fiscal and debt management;
- undertaking critical reforms that crowd in private capital to finance green infrastructure, digital technology, and climate-related investments through greater use of policy-based guarantees and insurance.

3

The Evolution of Budget Support

The earliest appearance of budget support was in the 1940s following the Second World War and establishment of the Bretton-Woods Institutions, but it gradually came to the fore as an instrument for international aid to developing countries at the end of the 1970s following the second global oil shock. Since then, it has evolved in significant directions to both differentiate the instrument to address multiple financing needs, as well as to adapt various design elements in response to evidence on performance.

Both the demand for and supply of budget support reflect conditions shifting global demand, as crises generally expand financing needs in low-income countries and shrink access to finance in global markets. Budget support has come to play an important role in providing countercyclical support during periods of crisis, but access varies significantly by country type, related to the quality of economic management, prevailing political winds, and income level.

This chapter builds on the historical context and global financial flows discussed in Chapters 1 and 2 and offers a detailed account of the trends and patterns in providing budget support over time, design elements as new instruments were introduced, and the evolution of conditionality.

The Growth of Budget Support in Official Development Assistance

Budget support has historically made up a significant share of development assistance. It has averaged about US$30 billion a year[1] in aggregate commitments across all development partners. This represents 10–13 per cent of total ODA, depending on the year. Demand for budget support as a fast-disbursing instrument spiked during times of crisis as countries came under increased fiscal pressure. Following the global financial crisis and the COVID-19 crisis, budget support as a share of ODA increased significantly and is estimated above 20 per cent since 2021 (Figure 3.1).

[1] Estimates in 2019 prices. See Appendix A on data and methods on how total estimates were derived. Appendix A, Table A.1 provides an overview of budget support by agency.

Retooling Development Aid in the 21st Century. Shahrokh Fardoust et al., Oxford University Press.
© Shahrokh Fardoust et al., (2023). DOI: 10.1093/oso/9780192882196.003.0003

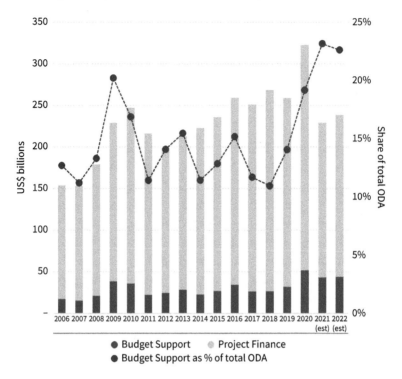

Figure 3.1 Budget support as share of total official development assistance, 2006–22

Source: MDB evaluation reports and annual reports; OECD DAC CRS; and World Bank Business Intelligence.
Note: Commitments in current prices; Values for AfDB, EU, and CDB and most bilateral partners for 2021-22 are projections.

Demand for budget support tends to be high given its fast-disbursing and more flexible financing for fiscal expenditures. However, supply has been limited not only due to limits on international financial institutions (IFI) financial exposure, but also due to limits imposed by shareholders on total supply as a share of commitments. Caps of about 20–30 per cent of total lending have been put in place reflecting the concern of some influential MDB shareholders that budget support may be riskier, less effective, and may displace project lending. Despite these limits, budget support has exceeded caps in periods of very high demand during economic crises. The World Bank abolished a previous ceiling when development policy financing was introduced in 2005 but maintains a notional ceiling on IDA-financed budget support. Given recent crises and increasing demand for and reliance on budget support, the rationale for these ceilings is being increasingly questioned.

MDBs have historically provided the largest share of budget support, covering about 85 per cent of total commitments. Of the MDBs, the World Bank is the largest contributing agency, specifically through countercyclical IBRD financing. World Bank budget support was particularly dominant during the aftermath of the global financial crisis as demand for high volume and fast disbursing financial support was met with considerable IBRD lending headroom. In 2010, following the global financial crisis, the World Bank is estimated to have provided 67 per cent of budget support globally. The IBRD capital increase in 2018 strengthened the World Bank's capacity to provide budget support, which is important, albeit insufficient given the enormous global challenges that cannot be addressed through investment lending alone (Chapter 6). Budget support through World Bank IDA financing is equally important when controlling for differences in GDP. While the average IBRD economy was estimated to be fourteen times larger than the average IDA economy, budget support commitments in IBRD countries were only four times the average of IDA countries. During the COVID-19 crisis, GDP-adjusted budget support commitments were 3.3 times higher in IDA countries than in IBRD countries. (World Bank 2022a)

Other multilateral banks or agencies such as the ADB, AfDB, CDB, or IADB also provide important budget support, but on a more select and regional basis. Combined, they averaged 31 per cent of total budget support contributions, with the EU contributing about 11 per cent of the total. During times of crisis, the World Bank and other MDBs combined, provide a disproportionately large response at 80 per cent or higher of total budget support.

Budget support from DAC partners countries was significant in 2006 at about close to 15 per cent of total commitments, driven by considerable contributions from the UK and Nordic countries. This has, however, fallen out of favour since. The budget support instrument has been used on a sporadic basis by non-DAC countries such as the UAE or Turkey through sizeable once-off transfers (Figure 3.2).[2]

There has been a shift in OECD DAC countries' support for the use of budget support as an aid instrument. Although traditionally many OECD DAC countries provided budget support, the volume for most partners was small. Budget support by the top three to five countries made up two-thirds of total budget support. Over time, this situation has become even more skewed toward fewer but bigger contributors (Figure 3.3).

---

[2] There remains serious measurement and definitional concerns from the OECD DAC credit reporting system data, which may capture transfers without reference to policy or institutional reform, potentially leading to an overestimate of commitments.

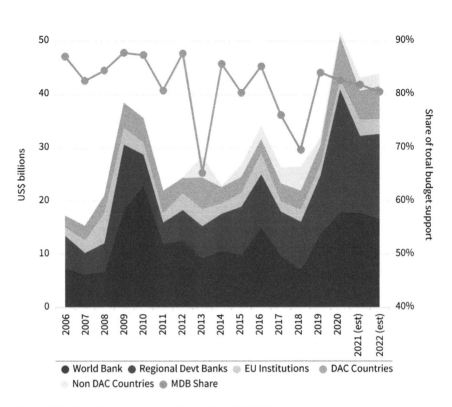

Figure 3.2 Total budget support financing, 2006–22

Source: MDB evaluation reports and annual reports; OECD DAC CRS; and World Bank Business Intelligence.
Note: Commitments in current prices; Values for AfDB, EU, and CDB and most bilateral partners for 2021-22 are projections.

Germany, Japan and France are the most dominant bilateral providers. During the covid-19 pandemic they have covered about 75 per cent of the total bilateral commitment volume of budget support. Transactions have tended to be high-volume operations to a select group of countries.

- While not allowing its main bilateral aid agencies (USAID or MCC) to provide budget support, the United States provides transfers to politically strategic allies. For example, the US government contribution to budget support was driven by their engagement in Jordan, specifically in support to a large cash transfer programme.[3] Limited budget support

---

[3] Sector budget support is considered a subcategory of general budget support by OECD DAC, as it constitutes a direct release to treasury. Most budget support by the US government is also classified as sector budget support.

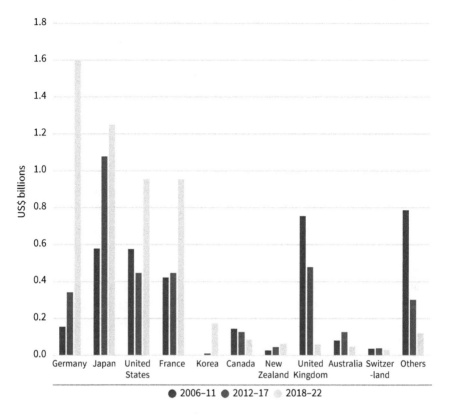

Figure 3.3 Budget support from OECD DAC countries donors, average commitments 2006–22
Source: OECD DAC CRS.
Note: Values in current prices.

engagement by the US government is for small island states such as Micronesia or the Marshall Islands. Japan has a more traditional and sizeable budget support portfolio. This includes the India Tamil Nadu Investment Promotion Program, the Mongolia Fiscal, Social and Economic Reform Development Policy Loan, and the Vietnam Economic Management and Competitiveness Credit.

- The Japanese budget support engagement has an embedded reform programme and tended to be aligned with the ongoing budget support engagement of the various MDBs. There are some large outlier budget support contributions by Japan to facilitate re-engagement with market economies and the MDBs following a period of isolation, such as the US$2 billion debt repayment facility for Myanmar.

France and Germany have increased budget support over time and are today amongst the most important bilateral providers. France has engaged in smaller scale budget support operations predominantly to former French colonies in West Africa, such as a recent US$112 million engagement in Cameroon and US$84 million in Gabon. Germany's use of the instrument was predominantly through the quasi-public Development Bank, Kreditanstalt für Wiederaufbau (KfW), to a few select countries such as a credit to Egypt for US$252 million in 2019, in support of a broad economic reform programme. Conversely, budget support has fallen out of favour with the United Kingdom and many Nordic countries. The UK has transitioned from one of the strongest proponents of budget support with over US$3 billion in the 2006–10 period to phasing out the instrument almost entirely. This trend also holds true for Denmark, Finland, the Netherlands, Norway, and Sweden, though on a lesser scale. Provision of budget support amongst bilateral partners has always been skewed to a few players providing the bulk of financing.

There has been a growth in budget support provided by non-DAC countries. In 2013, for example, the United Arab Emirates provided a $2 billion loan and a $1 billion grant to Egypt. In 2015, Abu Dhabi approved a $2 billion loan to Egypt and a $1 billion loan to Serbia, also classified as budget support by the OECD DAC. While these are large one-off transfers to recipient country treasuries, they tend to be isolated cases and the conditionality and policy reform content of these engagements is unclear.

Countries at different stages of economic development require a context specific engagement strategy. During times of crisis, it may be warranted to offer balance-of-payment support or a one-off budget support operation to offer urgently needed emergency support. During times of economic stability, budget support can be used to pursue a medium-term reform agenda through a programmatic engagement or tranches where reform content is progressively developed. Countries vulnerable to shocks can benefit from the insurance of contingent financing.

To make budget support suitable for a wide range of countries in different circumstances, multiple approaches have been developed. A programmatic engagement over many years may be useful for countries in support of a medium-term reform agenda. For some countries, engaging in-depth with a specific sector may be more appropriate than broad stroke budget support. In other instances, it may be necessary and appropriate to leverage budget support resources to crowd in private sector financing and, for countries prone to shocks, budget support can be used as an insurance mechanism to draw on funds without having to establish complex and costly contingency arrangements. In order to cater to these diverse set of needs, development partner agencies have developed a wide range of budget support modalities (Table 3.1). To motivate performance, a results-based financing instrument was introduced that also disburses directly to treasury (Box 3.1).

Table 3.1 Types of budget support

Type of support	Description	MDBs that use the instrument
One-off or emergency crisis support	One-off operations are single tranche, often in response to a specific financing need. Some partners have made special provisions to allow recipients to access funds rapidly during times of crisis or when in urgent need of foreign exchange. Exceptions to the conditionality framework may apply. One-off operations tend to be done in higher income countries or when a programmatic engagement is not possible.	ADB, AfDB, CDB, IAD, World Bank
Tranched budget support	A tranched operation is a single multi-year operation in which phased disbursement are made over multiple tranches.	ADB, AfDB, CDB, IDB
Programmatic budget support	A programmatic approach involves a series of sequential payments, typically annual, within a medium-term framework specified at the outset. That framework includes completed prior actions, monitorable progress indicators, and expected targets for subsequent operations. Unlike multi-tranche operations, in which disbursements are made based on promises for future actions, every single-tranche operation under a programmatic approach is approved following actual performance.	ADB, AfDB, CDB, IAD, World Bank
Policy-based guarantees	PBGs protect private lenders against the risk of debt service default by the sovereign government. Leveraging favourable credit ratings from the lender, PBGs allow the recipient to crowd in private financing at reduced interest.	ADB, AfDB, CDB, IAD, World Bank
Sector budget support	Support for sector-specific reform programs, but funds are released to treasury.	ADB, AfDB, CDB, IAD, World Bank
Subnational budget support	Budget support provided to states in a federal setting.	ADB, AfDB, IDB, World Bank
Contingency financing or drawdown options	The recipient has access to a contingent credit line where disbursement is made according to triggers that may be related to adverse economic events, unfavourable changes in commodity prices or terms of trade, natural disasters, or other national emergencies. An engagement with contingency financing provides a formal basis for continuing a policy-based engagement when no immediate need for funding exists.	ADB, AfDB, IAD, World Bank

Box 3.1   The emergence of results-based financing approaches

The World Bank was the first MDB in 2012 to introduce a programme for results (PforR) instrument. Instead of disbursing against policy and institutional reform, it links disbursement of funds directly to the achievement of specific programme results. Growing demand for the instrument has led to an increase of a lending cap from 5 to 15 per cent and eventually a removal of the cap entirely. Since 2012 there have been over 120 PforR operations, amounting to about US$20 billion in financing. Demand for PforR lending increased steadily between 2012 and 2018, when PforR commitments exceeded those of budget support. PforR operations may have been displacing budget support, given the inverse relationship during these years (Box Figure 3.1). The growth in PforR interest appears to have slowed with the COVID-19 crisis, reflecting the need for a fast-disbursing response.

PforR lending offers appeal to recipient governments, as they tend to be untied and fungible, with less donor oversight. PforRs also appeal to development partners as they aim to shift the focus from counting inputs toward incentivizing results and strengthening accountability. Aid payments are made on the basis of agreed metrics or indicators (IEG 2016f). However, their drawback is that they are not a net addition to total aid, but rather reduce financing from other instruments (Gelb and Hashmi 2014).

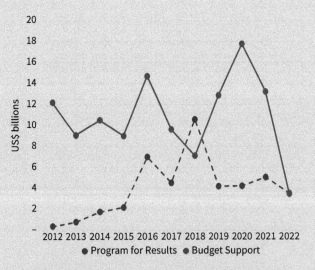

Box Figure 3.1   Budget support and results-based financing commitments by the World Bank, 2012–22

Source: World Bank Business Intelligence.

An output or outcome orientation can also be supported through project lending with performance-based conditions. This is, however, distinctly different from PforR lending in that it remains project finance against specific project expenditures. Funds are disbursed into a designated account, where they are earmarked. The funds are released when specific performance-based conditions, which can be policy oriented, are met. Typical examples include conditional cash transfer programmes that finance a share of the government's overall expenditures, which are often combined with specific measures designed to strengthen their effectiveness, transparency, and targeting. Although performance-based conditions in projects lending may not be suitable to support broader policy programmes, they can be effective in advancing institutional reforms in the programmes they are financing.

Budget Support during Times of Crisis

The origins of budget support date back to the 1980s, when the World Bank introduced structural adjustment lending in response to the oil price shocks in the late 1970s. These instruments were predominantly designed to address macroeconomic imbalances and were closely implemented alongside IMF stabilization programmes. As discussed in Chapter 1, subsequent phases saw a significant evolution of the use and design of budget support toward a more programmatic approach in support of longer-term structural reforms.

There remains, nonetheless, a critical need for providing support during times of crisis. Global crises are not infrequent — the food price shock of 2008, the global financial crisis in 2009, the crisis following the Ebola virus outbreak in 2014, the oil price shock in 2014, the COVID-19 crisis in 2019, and the crisis unfolding as a result of the Russian invasion of Ukraine — have fuelled demand for budget support, requiring a measured and appropriate response from MDBs. Correspondingly, historical trends show countercyclical spikes in budget support to counteract crisis (chapter 1, figure 1.1). This is also reflected by the average loan size of operations during times of crisis. The World Bank records that between 2006 and 2021, one-off operations were on average 37 per cent higher than programmatic operations, a difference that is more pronounced in IBRD than IDA countries. Naturally, the share of one-off operations was also higher during crisis periods.

The choice of instrument reflects the nature of need, particularly in times of crisis. Sudden crises that are short term and transitory in nature are better supported through one-off operations. One such example is the ADB US$1.5 billion budget support operations to the Philippines to help finance the COVID-19 response (Asian Development Bank (ADB) 2020). Similarly, the World Bank had numerous COVID-19 response operations and made

adjustments to reduce preparation time. A rapid response to the unfolding crisis in Ukraine is another example of how the instrument was used
(Box 3.2). Programmatic engagements have also been used, especially when
the crises are related to longer-term structural effects, as was the case with
the 2008–09 global financial crisis. There are also examples of restructuring
existing programmatic engagements to allow programmatic budget support
to address arising issues. For example, during the onset of the COVID-19
crisis, existing engagements were adjusted to tend to the arising emergency.

Box 3.2 Supporting Ukraine during conflict

Budget support can be an effective aid instrument to deliver fast-disbursing
resources during times of urgent need. One such example is the use of budget
support in response to the Russian invasion of Ukraine and subsequent collapse
of public services. The EU swiftly assembled a Macro-Financial Assistance (MFA)
package of Euro1.2 billion. This disburses directly to the Treasury and has some,
but limited, structural reforms. This emergency MFA package builds on a long-
standing programmatic engagement between the Ukraine and the EU, with lending
on favourable terms. Reforms supported by the MFA engagement are related to economic resilience, public financial management, governance and the rule of law, and
improving the business climate (European Commission 2022).

Similarly, the World Bank is providing a US$723 million budget support pack-
age consisting of loans, guarantees, grants, and parallel financing arrangements.
The fast-disbursing World Bank support is complementary to the EU MFA package
and is intended to help the government in fostering de-monopolization and anti-
corruption institutions, strengthen land and credit markets, and bolster the social
safety net. Budget support is aimed at supporting the government to provide critical services that are at risk, including wages for hospital workers, pensions for the
elderly, and social programmes for the vulnerable (World Bank 2022).

There is evidence that budget support is associated with improvements in economic policy. Moreover, Smets and Record (2022) find that the average positive
effect of budget support on the quality of economic policy in countries going through
deep economic crisis is three times higher (discussed in more depth in Chapter 4),
offering evidence that crisis is also an opportunity for reform progress. Such an
engagement, however, also requires safeguarding against additional risks, such as
the misappropriation of budget support funds after a forced regime change.

One precondition for the provision of budget support for many partners,
including during crisis situations, includes an adequate macro-fiscal environment and confidence in the sustainability of the debt exposure (see Chapters 1

and 5). In the absence of this, an active IMF programme that addresses these macro-fiscal concerns may justify an engagement. When such a programme is not in place, however, it has historically been difficult to engage. For example, in 2021, adverse macroeconomic conditions left Zambia unable to pay its debt. While the World Bank was committed to supporting the government in maintaining basic service delivery functions, it was unable to do so through budget support, following failed IMF programme negotiations. Instead, borrowing through investment project lending for highly fungible items such as wages has been pursued which is similar in many respects to budget support (World Bank 2021).

Contingency financing or drawdown options were introduced to the set of budget support instruments to act as an insurance mechanism. As explained in Table 3.1, the recipient has access to a contingent credit line where disbursement is made according to triggers that may be related to the crisis. As such, they are an attractive option for access to resources without the need to set up costly contingency funds. Following the World Bank's lead in 2007, contingency financing budget support instruments have now been introduced across most MDBs. For example, in 2012, the World Bank approved a US$1 billion deferred drawdown option (DDO) budget support operation, which provided finance to augment Romania's fiscal buffer. Debt management considerations and the unexpected sharp increase in the geopolitical tensions in neighbouring Ukraine, leading to considerably heightened risks market volatility, prompted the government to request the withdrawal of the funds as a precautionary measure (IEG 2017).

Contingency financing through budget support has become increasingly common to protect against catastrophic events. The IADB makes use of the contingent credit facility for natural disaster emergencies where the loan is disbursed after the IADB has verified the occurrence of a disaster event (Bruce 2019). During the COVID-19 crisis, the IADB and World Bank expanded the risks covered under their facilities to include public health risks and COVID-19, such that countries were able to draw down the option and accelerate access to resources (World Bank 2022; IDB 2020). There has been a lot of variability in use of the DDO feature in World Bank IBRD countries. At its inception in 2008 and 2009 there was substantial interest, and almost 30 per cent of total budget support was committed for DDO type operations. This waned in 2010 and 2011 but spiked again at almost 40 per cent in 2012. Since then, interest in the DDO approach continued, but at a lesser scale. The COVID-19 pandemic spurred a surge in Catastrophe DDO disbursements, which provides contingent budget support in case of a clearly predefined catastrophic event, including for the first IDA countries that became eligible in 2019. In total, only about 8 per cent of total World Bank budget support used DDOs since the option was introduced.

Pursuing Medium-Term Programmatic Support

A central premise of budget support is to support policy reform over the medium term. As described in Table 3.1, a multi-year tranched engagement or a programmatic engagement can facilitate this. A programmatic engagement involves several operations within a multi-year framework, with sustained and sequenced reform elements, that may support a multi-donor platform, and be tied to a joint reform dialogue. The introduction of a programmatic engagement only happened in the late nineties and was mainstreamed through budget support operations and poverty reduction support credits (PRSCs) in support of longer term pro-poor social sector reforms and a renewed emphasis on public financial management. Most other MDBs introduced a programmatic approach alongside the World Bank in the early 2000s (Chapter 1).

At the time of the introduction of PRSCs, there was an implicit expectation amongst some that the instrument would gradually become the dominant aid vehicle and replace sectoral investment engagement (World Bank 2005b). Bilateral partners such as DANIDA developed roadmaps on how to transition from project financing to sector budget support and eventually general budget support, with the vision that a mutually agreed budget with a pro-poor outlook in a fiscally sustainable manner would provide the basis for a sustained partnership and more effective aid. In this setting, a policy action matrix between the government and partners was agreed on to support the medium-term reform agenda.

During these years, the potential replacement of project lending was discussed in the World Bank in several Country Assistance Strategies. An IEG evaluation of PRSCs found that it was discussed in ten out of twenty-seven PRSC countries (Figure 3.4). Sectors where replacement was most explicitly discussed included the health sector, followed by education and nutrition. Evidence on actual replacement was however limited with evidence only coming from Benin, Cape Verde, Rwanda, and Senegal. In some cases, PRSCs temporarily replaced project lending, and in others the intention has not been pursued further given fiduciary concerns and disagreements from sector specialists. Ultimately, in most countries where replacement of sectoral investment was tried, the attempt was temporary (IEG 2010a). The complementarity of programmatic budget support with project finance has increasingly been documented in countries such as Armenia (Hicks 2010), thereby gradually shifting the narrative, which is discussed in greater detail in Chapter 5.

The budget support period from 2001 to 2008 was associated with the coverage of multiple sectors, requiring engagement across a wide range of

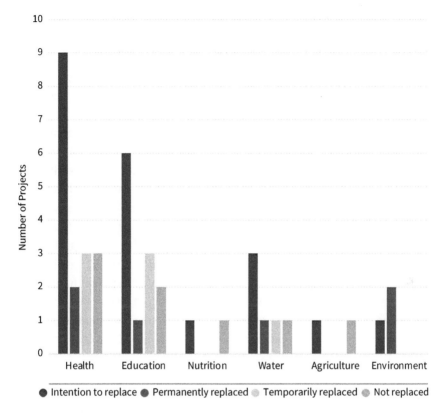

Figure 3.4 Intended and actual replacement of sectoral operations by PRSCs,
2001–08
Source: Authors, based on IEG 2010.

policy areas. Collaboration and pooling resources amongst partners have
efficiency upsides, but complex policy matrices reflecting diverse partner
preferences risk diluting the reform effort (European Commission 2018).
In Vietnam for example, the government was keen to make the reform
matrix as comprehensive as possible. The PRSC covered about seventeen
policy areas across the pillars of business development, social inclusion,
natural resource management, and improved governance (IEG 2015). Similarly, in Lao PDR, there was a wide-ranging effort to cover policy areas in
health, education, transport, rural electrification, water supply, and forestry
management (Grawe 2010).

As multi-donor general budget support engagements were perceived
to become politically complex and difficult to manage, interest in sector
budget support grew (Chapter 5). Sector budget support operations also disburse directly to the treasury but allow for a narrower focus and aim to

augment funding for key sector spending (additionality), often for health and educational spending. There is also evidence that sector budget support didn't face the same rigor in precondition requirements such as an adequate macro/fiscal framework. In Ghana for example, while partners withdrew from the programmatic general budget support engagement because of macro/fiscal concerns, sector budget support engagement in agriculture and environment were allowed to continue, thereby covering the potential revenue gap (European Commission 2017, IEG 2016a). Similarly, in Vietnam, budget support engagement in sectors became more dominant as interest in PRSCs waned. This is reflected in World Bank project data that show a doubling in the relative share of budget support operations led by sector teams from 15 to 30 per cent between 2008 and the 2009–13 period (IEG 2015).

Sectoral budget support appealed to donors but also led to problems in execution. The appeal of sector support was to allow donors to label their assistance as directed at specific causes, such as education, health, or gender equity emerging from the policy dialogue. However, it also posed challenges in securing greater local ownership and led to a more fragmented dialogue, in part because the policy dialogue was with line ministries (e.g. ministries of education or health), but resources pass through the ministry of finance with responsibility over fiscal policy and budget allocation (IEG 2015). The trend of leading budget support engagement by sectors has gradually been reversed, although sector engagement continues to play a dominant role in the policy reform engagement (Box 3.3).

Box 3.3 The role of sectors in programmatic budget support

A recent programmatic engagement with strong sector ownership is the Rwanda human capital budget support development policy finance credit by the World Bank. While it is co-led by the macro-fiscal team and sector teams, it is not sector budget support (i.e. funds are not earmarked to sectors). It builds reforms in a sequenced manner in mutually reinforcing policy areas. For example, in the health sector, the engagement first aimed to strengthen fiscal sustainability, then help determine the benefit package and lastly support allocation of resources by adjusting the payment mechanism to health providers (World Bank 2020d). These sequenced and mutually reinforcing actions were only possible given the medium-term orientation and phased approach of the engagement. Similarly, the EU aimed to support forestry and wildlife in Ghana through a set of sequenced and mutually reinforcing policy actions.

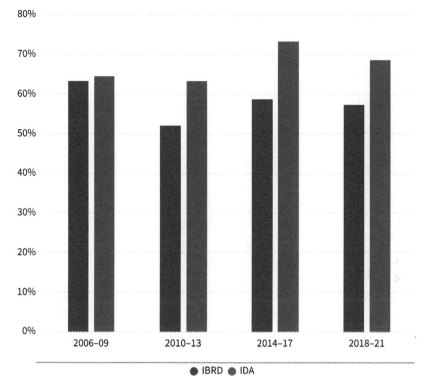

Figure 3.5 Share of programmatic operations in the World Bank IBRD and IDA budget support portfolio, 2006–21
Source: World Bank Business Warehouse.

The relevance of a programmatic engagement remains high, despite the gradual shift away from use of PRSCs over time (see Chapter 5). Over 60 per cent of all World Bank budget support lending continues to be programmatic in nature. Programmatic lending engagement in IDA countries is more prevalent than in IBRD countries. In IDA countries it peaked in 2014, when 90 per cent of all new budget support operations were programmatic in nature. This compares to 73 per cent of IBRD operations in 2018 (Figure 3.5). Programmatic support continues to be common across agencies. For example, Japan's programme for market economy, fiscal and financial reform, which aims to pursue medium-term reforms in the sector through a phased engagement.

Crowding in Private Finance

Budget support can be used as a vehicle to crowd in private finance. In addition to supporting reforms that improve the investment climate, budget

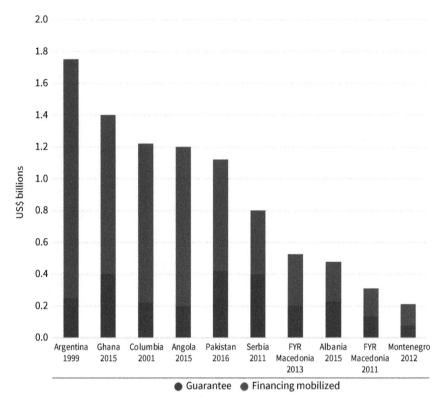

Figure 3.6 Using budget support to mobilize private financing through guarantees
Source: World Bank Business Intelligence.

support can also be deployed in the form of a guarantee, which can provide for risk mitigation to commercial lenders with respect to debt service payment defaults by government when the proceeds of the financing are applied to budgetary support (World Bank 2015).

Policy-based guarantees (PBGs) were used predominantly in middle-income countries (e.g. Argentina or North Macedonia). Until recently, low income and low-capacity countries in which credit ratings were weaker and financial markets less mature were not eligible. The first lower-income country to benefit from PBGs was Ghana, in 2015, when a $400 million guarantee was used to leverage one billion dollars in sovereign bonds from private banks. The ability to leverage private finance through policy-based guarantees has ranged significantly from 6:1 in Argentina in 1999 to 1:1 in Serbia in 2011. On average, the World Bank leveraged at a rate of 1:2.6 (Figure 3.6).

The use of PBGs to leverage private finance generated much interest during the 'billions to trillions' push (Wilson 2015), but the inherent risks of the approach have raised concerns (IEG 2016b), and deployment of the instrument (see Appendix B, Table B.1) has remained limited despite its potential and great financing need. Private sector flows and ability of the instrument to crowd in private capital are addressed in greater depth in Chapters 2 and 4.

Budget Support in Fragile and Conflict-Affected Settings

Budget support remains an important revenue source for many recipient countries. As a proportion of GDP, general government expenditure, and compared to private sector flows (see Chapter 2) its relevance has declined across high- and upper-middle-income countries. However, it continues to be an important source for countercyclical financing during times of crisis. In some middle-income countries, such as Ghana and Uganda, budget support has helped to sustain public service delivery by providing liquidity when government revenue alone was unable to cover statutory debt and wage payments (European Commission 2015, European Commission 2016, IEG 2016c).

In low-income countries, such as Rwanda, budget support continues to play a more important role, as reflected in its large share relative to GDP and general government expenditure. In 2016, for example, the World Bank, EU institutions, the African Development Bank, and Belgium together provided $677 million in budget support to Rwanda. This was equivalent to about 30 per cent of total government spending that year.

Budget support is also becoming increasingly important in fragile, conflict affected, and vulnerable (FCV) countries. Since 2012 World Bank budget support to FCV countries has increased on average from 0.7 per cent of GDP to 3.2 per cent of GDP. The number of World Bank budget support engagements has also increased significantly and now account for about a third of all budget support operations (Figure 3.7). The volume of World Bank budget support loans to FCV countries has also gradually increased from 15 to 24 per cent over the same time period. Average loan size for FCV countries was recorded at US$207.5 million and is significantly higher than that of a non-FCV IDA country at US$155.8 million. This was also the case in 2008 after the food price shock and in 2013 following the Ebola crisis, both of which affected FCV countries disproportionately.

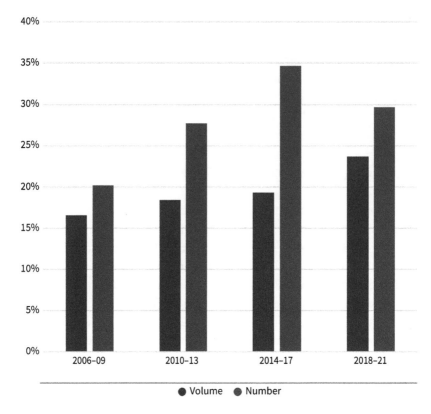

Figure 3.7 World Bank budget support lending to FCV countries, share of total budget support commitments and number of operations 2006–21

Box 3.4 Budget support in fragile, conflict, and violence-affected situations

Budget support has become an increasingly important instrument in countries affected by fragility, conflict, and violence (FCV), as it can provide much-needed liquidity and help advance policy and institutional reforms (World Bank 2022).

Budget support can be relevant in a wide range of FCV countries with very different contexts and development obstacles. Particularly in low-income countries, budget support has helped provide much-needed financing to maintain basic state functions, including maintaining a payroll for public employees, laying the building blocks of public administration, and helping to provide rudimentary public financial management. For example, budget support supported nascent fiscal institutions and basic fiscal management in the Central African Republic to help rebuild public trust in an environment of frequent conflict (World Bank 2022). Middle-income FCV

countries have a higher per capita income but may also benefit from critical policy reforms. Iraq is an example of a conflict-affected MIC that embarked on fiscal
transparency reforms that were nudged along with the help a series of budget support operations but then slowed down when increasing oil prices reduced the fiscal
stress. The unpredictable and volatile nature of challenges in FCV countries typically
requires a steady and incremental reform effort supported by a series of budget support operations. Such efforts help with wage bill reform, transparency, and better
public expenditure planning, but can be thwarted by policy reversal (as in the case
of Liberia) or catastrophic collapse of the political situation (as in Afghanistan).

Institutional Capacity of Budget Support Recipients

Countries vary widely in the strength of their policy and institutional foundations. To inform resource allocation criteria, the World Bank conducts annual
assessments of countries' policies and institutional performance. There has
been a gradual and moderate decline in the Country Policy and Institutional Assessment (CPIA) scores associated with World Bank budget support
since 2005. Dividing countries into three CPIA performance brackets (low,
medium, and high CPIA) shows that, since 2015, more budget support
engagements are in countries with a low CPIA score, a change from the previous trend where good institutional and policy performance was rewarded
through continuous and programmatic budget support. This pattern also
holds true for CPIA subdimensions, such as public sector management and
institutions and efficiency of revenue mobilization.

The decline in CPIA scores for LICs and LMICs seen over the last decade
(Figure 3.8) largely reflects the shifting composition of budget support toward
FCV countries and away from high performing UMICs which graduate from
IBRD eligibility. FCV countries, with both lower and lower-middle income
levels, carry weaker CPIA scores drawing averages down as their share of
budget support has grown, as noted above. Chapter 4 elaborates further on
the CPIA performance performance trends across country attributes.

Budget support is also increasingly being provided to countries with weak
public financial management (PFM) systems. A decline is visible for LICs and
LMICs in overall PFM quality as proxied by public expenditure and financial
accountability (PEFA) score quality, and particularly for LICs with regard to
budget credibility (Figure 3.9). Many IFI partners used to require adequate
PFM systems before they provided budget support to ensure funds would be
used for mutually agreeable objectives. This has receded in importance over

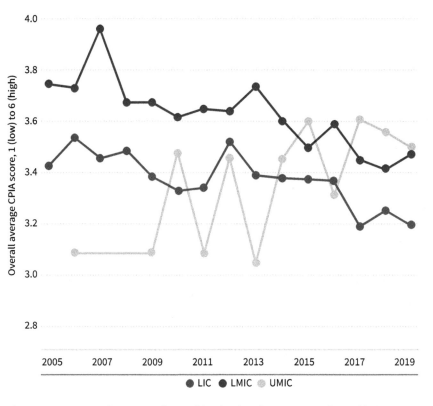

Figure 3.8 Average Country Policy and Institutional Assessment Score (CPIA group, 2005–19) for Budget Support Operations
Source: World Bank Business Intelligence and CPIA Data Hub.

the last decade, with the rationale that budget support can be, and is, used to strengthen PFM processes through tailored engagement in associated reform areas. Countries with relatively weak PFM systems such as Afghanistan, the Democratic Republic of Congo, Madagascar, and Yemen became eligible to draw on the instrument.

The Evolution of Conditionality and General Thematic Focus

Conditionality is a fundamental aspect of the contract around which donors and recipient countries operate. As discussed in Chapter 1, the design, use, and content of conditionality are integral features and can take various forms, including the following:

- Based on a set of mutually agreed reform areas, prior actions can be used as the legal condition for disbursement. These are deemed critical

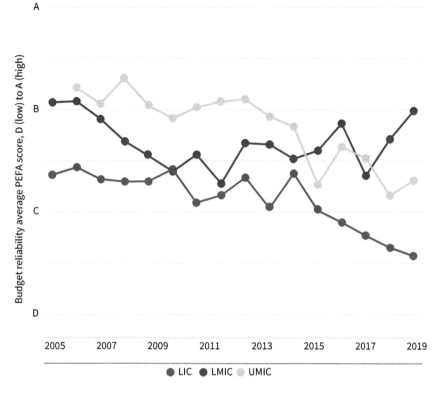

Figure 3.9 World Bank budget support lending by budget credibility score and country income group, 2005–20
Source: World Bank Business Intelligence and PEFA Secretariat.

to achieving the objectives of the programme and based on in-depth analytical work. They are often accompanied by technical assistance and project lending. The recipient provides legal evidence on the completion of the action before disbursement can be made.

- Tranche release conditions can be used as policy and reform measures that must be in place before a subsequent tranche can be released.
- In the context of a programmatic engagement, triggers can be used to document anticipated actions for subsequent rounds. Triggers are expected to become prior actions but are not legal conditions for disbursement in themselves.
- Benchmarks are the implementation progress markers of the programme that describe the content and results of the government's programme in areas monitored by the Bank. Benchmarks are not legal conditions for disbursement.

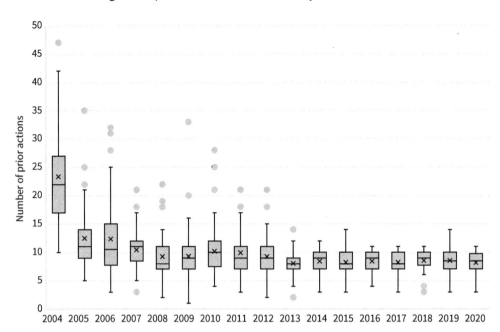

Figure 3.10 Prior actions in World Bank budget support operations, 2004–2020
Source: World Bank Operations Policy and Country Services prior actions database.
Note: The lines extending vertically (known as whiskers) indicate points outside the upper and lower quartiles, which are considered outliers.

The use of conditionality in budget support operations has shifted over time. In the early 2000s, it was commonplace to require a wide range of conditions across sectors. On average, the World Bank used twenty-four prior actions for budget support operations in 2004. Note that more conditions do not mean greater program rigor and depth. In fact an evaluation by the IDB suggests that programmes with larger numbers of conditions tend to have a greater share of conditions of low criticality or depth (IDB 2015). It was an explicit objective of the new policy lending instruments of the MDBs initiated after 2000 to reduce the complexity and burden of budget support conditionality (Chapter 1), and donors explicitly aimed to reduce conditionality as an aspect of the 2005 Paris Agreement. Development partners have since become much more parsimonious in the selection of policy conditions. The average number of policy actions for the World Bank fell to between eight and ten (Figure 3.10), with some programmes involving DDOs or PBGs having even fewer select conditions. Operations with thirteen or more conditions such as the Afghanistan Incentive Programme Development Policy Grant in 2021 (which aimed for flexibility by attaching separate amounts to be disbursed for each tranche release condition) have become outliers.

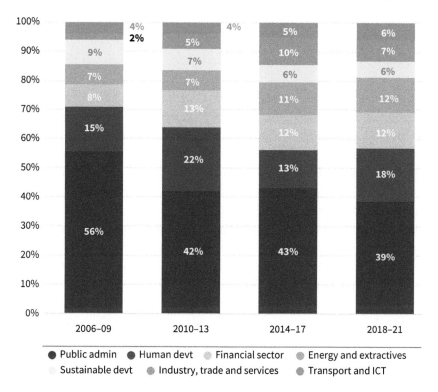

Figure 3.11 Sectoral distribution of World Bank conditionality
Source: World Bank Operations Policy and Country Services prior actions database.

The sectoral distribution of budget support has also changed over time. While conditionality relating to public administration continues to make up the largest share, it has fallen from 56 per cent of all actions in the 2006–9 period to about 40 per cent subsequently. Conversely, conditionality relating to human development, the financial sector, and energy and extractives have increased (Figure 3.11). There is some regional variation in the application of conditionality. While public administration absorbs the highest share of policy actions across all regions, it is most dominant in Africa and East Asia. Conditionality relating to human development is most commonplace in Europe and Central Asia and Latin America, whereas Middle East and North African countries have a disproportionately large engagement in the financial sector.

Reform of public administration is a principal and widely varying theme for conditionality, covering ninety-seven unique focus areas. These are predominantly concentrated on central government or federal agencies (80 per cent of conditions) although conditionality at the subnational level can be important, particularly in federated governments with significant responsibility delegated to the state or municipal level.

Under public administration, there has been an emphasis on public expenditure management, however with a notable declining trend. While 36 per cent of public administration conditions in the period 2006–9 focused public expenditure management, this was gradually reduced to 15 per cent in the 2018–21 period. Similarly, there has been a declining pattern in conditions for administrative and civil service reform from about 11 to just over 5 per cent in 2018–21. Nor has there been much focus on information communication technology reforms, including the important area of financial management information systems (Hashim and Piatti-Fünfkirchen 2018).

By contrast, transparency, accountability, and good governance have gained greater attention in design of conditionality since 2010. Other elements of public administration gaining emphasis include domestic revenue administration, tax policy, and debt management (Figure 3.12).

Conditions in human development include education, health and social support. Social support conditionality has gradually replaced engagement in education across human development. Health and social support sectors have been on a gradual declining trend over time. Health conditionality has again picked up since the COVID-19 pandemic, requiring dedicated actions for COVID-19-related support. For example, in a budget support operation to India, COVID-19-related conditionality required the government to establish a special health insurance scheme for health workers providing essential care/medical services to COVID-19 patients. Similarly, in the Dominican Republic, conditionality required the government to establish a citizen oversight commission for COVID-19-related procurement and contracting management. Education conditionality has been deprioritized. The education share of human development (HD) conditionality was reduced from 53 per cent in the 2006–9 period to 16 per cent in 2018–21 (Figure 3.13).

Within the HD sector engagement, the thematic orientation of social support was largely through social safety nets. While these only constituted 27 per cent of conditionality in 2006–9, this increased considerably in the decade to reach 46.4 per cent in the period 2018–21. This is in part driven by the need to protect the poor from COVID-19-related fiscal consolidation measures. Following COVID-19, in Ecuador conditionality supported the government to create an emergency cash transfer scheme for vulnerable households that are not covered by social assistance programmes. Health sector conditionality focused predominantly on health system strengthening, health service delivery, and health finance. Conditionality in health service delivery has

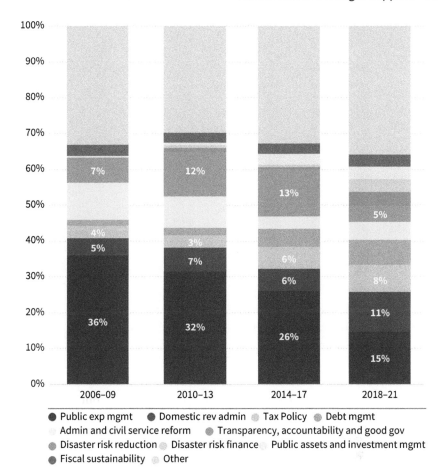

Figure 3.12 Thematic distribution of World Bank conditionality in public administration

Source: World Bank Operations Policy and Country Services prior actions database.

increased significantly from 6 per cent in 2006–9 to over 30 per cent in 2018–21. At the same time health finance conditionality decreased from 21 per cent in the 2010–13 period to under 10 per cent in 2018–21. In education, there has been a re-emphasis on quality of teaching. While teacher-related conditionality decreased rapidly from 16 to 9 per cent between 2006–9 and 2014–17, their share has increased to 26 per cent in the 2018–21 period. Conversely, work on education governance and school-based management has decreased from 28 per cent to 19 per cent over the same period.

Conditionality in human development has been supported increasingly through dedicated human capital development policy operations by the World Bank. These include programmatic human capital budget support

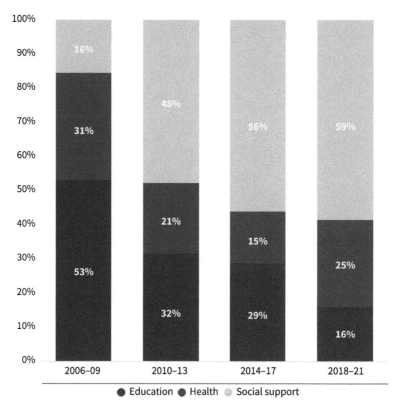

Figure 3.13   Sectoral breakdown of World Bank conditionality in human development
Source: World Bank Operations Policy and Country Services prior actions database.

engagements across regions in Peru, Rwanda, Pakistan, and Madagascar.[4] They take a lifecycle approach to address multisectoral bottlenecks in human capital development. Progress against malnutrition, for example, requires a well-coordinated approach across sectors and agencies in government. Conditionality in the Rwanda human capital DPF, for example, supports public financial management reforms that tag the budget across sectors for nutrition to make budget management processes more sensitive to cross-sectoral nutrition needs. At the same time, social protection conditionality aims to support targeting of the social assistance programme that will have spillover effects for the health sector through improved subsidization of health insurance.

---

[4] Peru investing in human capital DPF (P176387); Rwanda programmatic human capital for inclusive growth DPF (P171554); Pakistan human capital DPF series (P171568); Madagascar investing in human capital DPF (P168697).

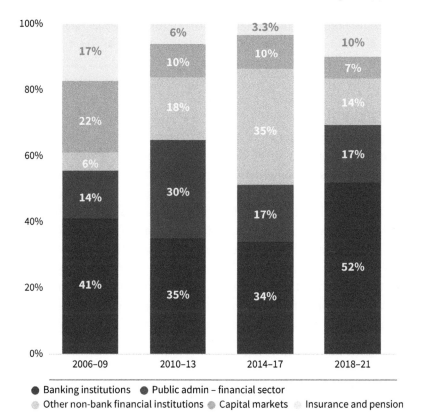

Figure 3.14 Sectoral breakdown of World Bank conditionality in the financial sector
Source: World Bank Operations Policy and Country Services prior actions database.

Conditionality in the financial sector include banking institutions, public administration in the financial sector, other non-banking financial institutions, capital markets, and insurance and pensions. The thematic focus of these has largely been on financial sector oversight and policy and banking regulation and restructuring. Conditionality for non-bank financial institutions has supported micro-small and medium enterprises (MSME) finance, financial inclusion, credit infrastructure, and housing finance. Capital markets used to make up about 20 per cent of financial sector conditionality but have been reduced significantly over time. Similarly, conditionality on insurance and pensions has been deprioritized over time (Figure 3.14).

Budget support lends itself to addressing cross-cutting development challenges such as gender equality and climate change that require close coordination across sectors and levels of government. The World Bank is tagging its budget support engagement for gender content and targeting climate co-benefits.

For gender tagging, a budget support operation is eligible if it has research-based analysis to identify gender gaps, specific actions to address the gender gaps; and a results framework to measure progress in closing identified gender gaps. The share of World Bank budget support operations tagged for gender has increased from 24 per cent in 2017 to 70 per cent in 2021, with considerable regional variation. The first dedicated gender budget support operation 'Albania gender equality in access to economic opportunities' was approved for Albania in 2019. The World Bank notes that this approach has helped align diverse stakeholders around a reform agenda, which has worked well to support the inclusion of gender-focused prior actions, and supporting analytical work critical to build awareness around gender gaps and their impact on development and economic growth more broadly (World Bank 2022a). While lending has become more gender sensitive, explicit conditionality on gender remains limited. There have been only thirteen prior actions in the 2014–17 and 2018–21 period each. The World Bank (2022a) also notes that budget support operations were used to address gender-based violence across all regions, including by addressing intimate partner violence, sexual harassment in employment, and child marriage, as well as through fighting the negative impact on female labour force participation.

Budget support is also a central vehicle for the World Bank to address adaptation to and mitigation of climate change. Through country climate and development diagnostics, budget support operations can support better planning and policies to help countries reach their climate objectives. These can be used to inform, prioritize, and sequence climate action. The World Bank estimates climate co-benefits in its operations and is committed to achieving at least 35 per cent of lending in co-benefits, calculated as the share of budget support financing that contributes to climate adaptation or mitigation. In 2021, the World Bank climate co-benefits reached 32 per cent of total financing, which missed the target in part due to the emphasis on COVID-19-related lending. Budget support resources, however, remain fully fungible, and it cannot be determined whether and how budget support resources from co-benefits are channelled toward climate action.

The average climate focus of World Bank operations has steadily increased over time. Prior actions have become considerably more sensitive to climate needs, with about 80 per cent of actions being relating to climate adaptation and mitigation (Figure 3.15). Climate action is predominantly taken through engagement in energy and extractive industries. Operations have included a diverse set of policies and institutional reform for climate action, including transforming fiscal policy to support climate goals such as carbon pricing, tax incentives for lower emitting technologies, getting energy prices right

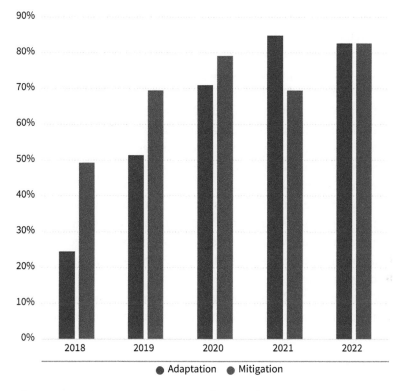

Figure 3.15 Prior actions sensitive to climate adaptation or mitigation
Source: World Bank CPAD Database (2022).

and removing significant subsidies, supporting long-term strategies, main-streaming climate in public financial management, and greening the financial system and long-term resilient decarbonization. Similar to gender equality, explicit climate conditionality, however, remains limited.

Conclusion

The use of budget support as an aid instrument has ebbed and flowed over the years. While it is not the primary vehicle to deliver aid, it remains an important one. About 10–13 per cent of ODA has been delivered through budget support, reaching 20 per cent during times of crises.

Budget support remains the ODA vehicle of choice for many recipient countries, reflecting demand for fast-disbursing and fungible instrument. However, supply has been limited in some MDBs as it is perceived as riskier, less effective, and displacing project lending by some constituents, leading to some of them imposition of caps on total commitments. However, given the favourable evaluation of its budget support effectiveness (discussed in Chapter 4) and the increasing need for budget support in countries affected by the recent crises, caps are becoming increasingly redundant.

MDBs have provided the largest share of budget support, covering about 85 per cent of total commitments. Of the MDBs, the World Bank—specifically through IBRD financing—is the largest contributing agency. There are some DAC countries that continue to provide budget support, though this has become less systematic over time. There are some isolated cases of non-DAC countries providing budget support.

Financing volumes fluctuated significantly, particularly as a result of one-off balance-of-payments support to middle-income borrowers. Much of the variations in financing volumes reflect short-term countercyclical financing to middle-income countries during times of economic crisis and constrained access to capital markets.

Many different modalities of budget support have been developed to cater to country circumstances. This flexibility of the instrument has helped maintain its relevance during times of crisis, the need to crowd in private capital, or help insure against natural disasters or other emergencies.

Pursuing a programmatic engagement has remained relevant as a means to support policy reform over the medium term, especially in lower income countries. The continuous engagement allows for supporting a sequenced reform programme to complement investment lending. In low-income countries almost two out of three World Bank operations are consistent with and complementary to a medium-term programmatic engagement.

Budget support has been increasingly used to support fragile and conflict-affected countries to provide much-needed liquidity and help advance policy and institutional reforms. About a quarter of World Bank budget support lending is currently in support of FCV countries.

In the early 2000s, adequate institutional and public financial management capacity was considered a *sine qua non* of eligibility for budget support. This requirement appears to have become less important as donors have extended access to budget support to an increasing number of countries with limited capacity, as measured by CPIA and PEFA scores. While it may provide resources to countries most in need, it also makes it more difficult to make the case for prudent resource use in line with mutually agreed priorities.

The use of conditionality has shifted over time. Development partners have acknowledged the need to be more parsimonious in choosing relevant actions to keep reforms manageable and avoid diluting the engagement space.

The sectoral distribution of conditionality has also changed over time. While conditionality relating to public administration continues to make up the largest share, it has declined significantly in favour of conditionality for human development and energy and extractives. Public expenditure management and civil service reform actions have declined, whereas domestic revenue administration, tax policy, and debt management have picked up significantly, especially since 2015. Conditionality in human development is heavily tilted toward social support. While health-related conditionality has increased due to COVID-19, education-related conditionality is becoming increasingly rare. In the financial sector, conditionality relating to banking institutions has become more prominent, especially with regard to financial sector oversight and policy and banking regulation and restructuring.

Budget support has been deployed increasingly to address cross-cutting development challenges such as gender equality or climate change. While the World Bank is tagging for gender engagement and estimating climate co-benefits, actual conditionality relating to those areas remains limited.

There is no comprehensive and up-to-date database capturing budget support from all sources. This makes it challenging to assess financial flows and the relevance of the instrument in the global aid architecture. Greater transparency and independent verification are fundamental building blocks for strengthening the effectiveness of the instrument and its relevance for country engagement.

4
The Performance of Budget Support

Supporting policy and institutional reform is one of the key objectives of budget support. The mere transfer of financial resources to a recipient country's budget, even when conditioned on certain policy actions, does not guarantee reform success (Svensson 2003). For instance, policy and regulatory reforms may fail to be implemented or sustained because of political economy considerations or redistributive concerns (Alesina and Drazen 1991). Sound evidence and analytical work may be lacking about the costs and benefits of policy change, making it difficult to design effective development policy operations (Deiniger, Squire, and Basu 1998). Uncertainty regarding the outcome may prevent policymakers from committing to engage in costly reforms (Fernandez and Rodrik 1991). All these factors may limit the effectiveness of policy-based lending.

On the other hand, development agencies—especially the multilaterals—have a long tradition in providing budget support and often take a leading role in producing development policy knowledge (Clemens and Kremer 2016). They are often engaged in policy dialogue, which may help in influencing policymaker beliefs regarding the benefits of reform (Smets 2020).[1] Furthermore, around the turn of the millennium, donors started to modify their approach toward policy-based lending, including strengthened country ownership of lending programmes by using countries' own development strategies, reducing the average number of conditions in loans, and moving from ex ante toward ex post conditionality (see Chapter 1). These modifications of policy-based financing appear to have had positive effects.

This chapter examines the performance of budget support in terms of reaching its development objectives and goes on to analyse which factors make policy-based lending successful at the programme level. It also reviews the literature on the policy impact of budget support at the country level

---

[1] The evolution of beliefs depends on local context and past experience, while they also fulfil important psychological and functional needs (see Benabou and Tirole 2016). Furthermore, a burgeoning literature shows that beliefs matter for policy choice, potentially leading to policy inefficiencies (Rodrik 2014). Informative and non-informative communication may, however, help in influencing inaccurate policy beliefs. See Smets (2020) for more detail.

Retooling Development Aid in the 21st Century. Shahrokh Fardoust et al., Oxford University Press.
© Shahrokh Fardoust et al., (2023). DOI: 10.1093/oso/9780192882196.003.0004

and presents some new empirical evidence that extends the latest research to fragile states and low-income countries.[2]

At the programme level, conventional evaluation metrics indicate that budget support has performed as well as traditional project financing in meeting its development objectives. The analysis presented in this chapter shows that factors at both the donor and recipient level matter for reform success but that much of the variation remains unexplained.

At the country level, a review of the recent empirical evidence indicates considerable heterogeneity across countries in terms of policy impact. Budget support targeting reforms in economic policy has been found to be successful, while addressing certain public sector governance and social policy concerns has proven more difficult. Recent research also finds that there may be diminishing policy returns to budget support and that the process of policy dialogue is important. Empirical analysis suggests that policy lending can be highly effective in times of crisis. The evidence presented in this chapter indicates that the policy impact also depends on the country context.

As discussed in Chapter 1, in addition to supporting policy and institutional reform, budget support was long considered the preferred mechanism to implement the principles of the 2005 Paris Declaration on Aid Effectiveness, which concluded that aid needed to show strong country ownership, be more predictable, use country systems, and be harmonized across donors to reduce transactions costs. Long before the Paris Declaration, it had become clear that without a strong commitment from the recipient country, development assistance was unlikely to be effective (see World Bank 1998). To facilitate medium-term fiscal planning, aid flows needed to become more predictable for recipient countries. Instead of relying on their own implementation arrangements, donors should support strengthening and using recipient country public financial management (PFM) systems and have a clear focus on results. Donor proliferation increased transactions costs, including through duplication of conditionality. Development aid needed better coordination and streamlining among donors (better 'harmonization and alignment').

Budget support emerged as the most promising aid modality to implement these principles. Countries would formulate their own development

---

[2] The World Bank's policy-based loans are the main focus of this chapter. Three reasons motivate this choice. First, most academic research focuses on World Bank lending and not so much budget support by other multilateral or bilateral agencies (see Bulman et al. 2017 for a notable exception). Second, the World Bank is by far the main provider of budget support. Third, recent research indicates that results on the success of World Bank lending generalize pretty well across donor agencies (Briggs 2019).

strategies and policy reform needs, and donors would support them by trans-ferring financial resources to the recipient country's budget. In the context of medium-term support, reform progress would be reviewed regularly, and financing adjusted gradually, responding to transparent performance measures. To align reform efforts with implementation capacity, the idea was to choose only those reform actions that were critical for achieving development results (World Bank 2015). Whenever possible, budget support would strengthen PFM arrangements. In countries with support from a multitude of development partners, harmonization along a common accountability and results framework should foster coherent (policy) interventions.

Drawing on independent evaluative evidence, this chapter discusses the effectiveness of budget support as a tool to implement the Paris Declaration. It finds that, in the right context, the principles of the Paris Declaration improve development effectiveness.

The rest of this chapter is structured as follows. The next section discusses budget support performance at the programme level. Section 2 investigates the policy impact at the country level. Section 3 critically reviews the effectiveness of the Paris Declaration principles and examines the contribution of budget support as a tool to implement the Paris Declaration. The last section summarizes the chapter's main findings.

Budget Support Performance at the Programme Level

To evaluate the performance of budget support at the programme level, we rely on project evaluation metrics produced by the World Bank's Independent Evaluation Group (IEG). After a project is completed, IEG rates various aspects of it. In rating the outcome, IEG gauges the extent to which an operation's major relevant objectives were achieved. Its overall outcome rating is the main measure of a project's performance.

Between 2000 and 2020, 75 per cent of budget support operations were considered successful in reaching their development objectives (Figure 4.1). Compared to investment lending, budget support lending performed slightly better as only 74 per cent of investment operations were successful. Overall, however, the difference in performance between budget support lending and investment lending is small and not consistent over time.

Policy-based lending tended to perform better in International Bank for Reconstruction and Development (IBRD) countries, where 83 per cent of operations were deemed successful, than in International Development Association (IDA) countries and fragile and conflict-affected states, where

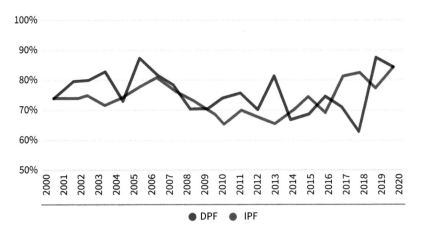

Figure 4.1 Performance of World Bank budget support and investment lending, 2000–20

Source: World Bank
Note: DPF= Development Policy Financing (budget support); IPF= Investment Project Financing. The figure shows the share of successful operations, i.e., the share of operations with an IEG outcome rating of 'moderately satisfactory', 'satisfactory' or 'highly satisfactory'.

just 69 per cent of operations were rate successful (Figure 4.2; see also World Bank, 2022). The lower policy and institutional quality in these countries may explain part of the difference. The weak performance rating for sub-Saharan Africa—where only 63 per cent of Development Policy Financing (DPF) performed moderately satisfactorily or better between 2000 and 2020—is also consistent with this reasoning.

What role do donor efforts or country conditions have in determining success of budget support operations? On the donor side, several aspects related to the design of budget support operations affect success. Policy-based loans are more likely to be successful when the design of an operation is informed by sound evidence and rigorous analysis (Fardoust and Flannagan 2013; IEG 2015; IEG 2016a; Knack et al. 2020; Smets 2020; Smets and Record, 2022). Moll, Geli, and Saavedra (2015) find that proper results frameworks are positively correlated with reform success. Investing resources in design thus seems to pay off. Indeed, Malesa and Silarszky (2005) find that preparation time is positively correlated with successful development policy lending. Smets, Knack, and Molenaers (2013) show that good preparation may also increase borrower compliance.

The development agency officials leading a budget support operation also have an important influence on performance. Although little is known about

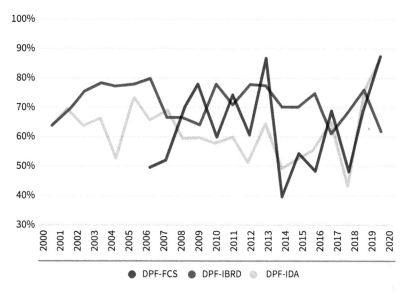

Figure 4.2 Budget support performance in IBRD, IDA, and FCS countries, 2000–20

Source: World Bank.
Note: DPF= Development Policy Financing (budget support); FCS = Fragile and Conflict-affected State; IDA=International Development Association (Low-income countries); IBRD=International Bank for Reconstruction and Development (Middle-income countries). The figure shows the share of successful budget support operations, i.e., the share of budget support operations with an IEG outcome rating of 'moderately satisfactory', 'satisfactory' or 'highly satisfactory'.

which competencies are required,[3] experience in designing a reform operation and appropriate policy dialogue skills is deemed important (Moll, Geli, and Saavedra 2015). For instance, effective policy dialogue may lead recipient policymakers to update their beliefs about the benefits of policy change, leading to increased reform commitment. Influencing policymaker beliefs may involve evidence and new information, but also non-informative dimensions of policy dialogue—such as a common work history—may lead to more successful policy reform (Smets 2020; Smets and Record 2022).

The privatization of Mozambique's telecommunications market illustrates the importance of project design and policy dialogue. Analytical work during the mid-1990s indicated a clear need for privatizing the telecommunication sector: by the year 2000 there were only 85,000 landlines and 51,000 cellphones in Mozambique, with high telephone charges and poor quality cellphones (World Bank 2005). Faced with the Marxist-Leninist FRELIMO party, it took the World Bank considerable time and effort to convince the

---

[3] In examining IEG outcome ratings, Limodio (2021) finds that project leader fixed effects explain a significant share of the variation in project outcomes. Relying on the curriculum vitae of project leaders, Limodio finds that a publication record, no degree in the natural sciences, no working experience with the IMF, a university degree obtained from the home country, and an MBA are positively correlated with project leader fixed effects.

Ministry of Planning to allow a second player into the telecommunications market. Several political advisors to the Minister of Planning claimed that only a state monopoly would serve the people. An extensive World Bank team succeeded in convincing the Mozambican government officials by showing them the positive impacts of telecom privatization, providing examples from all over the globe. This was instrumental in shifting the mindset. Also, additional in-country analytical work and a fine-tuning of conditionality helped to accommodate the operation to the local context and served to convince the government of Mozambique. After the negotiations, the government of Mozambique expressed a clear and firm commitment to implement the programmes: it created an independent regulatory body, revised the telecommunications sector law, and attracted a new mobile operator. By 2005, there were 800,000 mobile phone subscribers, and the quality of service improved substantially (World Bank 2005). Smets, Knack, and Molenaers (2013) argue that the extensive policy dialogue and accompanying analytical work facilitated belief change concerning the benefits of the reform, which increased ownership over the reform programmes (Hirschman 1965; James and Gutkind 1985).

On the recipient side, deteriorating economic conditions provide a window of opportunity for change (Krueger 1993; Alesina, Ardagna, and Trebbi 2006). In the language of contract theory, a deep economic crisis 'reduces the reservation utility' for engaging in reform.[4] After accession to the Eurozone, the Greek government built up large economic imbalances. By 2009 the fiscal deficit rose to 15 per cent of GDP, the current account deficit deteriorated to 11 per cent of GDP, while public debt reached 130 per cent GDP. These imbalances were externally financed and subsequently channelled in the economy through inefficient transfers, subsidies, and investments (IMF 2013). For instance, the Greek public sector was used as an instrument for patronage with high public sector wage differentials and an overly generous pension system (compared to the OECD average of 60.8 per cent, a Greek pension used to amount to 95.7 per cent of an employee's average lifetime earnings). Other frictions, such as indefinite labour contracts, compounded the crisis. Mitsopoulos and Pelagidis (2011) argue that weak political institutions and powerful interest groups were the main underlying causes for these apparent inefficiencies.[5] With the outbreak of the global financial crisis,

---

[4] The next section presents some empirical evidence that policy lending can be an effective instrument to support reform in times of crisis.

[5] These practices can be traced back to the 1980s, when Prime Minister Andreas Papandreou used public funds to reward previously deprived social groups and special interest groups such as the trade unions (Lynn 2011).

Greece's economy risked default and severe recession. In 2010, repeated downgrades of creditworthiness caused a sudden stop in capital flows and interest rate spreads near default levels. As a result, the government engaged in a large adjustment programme, led by the European Union, the European Central Bank, and the IMF. The main objectives were to restore fiscal and debt sustainability and to increase competitiveness. The programmes entailed cuts in public sector wages and pensions, tax increases, and structural reforms to enhance productivity. Although implementation of the adjustment measures took longer than expected and was marred by considerable social turmoil, the deep crisis did act as a catalyst for change.

Economic growth following the implementation of reform conditions is positively associated with project performance (Denizer, Squire, and Basu 2013; Smets, Knack, and Molenaers 2013). It is likely that short-term economic success helps increase the credibility of the reforms and sustain adjustment programmes by generating additional resources and muting political opposition. These findings suggest that the timing of engaging in policy reform support matters.

Budget support operations tend to be more successful in countries with high-quality policies and institutions (Dollar and Levin 2005).[6] A large body of literature shows that checks and balances on the executive or broad political representation promote investments in public goods, which in turn incentivize political leaders to build fiscal capacity and implement growth-enhancing policies (Besley and Persson 2011). Conversely, a lack of checks and balances on the political leadership may jeopardize reform efforts.

The 1987 structural adjustment credit in the Democratic Republic of Congo (DRC) provides a telling illustration of the importance of political ownership. In June 1987, the World Bank approved a Structural Adjustment Credit, including much-needed measures to reform the public investment programmes. However, even before the loan was declared effective, large inefficient investments were initiated outside the agreed-upon investment plan. Devarajan, Dollar, and Holmgren (2001) relate the failure to the DRC leadership and note that President Mobutu had no intention of making any change in the way he was handling the country. That is, while a broad consensus on the reform agenda existed between the World Bank team and government officials, the president completely disregarded the loan conditions and continued with discretionary spending, leading to the breakdown of the reform programme.

---

[6] Chapter 3 indicates, however, that budget support has not always been very selective in this dimension.

Although the evidence on budget support performance continues to grow, much remains unknown on what makes policy-based loans successful, especially on the recipient side. To illustrate this point, we regress IEG's rating of the World Bank and the borrower performance in supporting the operation on IEG's overall outcome rating. Both factors can explain 73 per cent of the variation in programme performance (the remaining 27 per cent may be related to external shocks knocking programmes off track), with borrow performance more important than **Bank performance** (Table 4.1).[7] World Bank effort in identifying and preparing an operation has a much larger impact than does its supervision, i.e., monitoring and resolution of threats to development outcomes. We also regressed a set of programmes leader dummies on World Bank performance and find that (time-invariant) task leader characteristics explain about 36 per cent of the variation.

Much less is known about **borrower performance**. Table 4.1 shows that overall policy and institutional quality, growth spurts, and initial macroeconomic conditions are associated with borrower performance, but the R^2 of the regression model is only 0.0475. And a country fixed effects regression indicates that time-invariant country conditions explain about 20 per cent of country performance, leaving 80 per cent unexplained. Cultural traits and characteristics, policymaker beliefs, government capacity, the legitimacy of reform, citizen communication, and the role of identity politics are understudied but potentially important factors determining reform success. For instance, while evidence, analytical work and new information may influence policymaker beliefs (Hjort et al. 2021), it is important to note that information exchange does not always help in changing beliefs.[8] Furthermore, finding out the views of policymakers during policy discussions may not be straightforward (see Smets 2020).

Additionally, there are indications that (complementary) investment lending and technical assistance may improve the effectiveness of budget support operations (see, e.g., IEG 2013b). While sector knowledge and client relationships matter in this respect, there is a need to study in more depth how budget support could benefit from complementary operations and customized technical assistance. For instance, development partners often support the drafting of legislation and regulations with technical assistance. When doing so, a tendency exists to introduce best practice principles (Pritchett, Woolcock, and Andrews 2013). However, as local context and

---

[7] The coefficient estimates of this analysis represent endogenous effects and should not be treated as causal impacts. See Smets et al. (2013) on how Bank and borrower characteristics may interact.

[8] Cognitive limitations, behavioural biases, strategic ignorance, reality denial, and self-signalling may make beliefs resistant to many forms of information (Smets, 2020).

Table 4.1 Programme-level regressions

Variable	Coefficient	Robust standard error
Dependent variable: IEG Outcome rating		
World Bank performance	0.416	0.070***
Borrower performance	0.573	0.068***
R-squared	0.733	
Observations	280	
Dependent variable: World Bank performance		
Quality at entry	0.769	0.065***
Supervision	0.171	0.061***
R-squared	0.800	
Observations	247	
Dependent variable: Borrower performance		
Policy quality	0.110	0.066*
GDP growth year t	−0.007	0.007
GDP growth year $t + 1$	0.018	0.011*
Checks and balances	0.022	0.026
Inflation	0.001	0.00003*
Current account balance	−0.007	0.240
R-squared	0.0475	
Observations	197	

Notes: IEG = Independent Evaluation Group. Coefficients are estimated with ordinary least squares. Constants are not reported. Borrower performance model is estimated with bootstrapped errors. *** significant at the 1 per cent level, ** significant at the 5 per cent level, * significant at the 10 per cent level.

country capacity differs from society to society (Cardenas and Carpenter 2008), a best-fit approach towards technical assistance for regulatory and institutional reform may be preferable.

Budget Support Performance at the Country Level

This section reviews recent cross-country literature on the impact of budget support on recipient country policies.[9] It examines the effectiveness of policy-based lending in three important policy areas: public sector governance, social policies, and economic management. It also presents some new

[9] See Smets and Knack (2016, 2018) for an overview of the early literature on the impact of policy-based lending. Some of the earlier studies failed to find a positive impact of policy-based lending (e.g., Easterly 2005). Methodological choices and the period analysed (the adjustment lending era) may partly explain the differences in findings.

empirical evidence that extends the latest research to fragile states and low-income countries.

Budget Support and Public Sector Governance Reform

While there exists a literature on the impact of overall aid on public sector governance (PSG), the only quantitative study that looks at the policy impact of budget support in this area is Smets and Knack (2018). They show that policy loans can improve the quality of budgetary and financial management but have difficulty supporting anti-corruption or civil service reform. They identify a concave relationship between policy lending and the quality of public sector governance, indicating that conditionality may become detrimental after a certain point. The authors note, however, that most countries are on the upward sloping part of the reform curve. Finally, the authors find evidence consistent with backsliding of reform after loans are fully disbursed, which raises reform sustainability concerns (see, e.g., Collier et al. 1997).

Vietnam's 2007–12 Poverty Reduction Support Credit (PRSC) series illustrate the difficulties in supporting anti-corruption efforts. The government's approach to fighting corruption relied on technical measures to strengthen systems, reduce opportunities for corruption, and increase transparency. Through the series, the World Bank supported the operationalization of a steering committee against corruption with the power to suspend high-level officials, implementation of asset declaration requirements with penalties for non-compliance, and annual procurement compliance and performance audits. Important policy actions were dropped—such as a revision of the press law and measures to enhance access to information by the pubic, and implementation of other policy actions remained incomplete (IEG 2015). Only a small fraction of civil servants submitted asset declarations, and the declarations themselves were not disclosed to the public. An anti-corruption steering committee was established, but it was abolished after the PRSC series closed. As a result, corruption remained a major problem in Vietnam. For instance, according to 2012 survey data, 39 per cent of firms listed corruption as a major obstacle, up from 5.1 per cent in 2009 (IEG, 2015).

What can explain these mixed results? Implementing reforms is (politically) costly in the short term, especially in the public sector, which is often used as an instrument for patronage and clientelism. On the other hand, building a well-functioning state apparatus takes years, if not decades (Pritchett and de Weijer 2010). This time inconsistency problem—as well as the fact that results of reforms are not always tangible—makes it unattractive for many governments to engage in public sector governance reform. Political leaders are therefore more likely to undervalue such programmes, resulting in a low commitment to reform.

Generating the evidence needed to design effective policies and regulations is challenging, especially for public sector reform, which often requires a deep understanding of the local context and behaviour. Andrews (2009) distinguishes between reforms involving 'concentrated' and 'deconcentrated' sets of actors. Successful implementation of reforms is more difficult when it requires changing the behaviour and norms of larger and more disparate groups of agents, such as civil servants. Harun (2007) notes that senior civil service officials in Indonesia were reluctant to embrace new accounting standards because they shared the opinion that what worked before would continue to work in the future.

Budget Support and Social Policy Reform

A related pattern appears when looking at policies for social inclusion (gender equality, social protection, environmental sustainability). Bogetić and Smets (2017) investigate the association of World Bank policy lending with social development policies over the period 2006–14. They find econometric evidence that Development Policy Financing (DPF) targeting social protection and environmental sustainability were effective in influencing policy but that DPF related to gender equality and health and education reform had no significant impact on policies in those areas. Similarly, IEG (2016g) finds that environmental DPFs have generally been successful in reaching their objectives, especially when analytical work and technical assistance is available to support the design and implementation of policy reforms. Furthermore, environmental DPFs are more effective if they are informed by a good understanding of the political economy of policy reform.

In 2008–10, the World Bank supported Ghana's environmental governance reforms through a series of three DPF operations. While the economy was growing rapidly during that period, the country was facing natural resource degradation and social conflict due to poor governance, weak environmental protection, and limited community involvement. The programmatic series focused—among other areas—on climate change and social issues in mining communities, supported by analytical work that helped galvanize the attention of key policymakers. Policy actions included the drafting of a climate change strategy and the preparation of new guidelines on social responsibility in mining. As a result of the programmes, Ghana developed a national climate change policy, including a national climate change adaptation strategy, low-carbon development strategies, and a technology needs assessment. Industry guidelines for social responsibility were developed and fully implemented, resulting in the provision of corporate social responsibility (CSR) benefits to local communities. Benefits were often provided in-kind, but also took the form of profit sharing or a fixed unit amount.

Budget Support and Economic Policy Reform

With respect to economic policies—macroeconomic stabilization, fiscal management, trade, and business regulation—Smets and Knack (2016) find that the quality of economic management increases with the cumulative number of World Bank economic policy Development Policy Loans (DPLs), albeit at a diminishing rate. Also, in this thematic area evidence is found suggestive of backtracking of reform efforts.[10] Giordano and Pagano (2017) focus on the ease of doing business. They show econometrically that cumulative World Bank policy lending enhanced the business climate—with decreasing returns—especially in less developed countries.

Tanzania's structural reforms in 2003–05 provide a telling illustration of successful economic reform support. Following substantial debt cancellation under the HIPC initiative, the budget support series focused on debt sustainability. Furthermore, given fragmented labour market policies and elevated costs of starting a business, the budget support programmes also aimed to improve the business environment. Among other policy actions, the programmes supported the adoption of a national debt strategy, legislative amendments to ensure prudential debt management, a new business licensing framework, and new labour market legislation, covering collective labour relations, dispute resolution, and employment relations. As a result of implementation of those actions, debt service to exports dropped from 5.2 per cent in 2002 to 4.3 per cent in 2005, and output in the industry sector grew from 7.8 per cent of GDP in 2002 to 10.3 per cent in 2005 (IEG, 2013b).

Moll and Smets (2020) study the reasons for the diminishing returns to economic policy lending. They find evidence that longer policy engagements lead to lower impacts and show this may be related to a change from first-generation to more complex, second-generation policy

---

[10] In one econometric test, Smets and Knack (2016) drop all observations after the last economic policy loan has closed. If reforms are not sustained following completion of the loan, then the estimated effects should increase when the years following loan closing are dropped. The regression results indeed indicate a higher policy impact, suggesting some backsliding of reform after loans are fully disbursed.

actions.[11] They cite two other reasons why the initial years of policy engagement are most productive. First, government decision makers and Bank staff may favour the most impactful reforms first and move to refinements in later years. Second, there could be a trade-off between providing predictable budget financing and reform feasibility. Development policy lending has two main objectives: providing budget financing and supporting policy reform. Over time, countries may run out of (politically) feasible reforms (Eifert and Gelb 2006). When that happens, the World Bank may still want to close the financing gap by providing budget support but include (politically feasible) policy actions, albeit with a smaller reform impact.

The findings of Giordiano and Pagano (2017) suggest that the overall engagement with the recipient country and analytical work are more relevant than the funds transferred, a result corroborated by Moll and Smets (2020) and Knack et al. (2020). Different econometric findings have led those studies to come to a similar conclusion. For instance, Giordano and Pagano (2017) regress the Doing Business indicator on the cumulative number of DPLs and their cumulative value. They find that only the number of loans is statistically significant, leading them to conclude that overall engagement with the recipient country is more relevant than the amount of resources invested. Moll and Smets (2020) examine the impact of World Bank conditionality on the quality of economic policy. They find that the number of policy actions makes no difference. What matters is that there was at least one policy action that made a significant difference. They interpret this finding to mean that the process of supporting economic reform (including policy dialogue) results in improved quality of government policy. Knack et al. (2020) rely on a novel data set of World Bank analytical work and micro-level survey data from 1,244 public sector officials in 121 developing countries. They find that analytical and advisory products affect not only the direction of government policy but also its design and implementation, more so than the financing that budget support provides.

Relatedly, Hjort et al. (2021) provide recent empirical evidence on the contribution of analytical work for economic policy reform. Using experiments with Brazilian municipalities, the authors find that mayors revise their beliefs when informed about the findings of randomized impact evaluations (IE), especially if it involves studies involving large samples (suggesting that policymakers value high-quality work). More importantly, the authors go on to show that municipal leaders in Brazil were more likely to implement a tax

---

[11] They also show econometrically that unsuccessful DPLs—as rated by IEG—are not associated with improvements in policy quality. The finding that unsuccessful engagements are unlikely to improve policy suggests that financing alone is insufficient to induce change.

reform after being provided a research note that reported the results of impact evaluations gauging the effectiveness of the reform.

The literature thus suggests that policy-based lending has a positive impact on the quality of economic policies. One reason why economic policy lending is successful is the large evidence base and broad consensus on what works in this area (Khemani 2017). Sound evidence about the costs and benefits of policy reform can reduce uncertainty regarding winners and losers of reform, increase demand for public policies, and help persuade policymakers to act (Smets 2020). Some economic policy reforms (such as tariff reform) are easy to implement, as they may involve a single stroke of the pen. Engaging in economic policy change may generate tangible (growth) benefits, even in the short term. Therefore, governments may be more likely to engage in policy reform, especially when facing negative economic conditions.

Budget Support and Economic Crises

An economic crisis in developing countries often leads to acute financing needs and a cut-off from the financial markets (as happened to Greece in 2010). International financial institutions often step in with budget support to close any financing gaps. Limited bandwidth and capacity in times of crisis may be arguments against a push for reform. But crises offer a window of opportunity for change (Alesina, Ardagna, and Trebbi 2006). The COVID-19 crisis offers the opportunity to support reform, even though authorities in developing countries have often been overwhelmed responding to the pandemic.

To investigate the (policy) effectiveness of budget support in times of crisis, we estimate the model of Moll and Smets (2020) on a sample that includes only countries going through a deep economic crisis (defined as per capita growth contraction of at least 3.46 per cent, which is one standard deviation below mean growth).[12] The coefficient on economic policy lending more than triples compared with the full sample (see Appendix E), suggesting that budget support can be used to support economic reform in times of crisis.[13] Similarly, World Bank (2022a) finds evidence that crisis-related DPFs perform better than non-crisis DPFs, especially for IBRD countries.

---

[12] Moll and Smets (2020) distinguish between the marginal impacts of additional policy conditions within the current year and the length of the policy engagement with client countries. See Appendix C for a detailed description of the econometric specification used in Moll and Smets (2020). Data and method are explained in the Appendix D.

[13] For the other thematic areas, the coefficient on policy lending is significantly positive. However, the results are based on a limited sample of just forty-one observations and should therefore be interpreted with caution.

Budget Support and Country Context

The impact of policy lending in the three thematic areas differs across country contexts. We estimate the model of Moll and Smets (2020) on a sample of aid-receiving countries, a subsample of low-income countries, and a subsample of fragile and conflict-affected states. Table 4.2 summarizes the results.[14] They suggest that World Bank policy lending has improved economic management (CPIA A and B) and public sector governance (CPIA D) in low-income countries but not in fragile states. With respect to public sector governance, the marginal returns to policy lending may become negative if too many conditions are imposed. For low-income countries, the initial years of an engagement in both thematic areas are the most productive (negative length of engagement coefficient). In contrast, World Bank policy lending in the social sector seems to positively influence policy quality (up to a point) in fragile states (see also IEG, 2013b), but not in low-income countries or the full sample of aid-receiving countries. In fragile states, there is no econometric

Table 4.2 Country-level regressions

CPIA thematic area	Variable of interest	Regression results		
		Full sample	Low-income countries	Fragile and Conflict-affected countries
A and B[a]: economic management	Marginal returns	Positive	Positive	Not significant
	Length of engagement	Negative	Negative	Not significant
C: social and environmental policies	Marginal returns	Not significant	Not significant	Concave
	Length of engagement	Not significant	Not significant	Not significant
D: public sector governance	Marginal returns	Concave	Concave	Not significant
	Length of engagement	Negative	Negative	Not significant

Notes: CPIA = Country Policy and Institutional Assessment.
[a] For economic policy lending, there is evidence suggesting that the sheer number of policy conditions does not matter but that a policy engagement generates a positive impact. See Appendix C and D for detail.

[14] See Appendix F for the detailed regression output.

evidence that a prolonged policy engagement in the social sector becomes detrimental (the coefficient on length of engagement is not significant).[15] Similarly, World Bank (2022a) finds that policy lending can be beneficial in fragile and conflict-affected states, leading to greater policy improvement, albeit from a lower base.

Budget Support and the Paris Declaration principles

In 2005, the Paris Declaration laid out several principles to increase the effectiveness of development assistance. It identified ownership, financing predictability, the use of country systems, a focus on results, and donor harmonization as building blocks for more effective aid.[16] As discussed in Chapter 1, budget support was seen as the most promising aid modality to implement these principles.

The Survey on Monitoring the Paris Declaration was developed to track progress on the implementation of the Paris Declaration principles over the period 2005–10. It includes twelve indicators on aid effectiveness, including ownership, the use of PFM and procurement systems, financing predictability, aid coordination, a results frameworks, and mutual accountability (for detail, see OECD 2008).

Table 4.3 presents the pairwise correlations between the share of budget support a country receives and various indicators from the survey. It shows that on average, countries with a larger share of budget support have more effective development strategies (the survey's proxy for ownership), more enhanced results frameworks, and a better PFM quality. Not only is the PFM quality better, local PFM and procurement systems are used more often in countries with a larger share of budget support. Mutual accountability in such countries is more advanced, and there is more predictability in the delivery of foreign assistance. On average, aid is delivered in a more coordinated manner, except for donor missions and analytical work.

To examine whether budget support is more effective in countries that made progress on the Paris Declaration principles, we divided our sample

---

[15] The coefficient on length of engagement is positive but not significant at conventional levels ($p = 0.189$). It may be that in fragile states the productivity of long engagements in the social sector blossoms over time.

[16] Benfield and Como (2019) find that the principles seem to improve results where they are applied. Their findings are based on a geographically balanced review of several hundred studies and evaluations, at both the macro level and the individual project and programme level, that covered a range of sectors to see where the principles had been applied and what effect their application had had. These were sourced from international organizations, bilateral development partners, partner country governments, CSOs, academia and think tanks.

Table 4.3 Budget support and the Paris Declaration principles

Variable	Pairwise correlations (*p-values*)
Share budget support	1.000
IND 1 operational development strategy	0.320 (0.000)
IND 2A PFM quality	0.518 (0.000)
IND 2B procurement quality	0.175 (0.436)
IND 5A use of PFM systems	0.545 (0.000)
IND 5B use of procurement systems	0.561 (0.000)
IND 7 aid predictability	0.240 (0.002)
IND 9 coordinated aid delivery	0.659 (0.000)
IND 10A coordinated missions	0.043 (0.582)
IND 10B coordinated analytical work	0.100 (0.200)
IND 11 M&E frameworks	0.325 (0.000)
IND 12 mutual accountability	0.160 (0.041)

into two groups: countries that scored above average on country ownership and countries that scored below average. We then estimated the model of Moll and Smets (2020) for both samples over the period 2000–15.

In countries with enhanced ownership, the policy impact of budget support is positive for all three thematic areas; when ownership is limited, budget support does not have a significant impact on policy quality (Table 4.4). One notable exception is economic policy lending, which seems to be effective even in countries without deep development strategies. In countries with enhanced ownership longer policy engagements lead to lower impacts.

The rest of this section briefly discusses each of the Paris Declaration principles—country ownership, predictability, use of country systems, focus on results, and donor harmonization—and examines the contribution of budget support in implementing them.

Table 4.4 Subsample regression analysis: limited ownership vs enhanced ownership

CPIA thematic area	Variable of interest	Limited ownership	Enhanced ownership
CPIA A and B[a]	Marginal returns	Positive	Positive
	Length of engagement	Not significant	Negative
CPIA C	Marginal returns	Not significant	Positive
	Length of engagement	Not significant	Negative
CPIA D	Marginal returns	Not significant	Positive
	Length of engagement	Not significant	Negative

Notes: CPIA = Country Policy and Institutional Assessment
[a] For economic policy lending, econometric evidence suggests that the sheer number of policy conditions does not matter but that a policy engagement generates a positive impact. See Appendix C and D for more detail and Appendix G for detailed regression output.

Country Ownership

A large body of theoretical literature and many empirical studies show that policy reform support is unlikely to be effective without government commitment. Using principal–agent theory to analyse a sample of twenty-one developing countries, Killick (1997) finds that political consensus in the recipient country concerning the proposed reforms has a decisive influence on the effectiveness of conditionality. Devarajan, Dollar, and Holmgren (2001) present ten insightful country case studies from the World Bank's early experience with policy reform in Africa. Benfield and Como (2019) report that inclusive ownership of policies is key to success in many cases. Lawson (2014) concludes that the delivery mechanisms of budget support are fully consistent with the commitments in the Paris Declaration, the Accra Agenda, and the Busan Declaration. Budget support processes proved to be more closely aligned with government policies and processes than other aid modalities.

Financing Predictability

Lack of predictability hampers economic growth and development (Hudson and Mosley 2008; Aldashev and Verardi 2012). Partner governments consistently flag aid volatility as one of the top impediments to effective support; for ultimate beneficiaries, it is often the main source of their vulnerability (Benfield and Como 2019).

A lack of predictability in education funding in Zambia was cited as the main impediment to progress, hindering planning and forcing short-term teacher hires that impaired learning. In contrast, the public safety nets programmes in Ethiopia emphasized the importance of providing predictable cash transfers that could be counted on in terms of timing and size. They proved highly effective in preventing distress migration and helped re-establish faith in the state.

Overall, predictability of development aid is fairly high in more recent years. According to the Global Partnership for Effective Development Cooperation, 87 per cent of development cooperation was predictable in 2018, up slightly from 85 per cent in 2016 (OECD 2019). While the predictability of budget support initially left a lot to be desired, Lawson (2014) concludes that annual budget support disbursements were largely consistent with the amounts projected in the budgets and treasury plans of the recipient governments. They were thus significantly more predictable than other aid modalities. Budget support resources are increasingly used to support within-year additional expenses (Ministry of Foreign Affairs of the Netherlands 2018).

On the other hand, recent evidence indicates that donors have on occasion used budget support as a sanctioning tool, suspending disbursements in response to political events in the recipient country (Molenaers et al. 2014). Doing so reduces the financing predictability of the instrument. At the same time, there has been less progress in ensuring the medium-term predictability of budget support and other aid modalities in line with aid effectiveness principles. A rigid link between budget support and the IMF's conditions for its own disbursement may cause unnecessary volatility in resource flows.

Use of Country Systems

By definition, budget support operations rely on country PFM systems. Using country systems may generate several development benefits (Knack 2013). It reduces aid fragmentation and duplication of activities, increasing aid efficiency. It also helps develop effective institutions; setting up parallel systems could lead to poaching and erosion of governmental quality in recipient countries (Knack and Rahman 2007). Use of country systems is particularly critical in fragile states because it reinforces the accountability of the state, strengthens the policy and planning process, and builds sustainable capacity through learning by doing (Hart, Hadley, and Welham 2015).[17]

---

[17] Progress in using country systems, however, remains mixed (see, e.g., IEG, 2011; World Bank, 2021). For instance, in a sample of thirty-two aid-receiving countries with reliable PFM systems, only 48 per cent

On the other hand, given that it is not possible to track the end use of budget support funds, donors have been concerned that their funds may be misappropriated if the quality of public financial arrangements in recipient countries is poor. It has been hard to dispel the widely entrenched myth that budget support is inherently more risky than traditional project-level support. The basis for scepticism was rooted in the arguments about the fungibility of aid, aid capture by ruling elites, and the perceived higher fiduciary and procurement risk of budget support (Alesina and Weder 2002; Klitgaard 1990; Svensson 2000; Knack 2000; Djankov et al. 2008). Systematic evidence on the diversion of aid is limited, however. Anderson, Johannsen, and Rijkers (2019) document that aid disbursement to highly aid-dependent countries coincides with sharp increases in bank deposits in offshore financial centres known for bank secrecy and private wealth management but not in other financial centres. Their findings of an implied leakage rate of about 7.5 per cent are consistent with established patterns of aid capture. However, the research does not support the assumption that project aid is more difficult to divert than policy-based lending (although project lending disburses more slowly, against specific expenditures and is subject to procurement and other constraints). Indeed, aid-supporting investment projects correlate more strongly with money flows to tax havens than budget support, which disburses more quickly and uses recipient countries' financial management systems. In their survey of countries receiving budget support, Lister and Carter (2006) find no evidence that budget support funds were more affected by corruption than were other forms of aid. The comprehensive cross-country survey by Dijkstra (2018) also finds no evidence that budget support increased corruption, contrary to the expectations about the high fiduciary risk of budget support.

Therefore, to guide decisions on budget support, donors strongly emphasized the need to understand, assess, and strengthen the PFM systems of countries in which they considered disbursing budget support.[18] Most budget support donors seek safeguards at several levels. First, donors monitor and help strengthen government disbursement and procurement systems as

of aid to the government sector was channelled through the countries' PFM system. Knack (2013) finds that the use of country systems depends on the donor's reputational stake in the country, perceptions of corruption in the recipient country, and public support for aid in the donor country.

[18] Shand (2006), on the other hand, cautions against overcomplicating fiduciary issues and suggests that risks need to be compared with benefits. He draws attention to the fact that donors have to be realistic about how quickly the level of fiduciary risk can be lowered by improved PFM and procurement systems. Experience suggests that such institutional reforms only produce results in the medium term. See Smets and Knack (2018) for econometric evidence on how budget support operations have been able to improve the quality of PFM frameworks and policies.

well as accountability institutions such as supreme audit authorities and parliamentary scrutiny. Second, they monitor public expenditure allocations at the aggregate level. Donors also support anti-corruption plans, including a stronger role for budget transparency and accountability to taxpayers.

Focus on Results

Rather than focusing on inputs and processes, donors and recipient countries should manage resources with a focus on results. For recipient countries, doing so involves linking national development strategies with medium-term budget processes and results-oriented monitoring and evaluation frameworks that monitor progress against outcome indicators. For donors, it implies linking programming and resources to results that are aligned with partner country performance assessment frameworks.[19]

In the context of budget support, institutions have introduced a focus on results in several ways. First, budget support operations usually include results frameworks that link policy actions to final outcomes and results, measured by adequate indicators. The results indicators are intended to demonstrate whether the programmes' development objectives have been attained. Francisco, Moll and Smets (2016) find tentative evidence that the inclusion of results indicators in budget support operations contributes to improvements in policy quality. Moll, Geli, and Saavedra (2015) show that strong and consistent results frameworks tend to make budget support operations more successful. IEG (2015) cautions, however, that designing results frameworks in budget support operations and their evaluation remain challenging.

A second aspect of a results focus involves choosing only those policy actions that are critical for achieving results, such as strong policy actions with sufficient institutional depth to trigger sustained reform (e.g., laws, regulations, directives). Moll, Geli, and Saavedra (2015) show that budget support operations with a larger share of weak policy actions—process-oriented actions such as plans, studies, and terms of references that do not have regulatory implications—tend to be evaluated as less successful. IEG (2015) notes, however, that the criticality of policy actions is context specific. In some cases, the submission (and subsequent adoption) of a law may be necessary for institutional change; in other circumstances, lower-level actions

---

[19] In its most extreme form, a focus on results involves the disbursement of aid contingent on meeting certain results/outcome targets. Donor agencies have experimented with various forms of performance-based aid, such as the World Bank's PforR (see Clist (2016) for a critical review of the instrument).

are critical. Moll and Smets (2020) find econometric evidence to suggest that a long-term engagement and continued policy dialogue are more important than the number and type of policy actions. Further research is thus needed to understand the criticality of policy actions and how criticality interacts with country context and sustained policy dialogue.

Donor Harmonization

Fragmentation of development assistance impairs results, leading to gaps, overlaps, missed collaboration opportunities, and higher transactions costs (see, e.g., Klingebiel et al. 2016).[20] The evidence shows that good partnerships are essential for bringing in more resources, increasing impact, and establishing checks and balances (Benfield and Como 2019). In Rwanda, for example, government requirements for development partners to specialize led to sharper focus, higher impacts, and lower administration costs, and it gave civil servants more time to focus on their core business.

Cooperation by aid agencies in the context of budget support has had a positive effect on donor harmonization and alignment of other aid modalities. Particularly in aid-dependent countries, this coordination took on institutionalized forms, such as budget support forums that provided platforms to discuss cross-sectoral issues.

Formalized donor coordination in budget support operations can also have negative effects, however. Wide differences in disbursement arrangements, tranching, and conditionality among donors could lead to conflicting signals and unpredictability in resource flows. This was exacerbated when donors encountered problems in recipient countries, such as corruption scandals or unacceptable political situations, to which they reacted in different ways, as discussed in Chapter 5.

Conclusion

Budget support was conceived as an instrument to support important policy reforms, while it also became the preferred mechanism to implement the principles of the Paris Declaration. This chapter has shown that budget support has a positive impact on the quality of recipient country policies. A thematic analysis reveals, however, that quite some variation exists in the

---

[20] In some sectors, however, such as education, fragmentation seems to be beneficial rather than detrimental for development outcomes. See Gehring et al. (2017).

policy impact of budget support. Supporting economic policy reform (debt management, trade and business regulation, monetary policy) has been more effective than certain areas in public sector governance and social policy. A lack of credible evidence on how to design public sector reform programmes and deep-rooted political economy constraints may partly explain the observed differences in performance.

Empirical findings also indicate there may be decreasing returns to policy lending. Recent evidence suggests that longer policy engagements lead to lower impacts which may be related to a change from first-generation to more complex, second-generation policy actions. Furthermore, recent studies show that the overall engagement with the recipient government, including policy dialogue, programme design, and sound analytical work are more important for reform success than the provision of financing and the supervision of reform programmes. Next, the timing of policy reform support and institutional quality of the recipient country are found to matter, but less so than programme-level factors. Moreover, this chapter has presented evidence that even in fragile and conflict-affected states, budget support can be effective. This may put into question the need for selectivity in providing policy-based financing.

It is important to note that much remains unknown regarding how to support policy reform. Cultural traits and social norms, policymaker beliefs,[21] citizen communication, the role of media markets, and task leader characteristics are potentially important factors for reform success which require further research attention. Furthermore, there is also a need to investigate how investment lending and technical assistance may help in improving the effectiveness of budget support operations.

This chapter has argued that, in the right context, the Paris Declaration principles of ownership, predictability, reliance on country systems, focus on results, and harmonization improve development effectiveness. Budget support, in turn, has the potential to be an efficient and effective way to support a country's own development strategy. Next, while the predictability of budget support initially left a lot to be desired, it increased over time and improved significantly compared to other aid modalities. Given the perceived fiduciary risks of budget support, strengthening and using country PFM systems has become an important and effective element of budget support operations. Furthermore, budget support operations have become increasingly focused on results, which may contribute to improvements in policy quality. Finally,

---

[21] The study of political beliefs and policymaking is traditionally the realm of the social sciences. However, recent research in computational and neurocognitive science on ideological thought may offer complementary insights (see, e.g., Zmigrod and Tsakiris, 2021).

cooperation amongst aid agencies in the context of budget support tended to have a positive effect on donor harmonization and alignment of other aid modalities. Increased harmonization may also have negative effects, however, such as decreased predictability of resource flows.

To conclude, the policy and aid effectiveness benefits of budget support clearly outweigh its risks and unintended consequences. Budget support operations have been shown to improve the quality of policy in different thematic areas and country settings, including in fragile and conflicted-affected states. Furthermore, in the right context, budget support is an effective and efficient instrument to put the Paris Declaration principles into practice. On the other hand, budget support is vulnerable to risks, primarily of a political nature, that can threaten its viability. Additionally, much remains unknown on how to effectively support policy reform while budget support has a limited impact in complex areas such as civil service reform. Finally, if ownership is lacking, providing conditional financing generally does not lead to sustained reform.

5

Promise, Disenchantment, and Sobriety

Learning from Experience with Budget Support

Fluctuations in the use of budget support over the last two decades over-shadowed ebbs and flows in its popularity as an instrument of development financing. Although periods of severe economic distress, such as the financial crisis 2009, saw peaks of fast-disbursing policy-based financing, particularly for middle-income countries cut off from alternative financing sources, the use of the instrument declined during the 2010s, including by most multi-national development banks. The initial promise of budget support for lower income countries eventually turned to disenchantment, particularly as bilateral donors largely disengaged from its use as the instrument of choice to further global development aspirations.

Why did budget support not become the aid instrument of choice? To what extent did budget support fall short of the high expectations of a decade ago?

This chapter examines the lessons from the broad reversal in donor perception following the initial years after the Paris Declaration's strong support for expanding use of budget support, as most European governments rolled back support for it or eliminated it from their foreign assistance programmes, despite the strong evidence in support of its effectiveness presented in Chapter 4.

This chapter identifies some of the reasons why budget support fell out of favour. They fall into four broad categories: aid coordination and the Paris Agenda, domestic conditions in recipient countries, internal factors of donors, and changes in the prevailing development paradigm. The recent resurgence of interest in budget support in response to the COVID-19 pandemic offers an opportunity to address shortcomings that led to its falling out of favour.

Retooling Development Aid in the 21st Century. Shahrokh Fardoust et al., Oxford University Press.
© Shahrokh Fardoust et al., (2023). DOI: 10.1093/oso/9780192882196.003.0005

Aid Coordination and the Paris Agenda for Aid Effectiveness

Budget support remains a key instrument for delivering development resources. Its performance compares favourably with that of other aid modalities.

Budget support promised a country-owned development process with strong alignment between donors and recipients: countries formulated their own poverty reduction strategies, and donors paid a portion of the budgets underpinning their priorities if they agreed with them. By relying on a country's own processes rather than setting up parallel systems, budget support was also supposed to strengthen public financial management (PFM) systems along the way.

What happened? Looking back at the last decade, some of the discrepancies between the promise and the reality of budget support can be traced back to the evolution of the aspirations embedded in the Paris Declaration.

The Political Economy of Aid Effectiveness

Despite their global aspirations of strengthening country ownership, and thereby reducing donor domination and aid fragmentation, the Paris Principles on Aid Effectiveness were perhaps too limited by postulating an alignment of interests between principals—the donors and agents—the recipient countries (Box 1.2). The issue was not so much that the aspirations of the Paris Declaration principles were unrealistic, but that they overlooked underlying political economy challenges from the outset. The donor community embraced budget support as a useful instrument to deliver on the principles of ownership, alignment between donors, and managing for results. But they sidestepped the inherent tension of conditionality by using the concept of 'mutual accountability' between donors and partner country governments. Koch et al. (2017) argue that the guiding principles of ownership and alignment aimed to do away with the problem of the diverging preferences of donors and recipients as well as among donors by eliminating donor preferences from the aid relation. Moving recipients' preferences to centre stage and committing donors to align their aid to these preferences and the resulting priorities obviated the need for conditionality or fragmented aid systems through ring-fenced systems set up to enforce individual donor preferences.

The half-hearted implementation of the Paris Declaration principles demonstrated that the overly technical approach to harmonization and donor coordination reflected in the Paris declarations' commitments ignored important political determinants of the collective action problem on each side of the donor-recipient relationship (Koch et al. 2017). Perhaps not surprisingly, little progress was made in implementing thorough review processes for mutual accountability that benefit from broad participation (OECD 2011c).

Erosion of the Poverty Reduction Strategy Paper Process

The approach of the Paris declaration to simultaneously tackle the principal-agent as well as the collective donor action problems underlying aid effectiveness by discounting donors' vested interests was enshrined in the Poverty Reduction Strategy Papers (PRSPs). Introduced by the World Bank in September 1999, as part of the Highly Indebted Poor Countries (HIPC) initiative, PRSPs were meant to be a key step in receiving debt relief (Bourguignon and Sundberg 2007).

PRSPs were never officially abandoned and are still officially required as a precondition for debt relief. But the approach fizzled out, despite some successful outcomes and initiatives. Most of the criticism pointed to examples in which the approach fell short of its core principles:

- From the beginning, the approach was driven by the IMF and the World Bank and did not quite fit the framework of the MDGs.
- Several countries had difficulties formulating a coherent strategy, following through with the promised polices on a sustained basis, and reaching the expected poverty reduction strategy outcomes. The challenge involved not only developing a long-term vision for a country's development that is shared by key stakeholders but, more importantly, operationalizing concrete measures to underpin a viable strategy that moves beyond wishful thinking.
- The process of formulating a poverty reduction strategy as a precondition for financing raised fundamental questions as to what extent a country's development process can be planned and prescribed by policymakers. The PRSP approach showed the limits of a 'plan-and-execute approach' favoured by 'planners' (who 'determine a big plan to reach the big goal and throw an endless supply of resources and a large administrative apparatus at that big goal')—as opposed to a 'search-and-amplify approach' to development 'searchers' (who 'are just on the lookout for favorable opportunities to solve problems') (Easterly 2006). The World Bank and IMF were criticized for supporting PRSPs that served their own institutional needs for three-year funding envelopes but were completely divorced from the MDGs or a focus on longer term targets.
- What mattered for the effectiveness of poverty reduction strategies was also the administrative location of the planners. PRSP units often had no

direct influence in setting the budget, as they were located in planning ministries that were separate from finance ministries and detached from the line ministries.

- The PRSP process came under criticism for imposing aid conditionality rather than supporting home-grown policy programmes. In several recipient countries, meaningful participation of the population in formulating the PRSP was undermined by the absence of a thriving civil society. The long-term nature of the PSRP commitments also ignored parliamentary processes, particularly when they extended beyond electoral cycles. As Lazarus (2008) points out, the classical paradox of aid is at the heart of the PRSP participations: if it can work in a country, it is not needed, and if it is needed, it cannot work. The process succeeded where it coincided with a national project for poverty reduction that was both articulated by political leaders and widely shared by citizens (as in Vietnam and Uganda); it was less effective when recipient societies were atomized or weakly politically organized.

- PRSPs increasingly became a bureaucratic burden that was not necessarily helpful for advancing the actual purpose of developing country-owned documents. Recipient countries were required to produce documents of almost 200 pages written for an external donor community, often in parallel with established domestic planning documents, with extensive support from donor-financed consultants. For the World Bank and IMF staff, it required extensive negotiations of the Joint Staff Assessments required for each PRSP.

- Donors confronted a dichotomy between the promise of aspirational plans underpinning their promise of scaling up foreign aid and the reality that resources were much more constrained and required a prioritization that was not necessarily in line with the PRSP.

- Over time, the PRSP approach gave way to a less formulaic approach that recognized differences in national priority-setting exercises to map out country programmes.

Overloading of Conditionality through Donor Coordination

Budget support offered the promise of donor coordination, but it often resulted in coordination overload and onerous conditionality. Instead of simplifying and streamlining the policy dialogue, bilateral donors tended to maximize their leverage on specific policy actions. Particularly in countries where budget support was the predominant form of aid, donor groups emerged as the principal forum for the coordination of conditionality. During the heydays of budget support in Mozambique, for example, up to nineteen bilateral and multilateral donors crowded the policy agenda, requiring time-intensive and costly coordination by a troika of donors in charge of designing and monitoring conditions for tranche disbursements in line with specific donor preferences. As a result of these 'cartels of good intentions', budget support became very transaction-heavy and perhaps less aligned with countries' own priorities.

Political Conditionality

Although budget support serves primarily as an instrument to support development, it has also been used as a vehicle of foreign policy. Depending on their political preferences, some donors thought it important to include conditionality that went beyond economic and structural reforms to include political issues, democratization, and human rights. Particularly among bilaterals, there has been a long-standing practice of using aid as a tool for political reform and human rights promotion (Selbervik 1999). Adding good governance as a secondary objective after poverty reduction was not highly realistic and potentially undermined the effectiveness of the fight against poverty (Netherlands 2012). According to the OECD/DAC guidelines, 'political conditionality should not be specifically linked to budget support or any individual aid instrument, but rather should be handled in the context of the overarching political dialogue between a partner country and its donors' (OECD 2006). This admonition notwithstanding, the frequent use of conditionalities of political conditionality resulted in budget support suspensions linked to underlying political developments. As a result, recipient countries may perceive budget support as at higher risk of being interrupted than traditional investment projects. Molenaers et al. (2015) find that multilateral influence, voice and accountability, democratic performance, ideological proximity, the number of donors, aid dependence, and economic growth tend to be associated with suspensions of budget support. The largest share of suspensions (41 per cent) was associated with regime issues (such as electoral fraud, repression of opposition movements, major human rights violations). Corruption issues were raised in 31 per cent of cases.

Incoherent Donor Responses

Donors typically interpreted and responded to unfavourable news in different ways, often driven by foreign policy concerns. Some withheld aid, others continued the political dialogue through uninterrupted disbursements or tried to bring about policy changes by adding political conditions to budget support. Even donors that were originally strong supporters of budget support found it increasingly difficult to defend to their parliaments aid that was paid directly into the budgets of countries seen as corrupt or unwilling to reform. The evaluation by Netherlands (2018) suggests that although there can be good political grounds not to allocate budget support to a country, financial incentives or threats to suspend aid turn out to be ineffective. This not very surprising conclusion had led to the reformulation of the concept of budget support around the Paris Principles on Aid Effectiveness in the first place.

Domestic Factors in Recipient Countries

The international aid architecture was not the only source of disenchantment with budget support. Concerns about recipient countries also played a role:

- *Political problems.* A range of domestic issues started emerging in countries receiving budget support during the heydays of the instrument, around 2008. They included fraudulent elections, political repression, and human rights violations, often in African countries. High-profile events such as in Ethiopia in 2006 undermined confidence in the wisdom of supporting the budgets of some countries and compelled donor withdrawal.
- *Corruption and fiduciary concerns.* Scandals involving public funds (such as in Uganda in 2012 and Mozambique in 2015) showed that budget support did not automatically improve public financial management systems, despite a heavy focus on institutional strengthening and accountability in public finance. Concern about the adequacy of PFM systems were raised even in some high-capacity countries such as Zambia, where budget support was provided over decades, although many fundamental public financial management systems were not in place. The treasury single account was not comprehensive in its coverage, and the financial management information system has not been sufficiently deployed to sectors and across levels of government. This created efficiency concerns in the management of public funds as well as challenges in expenditure control and accountability (Hashim and Piatti-Fünfkirchen 2016). At the same time, donor parliaments exercised greater fiduciary scrutiny. However, suspending budget support in response to corruption, violation of human rights, or unfair elections rarely led to the reforms donors would like to see. The fact that donors

did not always act in harmony in such cases provided mixed signals to recipient countries (Netherlands 2012).

- *Criticality and complexity of incremental reforms.* The nature of conditionality may have contributed to reform fatigue. In some countries, successive governments tried, with limited success, to make headway on difficult reforms, such as the elimination of subsidies. More frequently, however, programmatic budget support for incremental reform often concentrated on small measures that were hard to understand and easy to reverse. A focus on public financial management may have helped strengthen confidence in the reliability of country systems, but it made it harder to explain why the reform measures were meaningful and critical to the country's development and poverty reduction agenda. In their evaluation of policy-based operations, the African Development Bank (ADB 2018) found that they contained many process-oriented policy actions whose outcomes were not always clear. The design of the operations did not indicate how policy actions were critical or related to the desired outcomes. The theory of change in the design of budget support operations may have been weak.

- *Lacking selectivity.* Countries that received budget support often did not meet the entry criteria of good governance. In line with the recommendations of the aid effectiveness literature, the promise of predictable aid flows through budget support was predicated on good country performance which allowed for an alignment of donor and recipient preferences in support of long-term poverty reduction. In practice however, as discussed in Chapter 3, donors from the outset starting channelling large sums of foreign aid without being particularly selective. The lack of selectivity in the choice of countries ended up compromising aid effectiveness and predictability, forcing donors to adjust by using budget support suspensions to sanction breaches in their trust relationship with recipients (Molenaers et al. 2015).

Internal Factors of Donors

One of the most important factors behind the post-Paris shift away from budget support and the disillusionment by most bilateral donors has been the change in the political climate surrounding development aid and budget support. A range of political trends affected attitudes:

- Political buy-in for aid effectiveness concerns along the lines of the Paris Declaration principles waned. Despite continuing rhetorical support for aid effectiveness principles, the active political buy-in for aid quality dissipated over time, with many major donor countries failing to attend forums at the ministerial level (McKee et al. 2020). Although evidence suggests that the principles work, their broad nature allowed too much room for interpretation, which resulted in development fatigue brought about by the establishment of structures, initiatives, and processes intended to improve effectiveness that turned out to have little practical usefulness in terms of making development deliver more or cost less (Benfield and Como 2019).

- Budget support dropped out of favour with the conservative governments that came to power in several key donor countries where they replaced the social democratic development ministers of the original 'like-minded' Utstein group. Multilateralism, country systems and coordinated budget support gave way to a preference for bilateral aid and tangible project-based development assistance. Budget support became a more difficult sell to parliaments and taxpayers, who increasingly demanded tangible results directly attributable to bilateral aid that could be more easily communicated (vaccinations, kilometres of roads built, etc.). Debates were often driven without reference to the evidence base, aid effectiveness indicators, or end objectives. Following the election of a Conservative government in the United Kingdom, for example, the Department for International Development (DFID)—one of the most vocal and influential proponents of this aid modality—withdrew its endorsement of budget support and was eventually subsumed into the FDCO.[1] Other bilaterals (including Germany, Japan, and the Netherlands) and was eventually subsumed into the FCDO followed, joining long-term sceptics of budget support like the United States.

Internal Factors Affecting Multilateral Support for Budget Support

Incentives of budget support donors may be misaligned, which can also influence international institutions (see Box 5.1). Although the multilateral nature of international financial institutions makes them less susceptible to sudden political swings than bilateral donors, the role of donor shareholders on their boards permeates their policies, particularly as a result of replenishment of their soft loan funds (such as IDA). In addition, multilaterals are not free from internal factors that may affect their choice of instruments.

---

[1] DFID's new strategy emphasized greater reliance on modes of delivery that enable a clear demonstration of outcomes/results. It relied more on targeted forms of assistance, de-emphasizing budget support (Department for International Development 2015).

Box 5.1   Misaligned incentives of budget support donors

Budget support donors have their own set of objectives, which do not necessarily entail maximizing the effectiveness of policy advice. For instance, it is well documented that powerful donors strategically influence the decision-making process at international financial institutions (see, e.g., Kilby 2009). Also, for bilateral aid agencies, development assistance is partly driven by strategic and political considerations (Alesina and Dollar 2000). Next, donor agencies are often faced with spending pressure, which might endanger the longer time frame needed to design and test well-informed policies.

Furthermore, Manski (2011) lists a number of practices that incite budget support donors to provide policy analysis with incredible certitude instead of reasonable policy advice based on partial knowledge. Relatedly, Backus and Little (2020) illustrate the difficulty of policy experts to be upfront about policy uncertainty. Next, as promotion tends to be based on loan approval rather than loan quality, extrinsic incentives in aid agencies may be misaligned (Wane 2004). In addition, intrinsic, psychological factors may hamper the effectiveness of budget support. For instance, the simplicity principle in human concept learning could prevent us from embracing complexity (Feldman 2003), the pervasive bias of overestimating the likelihood of positive events could curtail accurate decision making (Sharot 2011), and biased beliefs in recipient country policymakers could prevent us from thoroughly analysing the political economy context (Easterly 2015). Relatedly, Banuri et al. (2015) and Vivalt and Coville (2022) document that staff of international financing institutions may be subject to confirmation and overconfidence bias when interpreting data on the effectiveness of development programmes.

These misaligned incentives are all the more worrisome because of the so-called 'broken feedback loop' (Svensson 2006). That is, there often exists political and/or geographical distance between the providers and the recipients of budget support. Because of this separation between taxpayers in the donor country and beneficiaries in the recipient country, the normal feedback process is blocked: citizens in the donor country are not well informed to sanction politicians about the impact of their aid programmes. The resulting lack of accountability may allow inefficient practices to continue.

The design and implementation of budget support in a country depends in part on whether the support is shaped by a parallel programme supported by the International Monetary Fund (IMF). The traditional division of labour on economic issues tended to leave the IMF in a leading role in the policy dialogue on macroeconomic aggregates while fiscal alloca-tion, allocative efficiency, and structural issues remained the domain of the World Bank. Particularly in crisis countries with large external financing needs, the IMF's dominance in the macroeconomic policy dialogue may have contributed to a focus on shorter-term policy measures designed to underpin balance-of-payments support in IMF-supported programmes rel-ative to longer term incremental measures associated with programmatic budget support. In lower income countries, the IMF has been offering long-term financing arrangements that typically include structural reform benchmarks.

Interdepartmental tensions may have played a role in the reluctance to fully embrace budget support. As budget support operations require coordina-tion across different policy areas, their preparation is typically managed by the equivalent of the economics department. Sectoral departments were left out and advocated their preference for sector-based operations rather than comprehensive budget-support approaches. The shift away from national budget support was also driven by, and reflected in, a greater emphasis on policy dialogue based on sectors, which tended to merge with more conventional sector lending (infrastructure, health, education, etc.) and a rediscovery of traditional bricks and mortar investment. In their examination of differential skills or capacity across departments, Moll, Geli, and Saveedra (2015) find a significant positive role of task team leader skills in the suc-cess of policy-based operations, particularly of economists relative to other professionals.

Aid Flows and Changing Aid Architecture

The context of aid has changed significantly in the years since the declaration of the Paris Principles on Aid Effectiveness (2005) that enshrined the ideas of using donor alignment, use of country systems and a central role of budget support in the following ways:

- *Expectations of sharply increased aid flows turned out to be unreal-istic.* The expected increase in overall development aid fell short of the doubling promised in Monterrey and Gleneagles. Although the volume of official development assistance (ODA) remained broadly sta-ble, its share in the overall resource envelope available to developing countries declined, as private capital flows increased, particularly to middle-income countries. Similarly, co-financing of budget support declined. ODA still represents a significant share of public resources for the poorest countries, which have not benefited from private capital inflows.

- *Vertical funds emerged.* As discussed in Chapter 2, the last decade saw the emergence of single-issue vertical funds that focus on a narrow theme (vaccinations, malaria, climate change). UN agencies such as the World Health Organization (WHO) have come increasingly under the influence of major individual donors that provide earmarked funding. Since 2000, two major vertical funds in the health field—the Global Fund to Fight AIDS, Tuberculosis and Malaria and the GAVI Alliance—provide new models of multilateralism. Evidence suggests that the earmarking of donor funding in international organizations undermines multilateral principles and that the new funding mechanisms in the health field compete with the operational roles of UN organizations. Browne (2017) finds that vertical funds tend to divert substantial resources into narrow, albeit critical, fields of healthcare, drawing resources and personnel in programme countries away from other areas.

- *New donors emerged.* Over the last decade, new donors entered the aid scene, as discussed in Chapter 2. The progressive rise of non-DAC providers of ODA, notably China, with specific motivations for development cooperation, added a new dimension of complexity to aid effectiveness. Bilaterals such as China, Korea, India, and Russia do not operate within the traditional ODA framework. Their assistance is an extension of their foreign policy. China's foreign aid is channelled exclusively through investment projects, with a heavy emphasis on infrastructure. Russia's approach could be characterized as chequebook diplomacy via foreign aid. New multilateral agencies such as the Asian Infrastructure Investment Bank (AIIB) and the New Development Bank (NDB) rely on project financing rather than budget support. At the same time, South–South cooperation emerged as a loose concept to denote development cooperation between emerging markets, notably Brazil, China, India, Mexico, and South Africa, to include not only grants and technical cooperation but also regional economic integration, trade, investment, remittances, debt relief, humanitarian interventions, peace-building, export credit lines, and other instruments and modalities of cooperation not included in ODA. Although South–South cooperation still lacks a common framework, clear criteria and methodologies to develop comparable statistics, it highlights the importance of non-financial contributions, and exchanges of solidarity including technology transfers, knowledge exchanges, and technical cooperation, as well as the important contributions that developing countries are making to global security, peace-building, good governance, environmental protection, regional integration, and other public goods, which do not sit squarely in the traditional realm of development cooperation (Besharati and MacFeely 2019).

- *New instruments were developed.* New results-oriented financing instruments such as Program-for-Results (PforR), Results-Based Financing (RBF), and sectoral reform programmes garnered interest because of their fast-disbursing nature, results orientation, and circumscribed financing sphere. Particularly in the absence of an adequate macroeconomic framework or a convincing reform programme, these modalities present a viable alternative to budget support.

Changes in the Prevailing Development Paradigm: The Search for a New Narrative

The perception and use of budget support has been shaped by several trends in the development discourse, which tended to shift away from long-term planning to eradicate absolute poverty that was at the core of the original use of the instrument at the turn of the century:

- *From grand aid schemes to targeted interventions.* The last decade saw a shift away from grand aid schemes towards a greater use of impact evaluation methodology to target successful interventions and take them 'to scale'. A stronger results orientation adapted to specific country circumstances gained currency at the expense of a standardized aid architecture built around large resource transfers and comprehensive country-wide poverty reduction strategies based on the standardized, albeit updated, macroeconomic building blocks of the Washington Consensus.
- *Emphasis on behavioural change.* An emerging body of literature focusing on the behaviour of economic agents led development practitioners to consider micro interventions to address incentives, policy and institutional reforms to shift rules and norms of conduct at the local sector, agency, or agent level. Smaller, local, well-evidenced programmes that could be scaled up were increasingly seen as a more effective way of drawing on the insights gained from randomized

impact evaluations/randomized controlled trials (RCTs) measuring interventions against poverty, on topics ranging from agriculture and health to governance and education. Highlighting the complexities of the daily decisions poor people must make with limited information and access to basic services, Banerjee and Duflo (2011) drew attention to the context-specific results and unintended consequences of anti-poverty projects. The evidence from randomized evaluations provides insights on small design tweaks that can significantly improve effectiveness based on a deeper understanding of local customs and culture.

- *Changing perspectives on poverty.* The selection of aid instrument has been influenced by the emerging narrative on poverty reduction, which focuses increasingly on the social dimensions of development, broadening a traditional focus on economic growth with grassroots and bottom-up approaches. These broader dimensions of poverty were explored in the 2000 *World Development Report*, which addressed opportunities for expanding poor people's assets. It argued that major reductions in human deprivation are possible; that economic integration and technological change can spur economic growth, equality, and poverty reduction; and that not only the evolution of markets but also the choices for public action at the global, national, and local levels matter. The 2006 *World Development Report* defined equity in terms of two basic principles: equal opportunities (that a person's chances in life should be determined by his or her talents and efforts, rather than by predetermined circumstances such as race, gender, social, or family background) and the avoidance of extreme deprivation in outcomes, particularly in health, education, and consumption. The report's main message was that, in the long run, the pursuit of equity and the pursuit of economic prosperity are complementary.

- *Tackling the global commons challenge.* The post-2000 aid effectiveness consensus is being supplanted by a convergence of views on the importance of addressing cross-border challenges such as climate change, migration, and pandemics, which call for platforms that transcend the traditional country focus of ODA. It is also being increasingly recognized that official international public finance flows are more effective when they are underpinned by an analysis of underlying political economy dimensions and development constraints and embedded in supportive policies that unlock potentially more significant private flows and domestic resource mobilization. It is also becoming clear that achieving the ambitious framework of the SDGs requires supportive development support that is aligned with developing countries' own goals.

Conclusion

Budget support was supposed to respond to concerns over aid effectiveness, with a focus on predictable resource flows to well-performing developing countries. The track record of the instrument discussed in Chapter 4 largely affirms its constructive role not only in well-performing low-income countries but also in fragile and post-conflict situations and middle-income countries. Even for countries that are not traditional recipients of development financing, the critical role of budget support in providing countercyclical financing during crises came into sharp relief in the aftermath of the financial crisis of 2008/9. Similarly, the Paris Declaration principles underlying the use of budget support as devised at the turn of the century, including country ownership, greater reliance on country systems, and better donor coordination are still valid, despite the weaknesses in implementation and significant changes in the international aid architecture over the past two decades.

At the same time, the discrepancy between lofty aspirations and the reality of budget support has given rise to renewed scrutiny of this financing modality. A range of factors drove the shift in the perceptions and use of budget support:

- *Expectations of sharply increased aid flows turned out to be unrealistic.* Total aid fell well short of the pledges made in 2005 at Gleneagles, and budget support bore the brunt of the shortfall. Additional financing for budget support did not materialize. Surges in funds coincided with financial crises, resulting in short-term financing with limited conditionality. Much of this lending was controversial (e.g., for middle-income countries such as Brazil and Mexico following the financial crisis) and criticized as short-term balance-of-payments financing rather than budget support.
- *Changes in the political environment included the political move toward more conservative governments, which were sceptical about its effectiveness and disinclined to continue financing policy reform.* A stronger results orientation contributed to scepticism toward budget support and a preference for traditional bricks and mortar projects with tangible, measurable results.
- *Fiduciary concerns and questions over fungibility as well as perceptions of greater vulnerability to corrupt practices undermined public trust in budget support.* While a mutually agreed budget with emphasis on poverty and service delivery sectors may be desirable, it also requires confidence in the budget execution system to ensure spending reaches

its intended recipients. A balance needs to be struck. One the one hand, mature PFM systems will provide confidence to budget support partners that funds will be used in agreement with budgets and stated priorities. On the other, PFM systems take years, if not decades, to build and there is growing evidence that PFM related actions are among the most effective (Smets and Knack 2016).

- *Providing budget support to countries with weak PFM systems constitutes a reputational risk,* as there is a higher chance of misuse of funds, elite capture, and inefficiencies. Although it may be possible to accept a degree of inefficiency in public sector management, weak PFM systems can also mean that stated policies, priorities, and plans are not reflected in budgets and that budgets are not executed as formulated. If this is the case, there may be ambiguity over whether development partner priorities are aligned with government priorities. If revealed preferences evidenced in the execution of the budget diverge grossly from plans and prioritize away from social sectors and pro-poor engagement, poor PFM practices become particularly concerning.
- *The erosion of the IMF- and World Bank–driven approach based on PRSPs diluted the role of budget support for low-income countries.* Over time, PRSPs came to be seen as onerous donor requirements that lacked government ownership and were prepared largely by World Bank and IMF staff. They were quietly abandoned.
- *The participation of multiple donors in popular recipient countries ('donor darlings') contributed to an overloading of budget support programmes with non-critical measures, reducing the effectiveness of donor coordination.*
- *New donors outside the OECD/DAC emerged,* with different aid frameworks, incentives, and objectives, raising new questions about the role of foreign assistance and aid instruments.

Drawing on this experience, several steps could reshape budget support as an instrument that retains public support and builds on its track record of development effectiveness:

- Make less exuberant, more realistic projections of likely sources of development financing from domestic and international sources, including supportive policies that unlock potentially more significant private flows and domestic resource mobilization.
- Increase understanding of recipient countries' political economy, development constraints, and specific development conditions.

- Systematically address fiduciary concerns.
- Focus conditionality on critical reforms that are recognizably significant and relevant to longer term development outcomes and public goods.
- Establish a clear division of labour among donors based on their financing and advisory capacity.

The experience with budget support suggests the need for greater nuance based on the country situation. Only a relatively small set of countries at some point in their development trajectory came close to the ideal model of a reform-oriented recipient country with low-income status, good governance, and a coherent strategy for poverty reduction that donors can subscribe to. Modernizing budget support would involve conditionality that is based on a realistic assessment of country conditions to finetune the support for realistic policy programmes. A fragile or conflict-affected country with weak institutions that is prone to corruption and high aid dependency may be deserving of aid, but it cannot be relied on to deliver the sustained reform and performance improvements required for consistent resource flows based on a programme of conditionality. At the other end of the spectrum, the apparent reform zeal of a middle-income country with intermittent access to financial markets may be short-lived and varies with its fluctuating resource requirements.

Modernizing budget support to meet the requirements of the coming decade will also involve adapting to the shifts in the prevailing development paradigm. Rather than supporting comprehensive country-wide poverty reduction strategies prepared for a donor audience, this would involve a more agile, evidence-driven, results-based, incremental approach with a stronger results orientation that can be continuously adapted to evolving country circumstances. A sharper focus on ultimate outcomes would allow greater flexibility and less intrusiveness in the specific steps to achieve goals. Continuous feedback loops and regular adaptation of policy programmes to a country's evolving reality could allow for more incremental approaches to reform that are not regarded as policy reversals. The narrow focus on the reduction of extreme poverty of the early aid effectiveness agenda should give way to broader considerations of addressing inequality and improving prosperity and quality of life. The SDGs offer an ambitious range of development objectives to be prioritized based on the needs of each country. The COVID-19 pandemic, climate change and the spill-overs of conflict and violence have highlighted the potential, and urgency, of using budget support to improve the global commons.

6
How Can Budget Support Meet 21st Century Challenges?

Major changes in the global financial landscape, massive shocks to the global economy, and the recognition of slow but inevitable changes being wrought by climate change have fundamentally altered the approach needed for development finance. Chapter 2 discussed the major emergence of private capital flows, remittances, and sovereign lending, alongside the receding role of foreign aid for most developing countries. At the same time the global pandemic and largest war in continental Europe since the Second World War have exposed the vulnerability of global supply chains and fanned new crises through macroeconomic interdependences: the highest inflation in nearly five decades in several high-income countries, a major debt crisis looms for many middle and low-income developing countries, and basic food security issues threaten the poorest countries now exposed to high commodity prices, fertilizer shortages, and debilitating climate shocks. This relentless barrage of shocks is forcing reflection about existing global institutions and has prompted calls by some major players to rethink the Bretton Woods Institutions and the international basis for collaboration and financing to manage crises in this 'post hyperglobalized' world.[1]

This chapter examines how to transform budget support to be a more effective instrument for development finance and address the changing global environment. Budget support has been an important instrument, helping countries adjust to shocks and supporting reforms to boost economic performance and improve service delivery. However, as the US Treasury Secretary noted in her Fall 2022 address to the annual meetings of the IMF and World Bank, the Bretton Woods institutions need to reform their "vision, incentives, operational approach, and financial model" in order to address the

---

[1] Hyperglobalization is a term used by Dani Rodrik to characterize the period of exceptionally rapid and unrestrained expansion of global markets and interdependencies. He views it as 'crumbling' due to contradictions and the impact of the 2008 financial crisis (Rodrik, Project Syndicate 2022).

Retooling Development Aid in the 21st Century. Shahrokh Fardoust et al., Oxford University Press.
© Shahrokh Fardoust et al., (2023). DOI: 10.1093/oso/9780192882196.003.0006

tasks bearing down on them in the new global environment.[2] Similar recent statements by the G24 and G20 cite the need to 'raise ambition in financing' and for the World Bank and IMF to review their financial model which at present threatens their effectiveness and credibility.[3] The COVID crisis and the Russian invasion of Ukraine, have served to uproot economic activity globally, thrusting tens of millions of vulnerable households below the poverty line. This is a major setback to aspirations of the Sustainable Development Goals (SDGs) to end extreme poverty. Attention to the existential threat of global climate change, disappearing biodiversity, ocean acidification and more threats raise prospects of massive financing requirements and an expanded need for financing to support policy adjustment, particularly in low-income countries. This changing financial landscape calls for reflection on how future foreign aid and multilateral development bank (MDB) assistance can best meet emerging challenges that will support resilience and sustainable growth which developing countries need to help achieve the SDGs.

Budget support should not be framed mainly around the transfer of funds to developing countries. While resource transfers are important, budget support is fundamentally about policy dialogue, technical support, and reform with country ownership. Joint problem-solving, including with analytic and technical assistance, aims to tackle key institutional and policy impediments to sustainable growth—distortions that impede efficient resource allocation, undermine market competition, or inhibit economic resilience and adaptation to systemic and structural change. Examples include reducing costly public subsidies such as to fossil fuels, advancing Nationally Determined Contributions (NDCs) to reduction of greenhouse gas emissions, or strengthening social safety nets to protect vulnerable households during periods of economic turmoil. Importantly, high quality growth cannot be measured solely in terms of augmenting GDP; rather, it is about growth that is *inclusive*—reaching low-income households through employment and opportunity to help break the transmission of intergenerational poverty, *sustainable*—focusing on long-term benefits that conserve natural capital and protect the environmental commons, and *efficient*—managing trade-offs to select the best path towards achieving greater prosperity. The MDBs and

---

[2] At both the Fall and Spring meetings of the IMF and World Bank, US Treasury Secretary Janet Yellen called for a 'reboot' of the Bretton-Woods institutions, noting that the World Bank was not set up to deal with crises, like climate change, that require investments at a scale it cannot finance, and the IMF wasn't designed to address global challenges like the 2008 financial crisis, or the COVID-19 pandemic, or the crisis induced by the Russian invasion of Ukraine (US Treasury 2022, International Monetary and Finance Committee 2022). As of this writing the Bank is preparing a new strategic 'Roadmap' in response to calls for greater ambition to tackle global public goods such as climate change.

[3] See the Group of 24 Communique of 19 April 2022 and the G20 Sustainable Finance Working Group 2021 Synthesis Report.

bilateral aid agencies have for the most part committed to these goals. Maintaining the focus of budget support and growth quality is challenging in the face of economic shocks and confounding political factors.[4] But evidence suggests it is a valuable instrument in the process.

Growth opportunities and the contribution of foreign aid need to be thought about in new ways in light of contemporary challenges, including digitalization and the emergence of new technologies, the urgency of global climate change, and growing inequality within countries that is exacerbated by the economic devastation wrought by persistent shocks. The disruption of trading patterns, supply chain constraints, the reversal of globalization, and food insecurity in the wake of the COVID crisis and war in Ukraine have further complicated the outlook for sustained and equitable growth and prosperity. These developments have emerged amidst the backdrop of a decline in foreign aid flows available to most developing countries. Against the evidence, evaluations, and experience discussed in the previous chapters, budget support on balance remains the most efficient instrument for transmitting fiscal resources to support high-quality growth due to lower transaction costs and faster processing time. But this requires that key conditions are met: there must be a sufficient analytic foundation for advancing dialogue; adequate country ownership based on close consultations and alignment with national development interests is indispensable, and the dialogue which forms the foundation of budget support programmes must be customized to the country's political economy and conform with local institutions, incentives, and procedures.

The shifting architecture of aid instruments and objectives discussed in Chapter 2 have been significantly shaped by trends in private financial flows, and point to the need to identify blended finance modalities that can successfully leverage private investment financing that will crowd in growth opportunities, particularly in low income countries. Structuring foreign assistance to catalyse private capital is not simple. But budget support can, through dialogue and technical support, help to address the private sector need for transparent business practices, competitive markets, and the rule of law.

The next section addresses the arguments for preserving budget support as a key instrument for advancing development and enhancing aid effectiveness. The second section responds to the arguments made by critics of budget support, primarily those raised in the previous chapter. The third section describes principal design challenges facing future use of budget support to

---

[4] For a rich discussion that frames the 'quality of growth' around the resulting distribution of opportunities, sustainability of natural capital, risk management practices, and governance see Thomas et al. (2000).

achieve its potential: addressing effective conditionality, mobilizing private development finance, and motivating collective action. The final section summarizes the principal recommendations for future design and deployment of budget support.

Why Budget Support Is Vital to Meeting 21st Century Development Challenges

The promise of budget support and arguments that lay behind support for increasing its role following the Paris Declaration remain relevant today. Indeed, apart from traditional economic support there are strong reasons for increasing the use of budget support to confront global challenges—those requiring national action but for which benefits accrue regionally or globally. The need to expand global public goods—clean air and water, safe travel and commerce, secure food supply chains, robust financial systems—has never been more pressing. Budget support can make a major contribution in providing the resources needed, sharing critical technologies, and incentivizing countries to act.

Budget support was rarely seen as a complete replacement for conventional project finance except perhaps in middle-income and high-capacity countries with access to private sources of infrastructure financing. The country-based model of the international financial institutions is country-specific, focusing on core infrastructure, human capital development, and capacity building. Budget support should play a key complementary role alongside project investments to focus on the critical policy reforms needed for fiscally and institutionally sustainable growth. The two types of support, conventional project assistance and budget support, aim to work in tandem in order to yield greater effectiveness and durable outcomes than when they are pursued independently. The same may be said of other financing instruments, such as results-based finance (see Box 3.1), or guarantees used to leverage private financing.

Central to the provision of budget support is a strong development dialogue and knowledge base. As discussed in Chapter 4, there is clear evidence that the stronger the analytic foundation in preparation and design of budget support operations, the better its performance and impact. Strong knowledge projects produced jointly and providing the basis for dialogue on budget support design are therefore critical to performance.

Budget support is a financing instrument that it is not appropriate to all country circumstances; the design of budget support and the conduits for its successful use clearly depend on country capacities and context. Table 6.1 provides a rough guide as to which approach may be most appropriate where.

Table 6.1 Mapping of budget support instruments to country circumstances

Country Type	Balance of Payments	Programmatic	Deferred drawdown	Policy-based guarantees	Subnational	Sector-based	Global public goods
Fragile LICs	N	N	N	N	–	Y	Y/N
Post-conflicts LICs	N	Y/N	Y/N	N	–	Y	Y
Weak capacity/governance LICs	Y	Y/N	Y/N	N	–	Y	Y
High capacity/governance LICs	Y	Y	Y	Y	–	Y	Y
Weak capacity/governance MICs	Y	Y	Y	N	–	N	Y
High capacity/governance MICs	Y	N	Y	Y	–	N	Y
Stable federated systems	N	Y	Y	Y	Y	Y	Y

Note: Y = suited to country type; N = unsuitable; Greyed = with qualification. LIC/MIC = low-/middle-income country.

In general, countercyclical balance-of-payments support remains a potent tool to support development priorities during periods of economic crisis. Even in conflict-affected countries that are trying to gradually strengthen their domestic institutions, such as Afghanistan or Yemen, there may be a need to meet payroll and maintain essential government services that merit using budget support. Multiyear programmatic budget support may be better suited to low-income countries and low-capacity middle-income countries, provided there is clear ownership for reforms that require long-term commitment and capacity building. Policy-based guarantees (PBGs) are best suited to higher capacity countries with more developed financial markets and access to international capital markets, although PBGs may also work in more challenging environments where there is strong and credible government commitment. Sector budget support, which typically supports multi-donor sector-wide programmes, is not well suited to middle-income countries with better fiscal capacity and management capabilities. Special-purpose budget support programmes, such as those that provide catastrophic risk insurance or target global public goods, should be available to all countries, with the proviso of greater care and oversight in the case of fragile and post-conflict countries.

Table 6.1 is not meant to be prescriptive, but rather to emphasize the broad spectrum of situations in which budget support can potentially be an effective development tool drawn from available evidence and experience. A further opportunity that could be added to the menu is support for policy and institutional reform even *without* budget transfers. This would sustain the policy dialogue particularly in middle-income countries in periods when there is no need for external financing by providing a 'seal of government policy approval' akin to that provided under IMF Article IV surveillance reports and advisory programmes without lending.

Based on the evidence and experience discussed in this volume, budget support remains a highly relevant aid instrument for several reasons:

- Budget support is *the most efficient instrument for transmitting fiscal resources to respond rapidly to crises,* and evidence suggests the impact of budget support is larger during crises (Chapter 4). Transaction costs are lower and processing time is usually faster per dollar transferred, but this requires a strong analytic foundation for advancing dialogue. Crisis management and response will be a persistent priority. Continuing periodic shocks to the global economy—including the current economic crisis induced by the COVID-19 pandemic—call for rapid responses to protect economic activity and the welfare of vulnerable groups. During the pandemic, non-official development assistance

(ODA) financial flows to developing countries declined substantially, and demand for budget support from the MDBs increased as countries struggled to respond simultaneously to pandemic and the induced economic downturn.

- Budget support has high potential to *help protect the global commons*. In combination with technical assistance, resource transfers to developing countries are needed to help build capacity and prevent or manage the next Ebola virus or novel coronavirus from unleashing the next pandemic. Governments are recognizing climate change as a front-burner concern and mobilizing for action. This directional shift will require resources to support a redirection of policies and a robust dialogue to underpin it, which budget support is designed to do.

- Budget support focuses on *institutions and policies to foster sustainable growth*. In addition to supporting infrastructure and human capital, effective aid to support growth ultimately depends on augmenting institutional capacity, increasing incentives to curtail costly behaviours, and promoting measures that improve durable governance and markets. Much recent literature on sustainable growth underscores the critical role of institutions and political economy (e.g. Acemoglu and Robinson 2019; Besley and Persson 2011). The long-run sustainability of assets—health clinics, roads, water and sanitation networks—depends on their effective operation and maintenance, which require sustained funding, robust institutions, and resilient social capital (Williamson 2000; Baliamoune-Lutz and Mavrotas 2009). Ensuring that public assets provide a future stream of social benefits to the population depends vitally on effective management of health clinics, the maintenance of roads, the sustained supply chains, and committed staff.

- Budget support serves as a *catalyst for private capital*. As discussed in Chapter 2, ODA will not fill the financing needs of developing countries to achieve the SDGs. Private capital will need to be tapped and directed toward developmental priorities. To attract such capital, countries will need to reform policies and institutions that have prevented markets from working efficiently. budget support can help to catalyse critical private investment flows to meet the SDGs.

- Budget support can *support policies for technology transfer and digitization*. Technological developments have made digitalization and the Internet critical tools for engaging in the global economy. Overcoming 'premature deindustrialization' in Africa (Rodrik 2015) to engage new labour force entrants in manufacturing and productive services will require expanded broadband access and technology to produce for integrated global markets. Automation, new processes, and new internet-based technologies will require technologies and broadband to support the 'servicification of manufacturing'—that is, the increased reliance on professional service inputs for global manufacturing, and the shortening of global value chains (Hallward-Driemeier and Nayyar 2018). Private sector investment will need to lead the expansion of broadband access and the building out of internet networks, but budget support can help create the policy and institutional environment needed to attract the investment capital needed. Budget support can also support the big data revolution, crowdsourcing, mobile banking, remote education, and many more applications.

Persuading the Sceptics

For budget support to fulfil its potential, it will have to address the challenges that contributed to persistent doubts regarding the instrument. Despite the overall positive evaluative assessments discussed in Chapter 4, sceptics are not convinced that budget support has a positive impact on public policy. Evidence in fact indicates that budget support has a positive impact on policies, although not with equal impact across all areas of policy reform. Customization of budget support to specific country circumstances therefore remains critical, as does the need to address the concerns that led to the disillusionment with the instrument discussed in Chapter 5: inadequate fiduciary oversight, declining political support by donors, aid dependency, lack of country ownership, fungibility, and weak donor harmonization.

Public Financial Management and Fiduciary Concerns

Budget support is implemented through the recipient's public financial management systems. The greatest concern of sceptics likely stems from this fact, which is the perceived high fiduciary risk and insufficient controls in place to ensure that financing will be used to achieve the donor's purpose (Herrling and Radelet 2006). This concern arises over the use of donor resources for its negotiated purpose through the recipient's public financial management (PFM) systems that becomes indistinguishable from domestic resources. In that sense, there are three main concerns:

(i) donor budget support resources are allocated against priorities in the budget and donors want to be broadly in agreement with this allocation;

(ii) donors want to have confidence that the stated allocations in the recipient budget will be implemented accordingly; and

(iii) donors want the domestic budget to be implemented with regard to efficiency and accountability.

Addressing these three concerns requires strong PFM systems that take decades to build and cannot be guaranteed. A medium-term budget outlook and meaningful budget preparation processes are required for agreement on resource allocation decisions that is guided by the legislative branch. Prudent implementation requires robust budget execution processes to be in place, including deployment and utilization of financial management information systems and adequate procurement capacity. Fiduciary risks can be mitigated through strengthening the internal audit function and guaranteeing institutional and financial independence of the supreme audit institution.

Budget support has been suspended in several instances when these principles were violated, as discussed in Chapter 5. For example, donors are reluctant to support governments if budget resources are being allocated toward conflicts or persecution of minorities. In these cases, budget support is often suspended, as has been the case in Myanmar, Uganda, Ethiopia, Rwanda, and others. Similarly, donors may not be supportive to countries making large capital expenditures in non-productive areas, and withdraw budget support accordingly (North Macedonia is a case in the early 2010s). Lastly, fiduciary concerns, or perceived fiduciary problems in government budget management, can lead to withdrawal.[5]

While this has led to the disenchantment with the instrument by many bilateral budget support providers, MDBs have deployed the instrument more generously in weak PFM environments (see Chapter 3). Being less rigid about the strength of domestic PFM systems allows donors to 'buy' policy reforms and provide fast-disbursing financial resources during times of need that may not be possible through project support. For example, this position made it possible for the World Bank to support policy reform through a human capital budget support operation in Madagascar (World Bank 2020c), despite human capital generally not being prioritized in the domestic budget. In North Macedonia, it was possible to support the government through a policy-based guarantee with the clearance of arrears, accumulated by investments in non-productive investments (IEG 2016d). Despite PFM

---

[5] This was the case following the 2013 Malawi Cashgate scandal, in which about US$32 million was embezzled, making it difficult for donor constituencies to continue to support such a regime until mitigating measures have been taken.

concerns in such contexts, provision of budget support may still be worth-while when valuable policy and institutional reform can be pursued under the programme. In weak PFM environments, donors have been successful in strengthening PFM reforms with associated conditionality as shown in Chapter 4.

This presents a conflict between the need for confidence in the prudent and effective use of budget support resources, while fiscal support is also needed in places where PFM conditions are weak. Public investment management assessments, public expenditure and financial accountability reviews, or fiduciary assessments help to inform specific PFM concerns and judgement.

Restoring Political Support among Donors

There was a shift away from budget support toward project finance after 2010, following the failure of most donors to fulfil commitments to double aid to Africa announced in 2005. As discussed in Chapter 5, criticism of budget support revealed a general distrust of intangible support through unmarked financial transfers. Donors preferred to support tangible projects that could be photographed, affixed with the national flag, and marketed to parliamentarians.

Convincing sceptics of the rich potential of budget support must be driven by evidence and recognition of the critical role institutional and policy reforms play in securing sustainable, long-term development objectives. Many policymakers are unaware of the strong performance of budget support. The contribution of combining tangible and intangible assistance in fostering sustainable results needs to be better understood and communicated. The US commitment to greater reliance on scientific knowledge and robust evidence to guide public policy announced in 2021[6] represents an important renewed direction for the United States toward rethinking the evidence on aid effectiveness, sustainability, and the use of budget support. A growing body of rigorous evidence from impact evaluation literature covering policy interventions, for example on public financial management and financial sector reforms, should serve to underpin credibility of budget support programmes and inform design. Bilateral agencies such as the US Millennium Challenge Corporation (MCC), the premiere US government development finance agency which provides only project finance, should reconsider the use of budget support to complement and secure more sustainable outcomes

---

[6] Presidential Memorandum (2021).

from foreign assistance. Similar hopes were noted by observers at the time of the Paris Accord (Herrling and Radelet 2006).

Dispelling Fears of Aid Dependency

Another charge made against budget support is that it induces dependency and can enable countries to delay reform by sustaining the status quo. In some cases it may indeed have done so. Uganda received decades of budget support beginning in the 1990s. It was able to sustain significantly higher public expenditure levels despite weak domestic resource mobilization and public revenue-to-GDP ratios that stagnated for several years at levels below the sub-Saharan Africa average. After a scandal involving embezzlement of aid money through the prime minister's office in 2013, most donors suspended budget support to Uganda. An in-depth evaluation of a decade of Ugandan budget support (2004–13) concluded that despite years of budget support, 'persistent, low revenue mobilization undermined sustainability of social sector outcomes, undermined budgetary credibility, and worsened the composition of public expenditures' (IEG and European Commission 2015). Other selective studies on support for reform find similar conclusions (Erbeznik 2011).

The evidence on budget support's success with reforms tells a different story (Chapter 4). Success rates, gleaned from reporting of the independent evaluation offices of the six major multilateral development banks that provide budget support indicate that the share of programme objectives that are successful are as high as they are for conventional project lending—across most institutions and country groupings, including fragile and post-conflict countries that qualify for budget support (Asquith, Fardoust, and Sundberg, 2023). In most cases, domestic resource management improved even during prolonged periods of programmatic budget support, and progress was made on poverty reduction and other indicators of human welfare. Although individual cases identify the challenge of perverse incentives to reform, there is little evidence that budget support delays reform, though there is some evidence of reform backtracking or slippage after implementation (Chapter 4).

Delivering on Country Ownership

Strong country ownership of the reform agenda is widely seen to be critical to the success of budget support programmes. Chapter 1 points out that this gave rise in the early 2000s to the view that programmatic budget support must be aligned with development priorities identified in national development strategies. Country ownership was a cornerstone of the 2005 Paris Declaration, but experience with 'poverty reduction strategy papers' that ensued was disappointing, as Chapter 5 details. The national strategy papers became increasingly viewed as an onerous imposition on countries that reflected the thinking of the MDBs and the IMF rather than homegrown national priorities and capacities reflecting local context and culture. The technocratic approach favoured by donors to communicate donor and MDB priorities was not deeply owned or legitimized in partner countries. Chapter 4 underscores the strong empirical evidence that policy reform is unlikely to be effective without strong government ownership.

Extensive consultation with government, civil society, and the private sector is now common practice in most donor agencies for the development and socialization of country strategies and for major projects. However, budget support operations tend to retain a more technocratic approach, working largely through Ministries of Finance and Planning, and bringing in the functional line ministries when specific policy reforms are in question. This needs to change if deeper ownership and community support for reform is to be mobilized to back needed social, institutional, and behavioural change. Reforms that have historically proven difficult, such as removing fossil fuel subsidies, adopting land registration and land taxes, or civil service reform, require broad public understanding and embrace by leadership if they are to be successful.[7] It is true that performance indicators on budget support operations, as summarized in Chapter 4, point to a relatively strong track record of delivery against programme objectives (around a 75 per cent success rate), similar to the success rate in project finance. But measured against these very difficult reforms that impose an adjustment burden on households and businesses, success is far more mixed, particularly with more difficult 'second generation reforms'.

Going forward, greater attention needs to be paid to local decision makers in both private and public spheres, and their contribution to finding solutions. External mandates alone will not work, particularly those based on 'global best practice' that are highly generalized. Engagement is needed with national and local governments, affected communities, and with the private sector to design and implement reforms fully cognizant of local norms and

---

[7] Evidence suggests that legitimacy of reform, persuasion in policy dialogue—both through information and through non-information based methods—and citizen communication are all important here (Smets 2020).

context. This will also require a blunt recognition that developing country governments may be captured by elites more interested in maintaining their own short-term self-interests rather than long-term development prospects of their population (Dercon 2022). In cases of grave misalignment between what is best for the country and the aspirations of entrenched elites, budget support is unlikely to be viable.

Embracing greater national ownership of development priorities will require addressing both the incentives that drive foreign aid agencies and the MDBs, as well as the quality of engagement and participation in programme design in recipient countries. Regarding the former, it has long been noted that internal incentives in aid agencies are predominantly driven by lending volumes and programme delivery, and less on outcomes and performance against national development priorities (see Box 5.1). A slower, iterative approach as advocated in this chapter may run up against the internal incentive system in international financial institutions. Gant charts and pressure to disburse funds on schedule can create tension between operations staff working against the clock and development experts who monitor progress against outcomes and impacts. Such tensions need to be managed constructively.

In countries where development challenges are complex and donor support has yielded poor results, an approach promoted by several development practitioners at Harvard's Center for International Development called 'problem-driven iterative approach' (PDIA) appear highly promising. PDIA focuses on problem-solving through facilitated consultation with multiple stakeholders and common purpose. It recognizes there are several 'unknowns' in complex problem-solving, and allows greater local ownership of the design and implementation process built around defining problems and objectives, understanding their root causes, and throughout implementation regularly monitoring performance to observe intermediate outcomes and reformulated solutions as lessons emerge and problems become better defined.[8] Context-based evidence and solutions, such as can be generated through randomized control trials and other experimental research, are also relevant for success in localized interventions. Such approaches help to find local solutions that support country ownership. Realism in timetables and pathways to getting reform scaffolding in place are needed.

---

[8] See Andrews, Pritchett, and Woolcock (2013) for a comprehensive discussion of the PDIA approach. Andrews (2021) provides a valuable discussion of what is often unknown in project implementation and a critique of the logframe and 'Theory of Change' approach to project development that is often employed in the MDBs, with special reference to education programmes in Mozambique.

Addressing the Fungibility Critique

A common criticism of budget support is that funds disbursed to the national Treasury can be readily diverted to non-developmental purposes, unrelated to 'reform'. Fungibility is a common criticism of all aid that is difficult to refute and not unique to budget support. Donor funds allocated to road construction may allow funds that would have gone to roads anyway to be used for other purposes.

Budget support aims to support public expenditure for development purposes. With transparent reporting, donors can scrutinize the whole of government fiscal envelope and readily assess budget allocations, revealed priorities, and development focus. Thorough public expenditure reviews, covering the quality of public financial management (PIMAs and PEFAs) and the sources and effectiveness of revenue mobilization, should be a prerequisite for standard budget support.[9] Such reviews help inform judgement about whether budget support is an appropriate instrument and provide both quantitative and qualitative insights into the alignment of public expenditures with development priorities.

Budget support underpins reforms to country systems, institutions, and the policy context for national development. The vital role of dialogue is to nudge fiscal support toward priority sectors and initiatives, and to help finance the adjustment costs and development requirements that doing so requires. In the event of an economic crisis, the focus of negotiated support will likely be short term and include fortifying social assistance programmes to mitigate adverse impacts—as has been true of recent budget support relief programmes following the COVID-19 crisis. For multiyear programmatic budget support, however, the fiscal dialogue must focus on medium-term, home-grown development strategies.

Fear about aid fungibility can place donors in a bind. They may reject aid to the central government for political reasons but want to support local public services for developmental and humanitarian purposes. The fungibility concern can be addressed only if budget support can (a) bypass national parliaments to reach lower-level government, (b) be limited to developmental purposes, and (c) demonstrate that it is additional to funds historically provided by the national government. Such circumstances are rare and require exceptional vigilance and monitoring, but some examples exist. In Ethiopia,

---

[9] For guidance on the scope and implementation of public expenditure reviews, as well as how they are to be conducted, see the World Bank website: http://www1.worldbank.org/publicsector/pe/befa05/PERs. htm. Full public expenditure reviews are periodically updated but may not be possible for programmes during crises.

for example, de facto budget support was provided from 2006 to 2014 through such a mechanism and supported decentralization. Although it was labelled as project support for 'protection of basic services', it replaced multi-donor budget support and directed budget support to local government budgets while restricting its use to development purposes (health, education, water and sanitation, rural roads, and agricultural extension). The net increase in local government expenditures was monitored in prioritized sectors (IEG 2013). Creative redirecting of resources should be creatively pursued where circumstances permit credible separation of developmental support to provincial or local governments.

Strengthening Donor Harmonization and Alignment

The background history of advocacy for donor harmonization and alignment was discussed in Chapter 1, and the effectiveness of the harmonization agenda is assessed in Chapter 4. The heavy burden donors and multilateral development banks imposed on developing countries through compliance costs and reporting requirements strained their very limited technocratic capacity. The aim of harmonization and alignment reforms by development agencies was to reduce this burden and provide coherence to country dialogue and coordinated reporting. Some progress toward this goal was made following the Paris Declaration (see Chapter 1). Problems became evident for many countries as chosen 'donor darlings' faced intrusive demands from multiple donors, discussed in Chapter 5 (Mozambique, Tanzania, Uganda, and Vietnam are notable examples). Chapter 4 also notes that harmonization may have some negative effects.

The value of advancing donor harmonization has not disappeared. It will still require sustaining a commitment to alignment across diverse donors. Greater coherence poses the challenge of managing discordant voices without derailing key messaging but preventing multiple agendas from proliferating. One approach would be to recognize leadership on budget support operations by the multilateral development banks, which are largely depoliticized and independent of colonial legacy and parliamentary fads. These institutions generally have the deepest analytic capability, the driver of dialogue and budget support design. Bilateral agencies, which are beholden to their home governments and taxpayer bases, could remain free to pursue their own areas of focus.

This division of labour could have implications for aid financing and allocation. Bilateral aid agencies, which have historically contributed a significant albeit declining share of budget support, would either pool budget support funds under multilateral development bank leadership or withdraw from budget support work and focus on project finance with more modest policy objectives. They could advance issues outside the budget support framework, such as gender equity, early childhood development, or climate change mitigation on a bilateral basis.

Addressing Core Design Challenges in Future Budget Support

The success of budget support depends on its design, the most important aspect of which is the selection and design of conditionality: the feasibility of key reform measures, their sequencing, alignment with elite interests within the domestic political-economy, and with the medium-term national development vision. Threading the needle between the need to balance and align the concerns of donors (principals) to visibly and measurably advance development outcomes and the priorities of country decision makers (agents) within their unique country context, about which they are far better informed, is challenging and vital to programme success (see Box 1.2). In this section, three specific challenges are discussed: the role of conditionality for incentivizing reform, the future contribution of budget support to mobilizing private sector investment financing for development, and the critical role of budget support in protecting the global commons for future generations.

From Conditionality to Concurrence

Conditionality is the core commitment device of budget support, indeed for all foreign aid, and has been a central issue, implicit or explicit, in each previous chapter. It is often contentious. It was the view of conditionality as oppressive, undisciplined, and out of touch with reality and capacity on the ground which led to calls for reform in the early 2000s, culminating in the 2005 Paris Declaration. Inherent tensions of conditionality were essentially wished away by lofty references to alignment with national development strategies, themselves technocratic and aspirational tools. Yet conditionality remains a major rationale for development finance, shaping the lengthy passage between constituencies leading from aid agencies to cities and villages[10]: between agency boards and the public aiming to demonstrate strong stewardship of taxpayer resources; between agency staff and their management

---

[10] Discussed in Bourguignon and Sundberg (2007).

operating within the incentive framework of the agency; between recipient governments and their own citizens, as they aim to demonstrate they govern in the national interest; between central government and local authorities where programmes requiring local implementation seek to balance local and national interests; and finally between authorities and their public, governed by local accountability mechanisms. The rules and conditions of budget support are invisible at the local level, but success may require their local translation and acceptance.

For conditionality to be effective, it should take the form of a credible concurrence between the financing institution and recipient country, based on jointly understood analytic foundations addressing the national institutional and policy context, and with a clear line of sight to programme objectives. The technocratic approach adopted by aid agencies is insufficient if it is not jointly understood, fit to purpose, cognizant of a country's political economy and fully relevant for counterparts within the specific country context. This requires a framing and implementation of conditionality that moves from conflictive conditionality to 'credible concurrence', in support of a realistic and consensual program customized to the country context. This is also underscored in Chapter 4, where the quality and depth of analysis underpinning budget support programmes is strongly correlated with development outcomes. High-quality analytic work aims to align the content of and commitment to budget support conditions, bringing stakeholders into the development process. It often needs to be accompanied by technical assistance to pilot and help to adapt new practices or technology introduced in programmes.

Chapters 1 and 3 discussed the evolution of conditionality from 'oppressive and undisciplined' to more focused and strategic. Evaluation metrics in Chapter 4 show that budget support has generally performed well. But the impression has persisted that it is not an effective instrument for spurring reform both because implementation often lagged the original aspirations of the policy programmes and because there are instances of serious failure. Chapter 4 cites instances that contributed to the disillusionment with budget support, such as Uganda in 2012 when evidence of widespread fraud led to the suspension of budget support; or Mozambique in 2013–14 when massive hidden borrowing exposed deep corruption in government. In neither case were the budget support operation nor the terms of conditionality at issue per se, but evidence of corruption was overwhelming, causing distrust of budget practices and the institutional practices to safeguard public finances. However, based on programme objectives, most budget support operations have been found to be successful. Lessons from experience with budget support point toward several steps to improve the underpinning, design, and deployment of conditionality.

- *Develop joint programmes to build greater ownership.* Joint ownership contributes to delivering on the development agenda, but requires alignment of conditions with local capacity and knowledge, development priorities, and the incentives of those in authority. This appears obvious, but policy prescriptions by donors often revert to repeating patterns, recommending generic 'best practices' often based on a simplified version of the Washington consensus.[11] Recognition of local institutional context and circumstances requires avoiding applying constructs from one country context to another, avoiding 'cookie cutter' approaches vilified in earlier critiques of structural adjustment. In other words, emphasis should be placed on the transfer of relevant knowledge, but not as a 'hegemony of ideas'.
- *Align incentives with the political interests of authorities and, where possible, with their constituents.* Related to the previous point, ownership relies on aligning interests, formal and informal, public and private, to improve the probability of reform ownership and success. This point is made abundantly by Dercon (2022), who refers to the 'underlying elite bargain' in foreign aid, perhaps most evident with budget support. The challenge for donors, in Dercon's words, is 'empowering citizens while nudging elite bargains towards development and growth'. He also acknowledges that in the face of persistent poverty donors can't simply wait for such nudging opportunities to arise. Aid agencies can't engineer change, and need to 'gamble on development', aligning support with those in authority who see inclusive growth to be in their own interest, while ideally forging greater elite accountability to their constituents.
- *Base reform actions and conditionality on identified dimensions of development effectiveness.* This is particularly true for 'first generation' reforms, reflecting their criticality, relevance, efficacy, additionality, and measurability (see Chapter 1). The emphasis on each of these dimensions and their measurement need to be grounded in a common understanding of the constraints to growth and to efficient public service delivery based on a common theory of change linking policy actions, implementation and behaviours to the expected outcomes.

---

[11] See (Pritchett et al. 2012). The authors refer to this practice as 'isomorphic mimicry' and provide multiple examples from MDBs and bilateral development agency experience.

- *Avoid fragmentation across agencies and agendas.* Conditionality needs to be coherent, focus on country priorities, and avoid fragmentation. This means avoiding the proliferation of donor wish lists to 'donor darlings' discussed in Chapter 5, whereby agencies commonly looked to advance selective policy concerns in programmatic budget support in the 2010s. Joint budget support financing made sense in simplifying and harmonizing procedures but did not lead to alignment. Joint support should not be used to add conditions to meet home constituency concerns. Donors need to accept more explicit delegation of lead responsibility to a single agency with deep local presence and analytic capacity.
- *Plan for exit strategies in high risk programmes.* Reducing or stopping programmatic budget support may be needed when there are clear and serious departures from programme objectives. Competing pressures, between internal disbursement incentives to meet financial targets and external pressures to end support when countries fall out of favour, run up against the recipient's need for fiscal predictability. One exit strategy that preserves an element of sanction but is less punitive is the European Union's use of two disbursement windows. Disbursements are divided between a stable medium-term window with periodic fixed tranches for disbursement and variable tranches that can be delayed or terminated to preserve incentives for meeting performance indicators (European Commission 2018).
- *Help facilitate greater private investment by 'de-risking'.* Private capital flows are increasingly important for development finance, with widespread recognition that the public sector has a role to play in strengthening the rule of law and improving the business environment in order to reduce sovereign and commercial risk facing investors. Support should be designed to help address business environment risk that inhibits bankable investments.

Continual learning and feedback is needed for budget support programmes dealing with complex institutional change, particularly on poorly understood or complex policy problems. The implementation sequencing and underlying incentives for reform measures are often not well understood. Ideally a strong monitoring framework can provide real-time assessment of progress to allow for feedback and programme adaptation. Many countries have limited capacity to carry this out. It is important to exercise realism and recognition of the costs frequent monitoring can impose, and the time required to adopt and implement institutional reform. Problem Driven Iterative Adaption (PDIA) is not a solution but an approach to real-time learning and adaptation that shows promise at the local level. While it has generally not been used with national level policy dialogue or with macroeconomic policies, the principle of iterating toward solutions should be considered in the dialogue process to assess performance, review and improve programme logic, and deepen systems resilience (Andrews et al. 2017).

Country Typology

Budget support is not appropriate to all countries under all circumstances. For some countries, budget support programmes are likely to quickly go off the rails, or never get on them. Two main dimensions affect the typology of countries and the confidence in the effectiveness of budget support. The first is political stability and the quality of governance, which reflect the institutions that manage public resources, professionalize an independent bureaucracy, and sustain systems of political checks and balances. The second dimension is demand for external support from authorities. Demand for budget support goes beyond the need to shore up fiscal space and accelerate growth. It encompasses political attitudes toward the multilateral development banks, toward the market economy, and geopolitics. Greater demand for assistance can be induced by emergencies without strong ownership. It needs to be distinguished from domestic motivation and demand for reform. However, evidence from Chapter 4 suggests that even in cases with weak ownership, economic reform can be successful.

Box 6.1 shows that no single instrument dominates. Agencies need to recognize the plurality of paths toward effective development assistance and reform. In extremes, the choice of aid instrument is clear: budget support fits well when a country's expenditure priorities align with public service delivery and there is confidence in country public financial management. Conditionality can be light and strategic. When incentives of authorities do not align, external financing is less important, and PFM is weak, the prospects for effective budget support are poor. Budget support is either unlikely to work and needs stringent conditions to address risks. Ring-fenced project finance to support vital public services or humanitarian assistance is appropriate, delivered through NGOs rather than country systems in extreme cases. There may also be cases where selective subnational governments have adequate systems in place, for example in federated systems with competent local government.

Many countries lie somewhere in between, with high needs but weak institutions, weak fiscal imperatives, fragmented authority, patronage systems, and few incentives to advance reform. In these cases, ambitious programmes to advance reform will often backfire, and measures to work in close collaboration with the regime are risky. Alternatives call for a more pluralistic approach. In these cases, foreign assistance, whether project or budget support, needs to be opportunistic and identify circumstances that are conducive. As mentioned above, where elite capture undermines the viability of coherent policymaking in the long-term interest of the country, a robust assessment of the political economy would come to the conclusion that budget support is not a viable option, arguing for solid analytic work rather than the provision of finance.

Box 6.1 Quality of institutions and the choice of aid instruments

Budget support is applicable in many country circumstances, but it is not appropriate in all countries and all circumstances. Box Figure 6.1 provides a simple illustration of country characteristics and the choice of aid instrument along dimensions of institutional capacity and how financially constrained or dependent they are on aid.

The choice of aid instrument in the diagonal corners is clear. In the top right corner there is confidence in a country's ability to use budget support effectively and address institutional and public service priorities, including during crises. Conditionality can be light and strategic or even absent. In the lower left corner, institutions are weak, political commitments have low credibility, and authority is less incentivized to pursue reform with low aid dependence. The prospects for effective budget support are poor, and budget support is either unlikely to be appropriate or it needs to be accompanied by stringent conditions to address the high fiduciary risks. Ringfenced project finance to support vital public services or humanitarian assistance is appropriate, delivered through NGOs in exceptional cases.

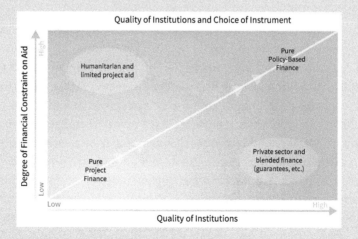

Box Figure 6.1 Quality of institutions and choice of instrument

continued

Box 6.1 *continued*

Where capacity is high and dependence on aid low (the lower right corner), budget support financing is needed during crises, with relatively modest conditionality, unless it is useful to advance contemporaneous strategic public sector priorities. Greater use of blended finance to attract private capital is feasible. These countries are usually middle-income countries with access to private capital markets for sovereign borrowing or investment by foreign investors.

The prospects for comprehensive public management reforms supported through budget support are greater in regimes with strong leadership and legitimacy through championing development and asserting their authority to advance reforms, such as Ethiopia and Rwanda. More ambitious conditionality over systemic reform has greater prospects for political ownership and sustainable success. The success of these country programmes suggests that working through country institutions with more centralized and autocratic regimes—accommodating the regime in power (Levy 2014 describes this as 'working with the grain')—can strengthen the technocracy and support checks and balance systems.

Competitive regimes are more fragmented, authority is contested, and opportunities to advance reform are limited, requiring an incremental approach. In these fragmented and less stable settings, aid may need to be limited to ring-fenced projects operating with heavy constraints on local institutions, possibly with support provided through civil society organization rather than government officials. This can provide more stable implementation arrangements to help focus on sustained service delivery and improve prospects that social assistance is distributed to those most in need.

In such cases, working with targeted sectors and combining project finance with policy-based finance to build coherent, targeted programmes to shore up public service performance and piloted systems is preferable. Foster and Rana (2020) document the experience with power sector reform from the 1990s and 2000s. Work with regimes that departed from the democratic ideal still can advance public service reform, but should strive to build greater stakeholder support and grassroots engagement to shore up accountability for quality service delivery. No one set of institutional patterns or sector organization was predominant, reflecting the need for institutional design that is flexibly tailored to local circumstances. The diversity of institutions, capacity, and political culture underscores the value of learning and accountability mechanisms.

Both international financial institutions and recipient governments must strive for realism, focusing on critical reforms that help achieve long-term development outcomes, including the sustainable provision of public goods. Identifying critical conditions requires deep understanding of local context and realism regarding the risks inherent in budget support instruments.

Mobilizing Development Finance

It is widely recognized that foreign aid cannot meet the financing needs of developing countries aspiring to achieve the SDGs. Incremental measures have been proposed by the Group of 20 (G20) that aim to relax the constraining limits on lending of the seven multilateral development banks by 'optimizing their balance sheets'—taking measures that will increase ability to lend without substantial damage to their credit ratings. The measures include (a) increasing their capital efficiency allowance for a higher leverage ratio and somewhat higher risk tolerance but retaining their AAA bond rating; (b) establishing an MDB 'exposure exchange' to collaborate on loan exposure types to help diversify against regional and sectoral concentration risks; (c) leveraging their equity in concessional windows to borrow on international capital markets; and (d) evaluating new instruments to share risk in non-sovereign operations, for example credit guarantees, hedging structures, structured finance, etc. (Independent Expert Panel, 2022). These recommendations are important, and some are already taking shape. But a huge financing gap for developing countries will remain, at a time when demands for greater investment to address climate change compounds the public investment shortfall for priority domestic development purposes.

Multilateral development banks and donors recognize the critical role of private capital in helping fill the SDG financing gap, estimated at nearly $2.5 trillion a year before the pandemic (UNCTAD 2014) and likely much higher (see Chapter 2). ODA and other official flows have declined as a share of GDP even as commitments voiced at successive Financing for Development Meetings since 2002 have pledged increases. Climate finance commitments made at the Third UN Conference on finance for development in Addis Ababa in 2015, and the 2022 United Nations Conference on Climate Change have shown more progress, but financing has slowed, not increased to meet the $100 billion target by 2020.

For many years, the solution to inadequate capital for development needs has been to call for a greater role by the private sector. Large private capital flows come predominantly through foreign direct investment (FDI), equity capital, worker remittances, and, more recently, private impact investments. Remittances alone are more than twice the level of total ODA flows.

The lion's share of these expanding private capital flows accrues to middle-income countries, while the poorest countries, with the largest development needs, have little access to capital. Low-income countries with natural resource wealth tend to attract FDI into the extractive sectors, but the resources generated often bring a host of problems and little growth in critical public services.

The often-heard refrain of development banks, bilateral agencies, and think tanks has been the need to leverage private financing for development through subsidies and guarantees that induce capital into markets that bear high real or perceived risk. The idea of going from billions to trillions, put forth in 2015 by the World Bank and other multilateral development banks, was that public resources could be used to de-risk and thereby leverage large private capital flows for development. The Millennium Challenge Corporation (MCC) launched three new facilities in 2020–21, each aiming to leverage greater private investment and new business technologies through selective use of grant capital.[12] Numerous reports argue for greater attention to advancing blended finance tools (see, for example, World Bank 2015; Badre 2018; Lee et al, 2018).

Experience has not matched expectations. Chapter 2 discusses this in some detail, including modest progress such as the creation of an International Finance Corporation (IFC) private sector window with partial risk guarantees, blended finance loans, local currency risk coverage, and a guarantee facility. But the promise of billions to trillions has fallen far short, particularly in Africa (Lee and Sami 2019). With few notable exceptions, the catalytic role of blended finance for 'de-risking' private capital flows has been disappointing, with just 37 cents of private financing for every $1 of public financing in low-income countries (see Box 2.5). One conclusion is that tolerance for risk by the private arms of development finance institutions is not very different from that of commercial investors (Lee and Preston 2019).

Many factors impede the aspirations of the billions to trillions agenda, including political risks; market failures, such as information asymmetries; and the lack of bankable opportunities as a result of the weak business environment in many low-income countries.

All of the leading areas that constrain private sector investment in low-income countries are the frequent focus of dialogue and action in budget support operations. Figure 6.1 shows the principal policy private investment

---

[12] The MCC has launched three facilities: the American Catalytic Facility for Development, for joint work with the US Development Finance Corporation; the Innovation and Technology Facility, which is partnering with the Small Business Administration; and the Millennium Impact for Infrastructure Accelerator, which is working in partnership with Africa50 to spur investment in Africa.

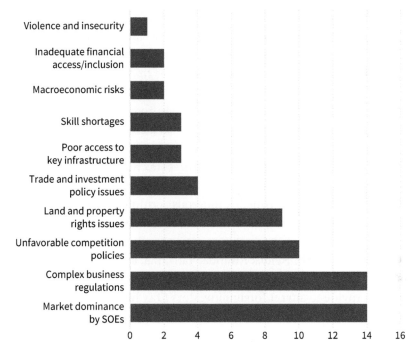

Figure 6.1 Principal policy constraints to private sector development
Source: IFC 2020. CPSD is the IFC Country Private Sector Diagnostic.

constraints as identified by the IFC. Market dominance by state-owned enterprises and unfair competition policies are major factors that prevent new market entrants, domestic or foreign, from risking investment capital. The complexity of business regulations and difficulty navigating property rights and land laws often give local and politically connected investors an advantage over foreign or smaller businesses, provided they are politically stabile. Analysis distinguishing fragile and conflict-affect countries from non-fragile countries identified political stability as the leading constraint, followed by access to electricity and corruption (Independent Evaluation Group, 2013).[13] Trade and investment policy can increase the risks of sourcing imported inputs or accessing external markets.

To this list one should add the need for predictability and credible policy signals from government and relevant public institutions by which private investors can make informed investment decisions. Circumstances change

---

[13] IEG (2013) draws on World Bank business enterprise surveys and notes importantly that prioritizing business climate reforms is necessary but insufficient for fostering growth in fragile country settings due to weak public implementation capacity, the absence of technical training in the workforce, and the prevalence of informality.

over time and policies often fall victim, undermining investor confidence. Stern (2022) argues persuasively that as circumstances evolve, technologies advance and learning occurs, policy revisions need to be 'predictably flexible'. That is, they need to be carried out in ways that can be anticipated and that people understand. Governments can aim to build in predictability about how policy will change as learning occurs and programs mature, which will help to reduce government-induced policy risk facing investors.

Providing public grants or subsidies to attract private investors is not new. Governments have long used tax expenditures (tax holidays), targeted infrastructure (export processing zones), or other incentives to attract investors. These practices have spawned numerous critiques about beggar-thy-neighbour practices that can become a race to the bottom as costs outweigh benefits and are often unsustainable or create contingent liabilities (Gurtner and Christensen 2008). Kenya, Rwanda, Tanzania, and Uganda together are estimated to lose up to $2.8 billion a year from the tax incentives and exemptions they provide to attract foreign investors (Tax Justice Network 2012).

A new approach to mobilizing private financing is needed that recognizes the scarcity and importance of public resources and applies it judiciously, with clear empirical justification, to incentivize priority investments in areas with measurable development impact. Concessional funds to support private capital should aim to facilitate more than individual transactions: They should address the underlying causes of high perceived risks. Addressing the underlying market failures—sovereign risks, weak access to finance, favouritism toward dominant state enterprises, weak judicial systems—lead to a more robust and sustainable environment for the private sector. The use of public resources to build a robust business environment should remain paramount.

Historically, budget support has advanced priority investments in substantive ways, for example by supporting programmatic work in parallel with conventional project finance with cross-cutting conditionality to address project risk. These efforts do not leverage private sector finance, but they often indirectly facilitate it, for example by strengthening regulatory institutions and the rule of law to establish transparent and more evenly applied business laws. It thus has the potential to transform private investment if tailored in new and innovative ways to address market failure or perceived risks that constrain new private investment. Such transformation is particularly focused where capital markets are poorly developed and sovereign risk is high or unrated.

Vehicles for blended finance include leveraged grant facilities; public–private partnerships; hedging instruments, including performance-based guarantees and performance-based debt buy-downs; and development impact bonds. Their performance record is mixed, in part because they rarely address the underlying causes of market failure and because the perceived and real risk to investors is high. Budget support used in parallel with these tools to advance critical policy and institutional reforms can extend the impact beyond the immediate transactions being facilitated.

Policy-Based Guarantees (see Box 2.3 on Ghana and Chapter 3) were introduced to cover private lenders against the risk of default by sovereign borrowers. PBGs are supported by both budget support and guarantee instruments. Interest in them is growing in part because they reduce country exposure to MDB balance sheets and provide opportunities to leverage private finance.[14]

These guarantees help countries improve credit access, diversify their creditor base, lengthen maturities, and lower interest rates, making them more attractive to borrowers (IEG 2016b and IEG 2021). To reduce risk, designers of PBGs need to pay more attention to the government's efforts to sustain robust macroeconomic and fiscal management and improve borrower's credit terms, particularly for the nonguaranteed portion of PBG-supported loans from private creditors. In these three-party transactions (development agency, private bank, the government), it is important for the agency supporting the transaction to work with the government to ensure competitive bidding, transparency, and due diligence with respect to private lenders.

Impact investment is another area with scope and promise for innovation. Historically philanthropic work and impact funds have tended to work in silos, with little effort to co-finance or coordinate dialogue to increase impact in line with country development priorities. Budget support instruments could serve to attract greater participation from, and collaboration with, impact investors by opening up the development dialogue around well-managed and locally owned objectives. Impact funds have become a major force in development finance, with total assets under management estimated at $505 billion in 2019 (IFC 2020). Budget support could complement and leverage private sector support of specific development needs (such as off-grid electrification, environmental protection, or access to water and sanitation), with impact investor interests supporting the roll-out and implementation of policy and institutional reforms to advance investor interests.[15]

---

[14] All PBGs are counted against the World Bank's capital. In contrast, only 25 per cent of the issued guarantee counts toward the World Bank exposure limit. PBGs are therefore attractive where countries are approaching exposure limits.

[15] Kharas notes somewhat fancifully an annual 1 per cent tax on the wealth billionaires would yield $130 billion per year, over 80 per cent of total ODA. See: dianeravitch.net/2021/12/02/homi-kharas-how-billionaires-could-solve-global-problems-with-a-1-tax/.

The challenge to scaling up impact investment is the absence of lenders willing to take below-market risks, a 'missing middle', according to Lee and Preston (2019). Impact investors seek development impact but expect risk-adjusted market returns. The development finance institutions, such as the IFC, also seek risk-adjusted returns to meet shareholder expectations. Missing are investors that will accept below-market returns in return for high development impact. Early-stage finance with adequate tenure, higher risk tolerant financing, and local currency instruments are largely absent in most low-income countries presumably forfeiting many viable and profitable investment opportunities. An independent fund could partner with the developmental finance institutions or impact investors to take on risks at below-market or even zero return in exchange for greater development impact. Such a fund would behave differently from existing funds: It would take on higher risk financial tranches focused on funding gaps; it would require different staffing, focusing on financial and development impact; and it would finance investments originated by development finance institutions. It would require clear metrics for monitoring outcomes and progress toward identified development objectives. Robust and credible monitoring systems for blended finance need to be created, drawing on lessons learned from the independent evaluation operations conducted by multilateral development banks. Creating such capabilities should be a priority for the decade ahead.

Motivating Collective Action

Strengthening support for the global commons is the defining challenge facing the world today. SDG 13, which calls for taking 'urgent action to combat climate change and its impacts', is intertwined with SDG6 (on clean water and sanitation), SDG7 (on affordable clean energy), SDG14 (on sustaining life below water), and SDG15 (on sustaining life on land). Addressing the sharp decline in biodiversity is entwined with, and possibly at odds with, ending hunger (SDG 2) through efficient food production or converting land to build infrastructure and industrial uses (under SDG 9). These challenges are complex and costly, but vital. They will require a dramatic shift in political priorities and in our collective behaviours if the world is to succeed in securing a safe and viable home for future generations.

The International Panel on Climate Change (IPCC) has laid out a goal of containing global warming to 1.5°C above pre-industrial levels. Meeting the goal will require reducing carbon dioxide emissions by an estimated 45 per cent by 2030 and reaching effective zero net emissions by 2050. The world is far off-track for achieving these goals, some argue irreversibly so. Some projections point to global temperatures rising by 3.2°C by 2100, with profound consequences for rising sea levels, declining biodiversity, and potentially catastrophic changes in global weather patterns.[16]

Budget support, the preeminent aid instrument built around dialogue, technical assistance, and policy reform, can be a potent ally to address support for the global commons. Strong shared dialogue, a global governance process, and real resources transfers needed for concrete action, are all vital for progress. Addressing climate change through concerted action to curb greenhouse gas emissions and promote rapid carbon sequestration will require much more than the single step of implementing an agreed carbon pricing regime that reflects environmental externalities, as Stern (2022) points out. It will require a whole range of public policies to maintain a positive investment climate attracting necessary private capital, effective and climate smart urban planning as urban populations swell, investment in new technologies and adoption of consistent regulations and standards.

The classic 'wicked problem'[17] posed by the challenge of preserving the global commons, with multiple incentives pulling in different directions under conditions of uncertainty, calls for budget support, operating in tandem with project funding. It will require rethinking financing and approaching solutions in an iterative manner, particularly since, for many policy changes, individual national action does not generate direct national benefits, such as reduction of greenhouse gases. Unlike the problem addressed by the Montreal Protocol, climate change is extremely complex and involves uncertainty around timing and impact. It is characterized by incomplete information, multiple forecasts, and evolving circumstances that are difficult to fully grasp by existing institutions. Uncertainty over the parameters of the problem gives rise to a wide range of forecasts, albeit all pointing to potentially catastrophic outcomes. Climate change is also complex socially and politically, with interdependencies across geographical areas; shared watersheds, habitats, and ocean resources that cross national boundaries compound the complexity of shifting human behaviour. But success with the Montreal Protocol provides lessons for tackling global warming (see Box 6.2).

Motivating collective action for addressing climate change will also require shifting from traditional economic analysis and characterization of risk as a 'departure from the norm' toward new norms requiring regular stress tests

---

[16] The UN Department of Economic and Social Affairs reports that greenhouse gas emissions must peak before 2025, and thereafter fall by 43 per cent by 2030 in order to reach the 1.5°C cap. Despite the drop in economic activity caused by the COVID-19 crisis, current commitments fall well short of meeting the 1.5° C target and emissions are rising as restrictions are lifted (unstats.un.org/sdgs/report/2022/goal-13/).

[17] Andrews et al. (2017) define 'wicked hard' problems as the most difficult tasks that are transaction intensive (a large number of agents need to participate), discretionary (the decisions made by agents are based on difficult-to-verify knowledge), and often not based on a known technology.

as risks evolve. This point is forcefully argued by Stern (2022) and Thomas (2023). Economists and policy makers must avoid forcing "a huge and non-standard challenge into a narrow and standard framework" for the sake of convenience. Multiple areas of market failure which are evident from analysis of climate change underscore the need to deepen economic analysis in terms of dynamics of development and of the nature and breadth of potential benefits from early action.

Box 6.2 Why was the Montreal Protocol so successful?

The Montreal Protocol, established in 1984, sought to arrest the deterioration of the ozone layer and expansion of the ozone hole above Antarctic. It is the only UN treaty ever ratified by all countries. Its success reflects five main factors.

- It addressed a problem that was well defined, and there was strong scientific evidence that helped forge a collective understanding of the threat that failure to control hydrochlorofluorocarbons (HCFCs) posed.
- It recognized the need for differentiated country commitments based on countries' income level and capacities. Reduction and phase-out dates were less aggressive for developing countries, which accounted for a much smaller share of HCFCs.
- It provided financial support to help countries meet their commitments. Under the terms of the treaty, a multilateral fund was created to provide financial and technical assistance to developing countries to comply with their commitments. Almost three-quarters of countries qualify for access the fund, which is replenished every three years.
- It put in place a monitoring and authorization system to track and report on compliance. Control over imports and exports of HCFCs is regulated under a quota and licensing system that tracks and reports on usage.
- It established an effective governance structure, which brought parties together under UN auspices. The fund is managed by a board consisting of an equal number of developed and developing countries. Its technical work is carried out by four multilateral agencies: the United Nations Environment Programme (UNEP), the United Nations Development Programme (UNDP), the United Nations Industrial Development Organization (UNIDO), and the World Bank.

Under such circumstances, country-based budget support with climate related conditionality requires a shared policy dialogue and stakeholder engagement. To date, pledged assistance to support management of climate change, protect marine fish stocks, or guard other global commons is far below estimated requirements to mitigate and adapt to global warming. Moreover, little of what is pledged has materialized, and none of it through budget support. Given the projected magnitude of temperature changes adapting to global warming will be costly and require internationally coordinated support. Dedicated funds to climate smart infrastructure will be key to offset fiscal costs of policy reforms and institutional reform needed to adapt to environmental change. Cost estimates have placed annual financing needs to address global warming in low- and middle-income countries at around $1.5–$2.7 trillion over the 2015–30 period (Vorisek and Yu 2020).

Budget support provides an opportunity for greater use of conditionality in support of nationally proclaimed goals to which governments have made binding commitments. In 2015, for example, more than one hundred countries committed to Nationally Determined Contributions (NDCs) to reduce their greenhouse gas emissions to meet the goal of the Paris climate agreement. Linking budget support to support for these goals in lower- and middle-income countries and providing access to low-carbon-emitting technologies, such as renewable energy generation and carbon capture technologies, could support changes critical to limiting global warming.

Some funds have been set up with environmental objectives, such as the Global Environmental Facility (GEF), which is housed at the World Bank and supports environmental projects. The Green Climate Fund was established by UN members under the United Nations Framework Convention on Climate Change [UNFCCC]), which supports climate change mitigation and adaptation activities. About $5.2 billion was pledged under the eighth GEF replenishment in April, 2022 including carry over from GEF-7.[18] Most of these funds are for country-level environmental projects, with past allocations to address biodiversity (32 per cent), climate change (20 per cent), land degradation (12 per cent), and treatment of chemicals and waste (15 per cent). The GEF set aside for global and regional climate change in 2018–21 totalled only $20 million, or 0.5 per cent of total funding (GEF, 2018). No funding through these facilities is provided using budget support mechanisms. While important initiatives, their funding is dramatically below estimated funding requirements for global climate change mitigation and adaption.

---

[18] Global Environmental Facility (2022).

Reform programmes that face entrenched incentive structures and resistance to the required behavioural changes will need greater community engagement, consultation, and local knowledge. Removing subsidies and reducing dependence on fossil fuel technologies is a massive undertaking, particularly in low-income countries, but also middle income (such as in Argentina which heavily subsidizes fossil fuels). In 2017, governments spent an estimated $5.2 trillion (6.5 per cent of global GDP) on fossil fuel subsidies (Coady et al. 2019). Estimates suggest that efficient fuel pricing would have lowered global carbon emissions by 28 per cent and deaths from pollution by 46 per cent while boosting government revenues by nearly 4 per cent (Coady et al. 2019). Benefits like these point to a market solution for cutting greenhouse gas emissions if externalities are priced in. Sustained budget support can support the necessary analysis and policy dialogue that the deep political, social, and distributive consequences of such a policy change will require along the transition path.

Distinct but not unrelated are efforts to support regional integration—to facilitate trade, develop regional power pooling and transport networks, or collaboration to combat desertification, etc. in regions such as Africa and Latin America. Integration in the subcontinent has been a vision of regional leaders for decades in recognition of the tremendous efficiency gains that could accrue by virtue of scale economies and infrastructure networks. Several subregional initiatives have been launched but with mixed or little success. Recently, efforts have gained momentum, including the African Continental Free Trade Area, founded in 2018, which holds renewed long-term promise to help integrate trade across its fifty-four African Union signatories. But it will take a great deal of further coordination, institution building and policy reform to bring this vision to reality.

Budget support has a role to play in regional integration to advance dialogue and support institution building. The World Bank first recognized the importance of dedicated funding for regional integration under the 13th Replenishment of IDA (2003–5). Regional integration projects were developed to support cross-border infrastructure and shared natural resources. Funding commitments totalled $17.5 billion over the 2010–20 decade (World Bank, 2020) and a further $7.6 billion has been set aside for 2021–23. The Regional Integration Programme represents as much as one-fifth of all World Bank lending in Africa, principally for regional infrastructure. One innovative regional budget support programme was approved and disbursed in 2020 to support market integration to six country members of the West African Power Pool (WAPP). The programme has yet to be evaluated but promises valuable lessons for support of power market integration to improve access, boost energy quality, and reduce costs to the fourteen members of WAPP. Budget support is also being used in conjunction with digitalization and trade elsewhere in Sub-Saharan Africa and in North Africa (e.g. Egypt and Morocco).

In summary, budget support can play a major role in supporting protection of the global commons for several reasons. As a tool for fostering policy dialogue conducive to collaborative problem-solving, budget support can serve to motivate needed reforms for sustainable problem-solving in tandem with investment projects. Public goods all have characteristics that require clear rules, management structures, monitoring, and governance. No blueprint for country approaches will fit all countries; the contextually driven and nationally owned approaches need to be features of budget support deployed for this purpose. Budget support can also help to finance technology sharing, nationally or regionally, that is needed to advance the NDCs to address climate change. Shared technologies are required to protect the global commons, many of which, such as shifting to renewable energy, are costly. Investment project financing is well suited to technology transfer. But the work of supporting new legislation requirements, sharing international experience, fostering new regulatory institutions, incentivizing local behaviour change, monitoring mechanisms, and providing the fiscal resources to create the context in which transferred technologies can be sustained, lies in the domain of budget support. It can help incentivize national action, particularly through grant financing to low-income countries, thereby mitigating the free-rider risk in such programmes (countries which do not fulfil their commitments nevertheless benefiting from the actions of others). Finally, if budget support can address the business environment in order to catalyse private financial flows, this will augment critical resources needed for development finance.

Recommendations for Forging More Effective Budget Support

This volume has reviewed the historical evolution of budget support as an instrument of foreign assistance to help countries cope with unforeseen crises, to support national development strategies in the interest of quality growth with sustainable poverty reduction, and to support the global commons, adapting to climate change and risks posed by pandemics or other trans-boundary events that require collective action.

Since the 2005 Paris Declaration on Aid Effectiveness, over $400 billion has been committed to developing countries as budget support. While large in absolute terms, this is modest with respect to total ODA flows ($2.6 trillion) or to total long-term capital flows ($4.7 trillion). However, it has played an outsized role in development finance, surging during periods of crisis to help with critical fiscal support, and providing sustained support to countries embarking on reform programmes to support structural change and economic growth. Budget support is a valued source of development finance that has been rationed overtime to avoid crowding out more traditional project finance.

Budget support is not without its critics, including among bilateral development agencies where political and intellectual winds have at times shifted attitudes toward aid and its instruments. Arguments are made by critics that there is insufficient control over how funds are spent, abetting potential corruption, that it may result in greater aid dependency and 'moral hazard' perpetuating indebtedness and cycles of default. Conditionality is seen by other critics as oppressive to the recipients, by some borrowers as too restrictive, and by yet others as an ineffective tool for reform.

Some of these criticisms have merit: Conditionality has been onerous in some programmes, particularly prior to the Paris Declaration. Moral hazard cannot be entirely dismissed, and there have been clear and well documented cases where corrupt regimes or counterparts have abused public confidence and stolen funds. But in contrast to these criticisms, independent evaluation of budget support across the MDBs and EU concludes that budget support has been a valuable tool for development. Using tools similar to those employed for evaluation of projects, budget support has exhibited similar or even higher rates of success than project finance (around 75 per cent success as reported in Chapter 4). Research examining cross-country differences further supports the relationship between foreign aid (including budget support) and growth performance. Many budget support operations have successfully advanced the objectives of national development programmes, supporting improvements in the business environment, improving the allocation of public expenditures, and strengthening public service delivery.

Since the MDBs and EU committed to new guidance and design for budget support in the early 2000s there have been new shocks to the global economy, new trends in financing, and growing recognition of threats to prosperity that will require collective action from all countries regardless of income level, and from both the public and private sectors. The shifting landscape of global finance and concomitant risks requires rethinking the role of budget support and its contribution to sustainable development in foreign assistance. We argue in this volume that evidence points to the need to not only the continued use of this instrument, but also consider its greater potential to address global economic challenges and support strategies to address global warming and crisis preparedness.

There are several recommendations that follow from the analysis here. They can be grouped into areas corresponding to the main uses of budget support: 1) as an instrument to help countries cope with the costs of unanticipated crises; 2) as support aligned with medium-term reform programmes to generate sustainable and high-quality growth; and 3) proactive support to mitigate threats to the global commons.

There are also cross-cutting recommendations, the central one of which is that rich countries should extend more foreign assistance for the purposes outlined above, and provide more of it in the form of budget support and, for low-income countries with relatively well-functioning institutions, in the form of grants and highly concessional credits. In the same vein, multilateral development banks must be adequately capitalized to address even a fraction of the enormous financing requirements of today's global challenges. There is no doubt that the need for assistance to address economic, health and environmental crises is growing. Rapid globalization has occurred alongside new risks and more virulent shocks which existing institutions lack capacity to adequately and comprehensively deal with. Budget support, underpinned by robust development dialogue and robust analysis, is the most efficient and effective mechanism to transfer resources required for responding to shocks, fostering economic development, and responding to the predominant threats of climate change and pandemics. Transparency and educating the public need to accompany the call for greater resources and sacrifice that is needed now to protect the welfare of future generations. It has been half a century since the UN general assembly called for rich countries to commit 0.7 per cent of gross national income in ODA, but fewer than half a dozen countries have met or exceeded that target since. In many countries, the public is ill-informed and sometimes deliberately misled about foreign aid and its contribution to national values and goals to which their citizens aspire.[19]

---

[19] It is often reported that US opinion polls consistently show that most Americans believe foreign aid is on average around 25 per cent of the federal budget, when in fact it has long been under 1 per cent. This includes military aid, although support to Ukraine in 2022 will likely nudge this higher. Comparative ODA figures published by the OECD in 2021 show US ODA/GNI was 0.17 per cent, while five DAC countries exceeded the UN target (Germany, Luxembourg, Norway, Sweden, and the UK) (OECD April 2021).

Budget support needs to be tailored to country circumstances and capacities, and based on robust, credible and broadly accepted information. This requires a deep understanding of the country's traditions, constraints and political-economy. To avoid use of cookie cutter approaches to reform dressed up as 'best practice', an active and frank policy dialogue with authorities based on solid analytic foundations is indispensable. So is the need to refrain from budget support when the conditions are not right. Rampant corruption, weak reform commitment, or entrenched elite capture undermines the value and acceptability of budget support as a commitment device.

Collaboration across agencies must seek to avoid duplication, enhance responsiveness to partner governments, and make use of existing knowledge and data. These are obvious but often overlooked. The United Nations family of agencies is a case in point where drawing on data, analytic, and coordination capacity should serve to depoliticize and reduce coordination costs. Examples include the UN International Labour Organization on labour markets, the Framework on Climate Change and Intergovernmental Panel on Climate Change on addressing global warming, or on health service delivery standards with the World Health Organization. Joint diagnostics with partner countries gain from drawing on the respective strengths of UN agencies and the MDBs.

Budget support has demonstrated success in satisfactory implementation and achieving set objectives across the full typology of developing countries, including in fragile and conflict affected countries (Chapter 4). But country needs and capacity to effectively use budget support vary, with fragile, conflict affected, and vulnerable states (FCV) in need of both tighter expenditure monitoring and strengthening public financial management (PFM) practices. Several non-FCV countries are also constrained in PFM quality and capacity, requiring care to incorporate targeted reforms and attention to credible ownership of reform. Strengthening domestic resource mobilization is another area where FCV and many low-income countries require programmatic support to gradually raise resource mobilization. Concerted attention, drawing on the metrics and monitoring of agencies working on these areas (Public Expenditure and Financial Accountability, Public Investment Management Assessment frameworks, Stolen Asset Recovery Initiative–UN StAR, etc.) should be built into budget support programmes.

Addressing Unforeseen Crises

The historical record shows the surge in demand for budget support that has accompanied global economic crises, driven by the critical fiscal need when economies falter: to support social safety nets, pay public salaries, and sustain key imports. Indeed a global shock first gave impetus to establishing the first MDB budget support instrument, when structural adjustment loans were introduced following the 1979 global oil shock. More recent history shows how development agencies have responded, increasing quick disbursing support following the Great Recession of 2008, the COVID-19 pandemic and Russia's war on Ukraine, two crises to which the MDBs and IMF quickly responded. Such crises will no doubt persist, but the capacity of MDBs to respond to multiple crises is being called into question, most immediately with the Russian invasion of Ukraine which set in motion inflationary pressures on global prices of grains and oils, fossil fuels, and fertilizers, seriously threatening the fiscal position of food and fuel importers. This is fully within the capacity of the Bretton Woods institutions to support emergency fiscal needs, including gap financing for social safety nets.

The global pandemic and Russia-Ukrainian war crises have seriously exacerbated a precarious debt sustainability problem in many developing countries, threatening default in the absence of rapid relief. Measures have been put in place for a debt service moratorium to help reduce the risk of default. But this also underscores the need for greater grant financing through budget support, or highly concessional funds that will not worsen the debt repayment obligations. Greater grant and concessional financing for highly indebted LICs is needed.

This raises the fundamental question about how to build greater international financial institution (IFI) financial capacity in order to bridge large-scale fiscal needs and help poor countries foster resilience to global shocks. Greater capitalization of the MDBs, which could target their need for risk insurance against losses, is one avenue. Capitalization efforts have occurred over the past decade, but in fits and starts, with little clarity on rules or metrics going forward. The IMF Resilience and Sustainability Trust approved in 2022 is a valuable initiative focused on resilience to external shocks and long-term financing of up to twenty years for structural reform.[20] It has yet to raise sufficient capital commitments, but efforts are underway and may benefit from channelling higher income country shares of the 2021 IMF allocation of 650 billion Special Drawing Rights (SDRs). With the IFIs playing an increasingly important role providing insurance against catastrophic loss, there should be an actuarial basis for sustained capitalization and rapid adjustment of financial capacity to address global threats.

---

[20] The Trust has yet to raise sufficient capital commitments, but efforts are underway and may benefit from channelling higher income country shares of the 2021 IMF allocation of 650 billion SDRs. See: https://www.imf.org/en/Topics/Resilience-and-Sustainability-Trust.

A new international effort to pool dedicated funds for crisis financing to go beyond current MDB capacity is needed. One laudable instrument the MDBs use is Catastrophe Deferred Drawdown facilities (CAT DDOs) which provide country-based insurance explicitly designed as rainy-day budget support for quick disbursement when crises arise. There was a modest increase in their development and use after 2017. But they remain very limited and absorb MDB headroom, pulling resources from other contemporaneous uses while imposing costs on developing countries during good times, both of which discourage their adoption.[21] A more efficient and equitable option would be to pool guaranteed insurance funds against regional or global shocks, managed through the MDBs, and possibly including managed stockpiles of vital buffer stocks (vital intermediate goods), with explicit triggers for rapid disbursement and replenishment. Explicit design rules that weigh country risk, current fiscal capacity, alternative financial access, and credible assessment of the commitment and capacity for reform will be required.

In times of crisis, budget support should prioritize speed of support over pressing conditions tied to new reform. Budget support provides rapid countercyclical financing at times when other financing sources are procyclical and less accessible, for example from commercial banks, oversees remittances, or even trade credits. Countercyclical support can be coordinated with the IMF, which provides short-term balance-of-payments support in times of crisis, whereas countercyclical support by the MDBs is more commonly focused on longer term structural measures to support critical social safety nets, key recurrent expenditure needs, and sustaining fiscal requirements to address the crisis, such as emergency medical spending in the event of a pandemic.

As is often said, crises do present opportunities. Financial crises may motivate or possibly force governments to change policies, for example toward capital controls and short-term capital exposure in businesses and the public sector. Pandemics can train new attention on national health policies, public immunization, and capacity to contain societal spread. Oil price shocks may provide the necessary impetus to move toward renewable energy production and incentives to reduce fossil fuel dependence. But pressing new conditions to advance new reforms, particularly measures unrelated to the emergency at hand, should not impede or delay provision of critical resources. Reform

---

[21] The World Bank retrospective on budget support (World Bank, 2022) discusses the role of Cat-DDOs and reports a large increase in commitments in 2018, and subsequent disbursements in 2020, the first year of COVID-19. World Bank management assesses the sharp drop in 2021 DDO commitments and disbursements as likely reflecting 'both countries' preference towards fast-disbursing DPF support and management's focus on providing financial support to clients in the wake of the pandemic'.

measures should be designed around emergency response measures and ongoing efforts to ensure strong public financial management practices.

Sustained Programmes to Support Policy and Institutional Reform

Sustained or programmatic budget support underpinned by policy dialogue and solid analytics is a core instrument of the MDBs in support of countries committed to implementing programmes of medium- and long-term reform toward inclusive and sustainable growth. Many examples of the types of reform programmes have been cited earlier, including strengthening public financial management to reduce potential corruption and improve fiscal performance, building capable and independent utility regulators to protect the public interest and ensure sustainability of supply, or addressing state enterprise reforms to encourage market competition enhancing a level playing field for private investors and businesses. Each of these areas requires a long-term time frame to put in place as incentives, practice and behaviours take root to make them secure and sustainable. Budget support is the principal instrument to addressing programmes of systemic reform, built on national development strategies.

Success in programmatic budget support depends largely on the alignment of views between aid agencies and recipient governments. As discussed in Chapter 4, the classic principal-agent model as applied to models of foreign aid has served to highlight the inherent tensions of conditionality. In protracted reform programmes, the alignment between interests of influential public and private actors (agents) and the objectives of foreign assistance agencies (principals) is key to staying the course. Policies and institutions present the formal rules and instruments for reform, but incentives and behaviours, often obscure and informal, determine how close to the prescribed path economic and social norms are hewn. Public and private actors themselves are never monolithic, and some actors will typically profit by the failure of others, necessitating understanding of the political economy driving reform, and agility to shift course or even stop support when interests get out of alignment. To shift from a tradition of 'conflictive conditionality' to the vision of 'credible concurrence' requires flexibility in implementing a thoroughly context specific programme with a clear line of sight towards longer term development results.

Programmatic budget support with calibrated 'off ramps' need to be built around adherence to coherent and transparent medium-term reforms, with transparent exit strategies. The MDB practice of using 'prior actions' and subsequent 'triggers' keeps this in view by requiring progress and reform momentum in advance of disbursement, while providing negotiated next steps to keep the programme on track. These next steps retain some flexibility as circumstances evolve but provide the central scaffolding and coherence for subsequent action. This practice has similarities to the structure of results-based financing (RBF, see Box 3.1) but built around results defined by measures for policy and institutional implementation (prior actions), and which evolve over time ('triggers' in MDB parlance), recognizing their greater complexity and measurement challenges. Budget support provided under European Union programmes uses a different approach of committing in the medium term to funding a programme of reform, but consigning them to two accounts: one of them is essentially guaranteed throughout the programme, while the other portion is subject to assessed progress with a given reform programme. Deviation from commitments to reform terminates the EU disbursements on the latter share.

It is important that partial or comprehensive financial off-ramps be retained, including transparent procedures for assessing progress (for example, based on independent and timely performance indices), and built around a regular dialogue with counterparts, including with civil society. Coups, conflicts, and backsliding (recently in Mali, Ethiopia, Sri Lanka, Tunisia, Guinea, Myanmar, and elsewhere) are cause for programme reassessment and, ultimately, programme termination. Measures required to reinstate programmes should also be transparent.

Programmes to support subnational reform should also be pursued vigorously in federated countries where subnational authorities have legally established responsibility over a range of public services. In unitary government systems where the central government retains responsibility effectively over all public policy and services, budget support must operate at the central government level. Whereas in federated systems the division of responsibility between state and national government provides opportunities to direct programmes to states or provinces where budget support can be based on mutual national and subnational interests aimed at strengthening state economic performance and governance reform in areas where the federal government lacks authority. In India for example, state government may need support for civil service reform, education and primary health policies, state-level infrastructure investment practice, land cadastre and property taxes, and a broad range of governance practices vested with state authorities. Budget support must conform to national budget practice, and to maintain incentives for reform it must provide fiscal resources that are additional to central government transfers under national laws. This comes with a cautionary note however, since a balance is needed between directing national funds to incentivize local reform with the need to maintain equity and fairness across states.[22] Subnational reform programmes should also be informed by a deep understanding of decentralization (deconcentration, delegation, and devolution) and lessons from international experience, which has garnered extensive interest both from donors, agencies and many governments.[23]

Building on experience in the early 2000s and early 2010s, multi-donor budget support operations help to pool donor resources for greater efficiency, but also require coherence and focus in leadership of the development dialogue. Past experience with multi-donor programmatic support has led to cases with fragmented reform efforts, multiple agendas that catered to donor preferences, and a lack of coherence in communicating with government authorities. In some cases, this led to a breakdown in multi-donor structures. The lesson from past experience is the importance of clear leadership with authority over the development dialogue and responsibility for avoiding festooning programmes with special donor interests. The MDBs are often best equipped to provide this guidance role due to deep knowledge base and access to expertise, but in some cases, donors with a long history and government trust may be well positioned to provide a strong leadership role.

Supporting the Global Commons

The world is still reeling in the aftermath of the COVID-19 pandemic and Russian invasion of Ukraine, but addressing climate change and the projected impact it will have on human welfare is the greatest existential question facing this generation and future generations on earth. 2021 was another banner year for global warming, setting new annual records for greenhouse gas concentrations, sea level rise, ocean heat, and ocean acidification.[24] Global forecasts by the Intergovernmental Panel on Climate Change, and negotiations around Nationally Determined Contributions to limiting greenhouse gas emissions under the Paris Agreement, underscore the gravity of the

---

[22] Experience with subnational budget support in India during the 1990s involved channelling large national development resources under World Bank and Asian Development Bank loans (obligations of the central government) to select states, some of which were considered better off than other states (Andhra Pradesh, Karnataka, Bengal, etc.). Eventually. this led to national opposition on equity grounds. Later efforts shifted budget support to other states with less access to financing, but also, critics argued, less capacity to deliver reform.

[23] See Bahl and Bird (2018) for an excellent online source on theory and experience with fiscal decentralization in developing countries.

[24] UN Framework Convention on Climate Change press release of 18 May 2022.

situation, the costs of inaction, and the need for collective resolve. There is deep uncertainty surrounding the specific trajectory of climate change impacts linked and failure to act, but pursing business as usual is expected to be catastrophic by most forecasts.

The resource requirements to tackle climate change and support global public goods (GPGs) far exceed current international resource commitments, and need distinct allocation principles. Some funds exist through multi-donor programmes committed to environmental needs (e.g. the Global Environmental Fund, or the GAVI alliance, a dedicated vertical health fund), but they fall far short of projected needs. The MDB system of country-based programming is well suited for country-based investments, for example to support progress with Nationally Determined Contributions under the Paris Agreement. But use of MDB country allocations to tackle protecting the global commons is not practical. First, funding for GPGs should not compete against country-based allocations for development finance covering education, healthcare, core infrastructure, and other needs. Second, allocation needs to be based on the magnitude of the problem and a feasible action programme.

Distinct and separate funding for GPGs should be pooled and allocated in ways that tackle key risks and maximize the public good, and without removing financing for country-specific development needs. These funds could operate in parallel with the MDB's development financing, drawing on their considerable analytic and technical assistance capabilities, and require a broad and representative governance.

The G20 Eminent Persons Group convened to examine Global Financial Governance in 2017/18 proposed dedicated trust funds to tackle GPGs through 'global platforms' that bring major country and institutional players together in each field. They proposed integrating these funds into the core country-based operations of MDBs, but coordinated by the designated UN guardian agency and the World Bank (given their broadest reach and greatest analytic capacity among the MDBs), and for regional public goods, entrust similar funds to operation through the regional development banks (RDBs). But integrating these funds with the MDBs would permit leveraging off their strategies and operations to avoid parallel structures and promote greater efficiency. Scale economies in operations, investing in development data and research, and building synergies with business alliance, NGOs and philanthropies, were arguments for vesting responsibility in the World Bank and respective UN agencies. The hope is that with these platforms in place, along with coordinating work with the private sector and NGO agencies, this would serve to mobilize financing for the vastly larger financing needs for GPGs in the future.

Where does budget support fit into this deeply uncertain future? Budget support provides an instrument for intergovernmental dialogue and inter-institutional dialogue governing the objectives and conditions around resource transfers to support GPGs. The work will be complex, costly, and controversial, requiring mechanisms for consensus-building and ownership of the necessary reform measures required to build the institutional framework and regulations needed for operation of carbon markets, monitoring performance, and implementing transfers and sanctions, should they be necessary.

Greater implementation of regional programmes dedicated to market integration in sub-Saharan Africa, the Middle East, and other regions where fragmentation is highly pronounced is needed to address coordination failure across countries and to reduce risk. Efforts should be prioritized if there is political demand and action on the part of countries with contiguous markets, shared watersheds, and networks. Regional funds are scarce and are the exception to country-based programming, due in part to political complexity and hence challenges with implementation. Funds need to be separated and dedicated to regional integration for the same reason as environmental funds—the prevailing political preference bends toward short-term domestic investment. Support for the African Continental Free Trade Area, developing the West African Power Pool markets, integrating regional trucking and transport routes to facilitate movement and access to ports, etc. are all tremendously important for African growth potential. Budget support has not been a major tool to date for facilitating regional projects, but budget support could play a facilitating role where policy dialogue, regulatory practice, and institutional coordination are major constraints to integration.

The IFIs need to sustain their internal organizational incentives to promote this work and ensure that staff are recognized for work to develop effective and efficient programmes. There are risks from siloed behaviours and 'sectoral chauvinism' that can serve to damage efforts to secure collaborative solutions, particularly those bridging private sector and public sector interests in multilateral development banks.[25] Strong collaboration between the public and private groups is needed, which historically has been challenging across private and public facing departments of the MDBs. Mobilizing the

---

[25] The 2016 Climate Change Action Plan notes that incentives for World Bank Group collaboration need greater alignment internally and with external funds and cross-sector operations, including shared budget across sector practices (World Bank 2016).

private sector to invest more in market integration, or mitigation and adaptation to climate change, has met with modest success at best. There must be bankable, viable investment opportunities to attract private capital. The dialogue and policy reforms that form the core of budget support could prove to be the tool which opens the door to greater catalytic success in mobilizing private capital and technology for environmental interventions, digitization, and regional integration investments.

Conclusion

In conclusion, this volume has argued that the key to aid effectiveness is the quality of dialogue and joint problem-solving between committed partners in development. Policies and institutions matter, and budget support is the main development instrument for addressing overarching policy and institutional reform. Evidence supports the conclusion that budget support is impactful, helping to shape reforms and improve public services and economic performance, although not in all countries and circumstances. Continued learning about context specific drivers of policy change and how budget support can contribute to welfare-enhancing reform remains a priority. Financial transfers help secure a voice at the policy dialogue table and play a critical role, particularly during global crises.

The chapter addresses the concerns of critics, and addresses the major design issues that pose challenges to effective use of budget support. This includes a shift from conflictive conditionality to credible concurrence to support and incentivize effective reform, concluding that the quality of dialogue, contextualization, analytic underpinnings, and agility to learn and pivot when necessary are important for success. The chapter also explores the typology of countries with regard to choice of aid instrument, recognizing that budget support is not appropriate in conditions with very weak instructions alongside low political commitment to reform. Discussion of design challenges also turns to the importance of furthering efforts to mobilize private capital for development purposes, a challenge that has met with great expectations over the last decade. Using scarce concessional financing to address market failures and thus 'de-risk' private investments enough to induce private investment flows holds promise but has met with limited success. The chapter argues for use of budget support to address underlying risks and areas of market failure in developing countries in order to improve the business climate (rule of law, competition, regulatory environment) as an important element of de-risking. This needs to be on a systemic basis, rather than on an individual transaction basis, in order to be sustained and impactful.

Finally, the chapter advances priorities for considering expanded use of budget support in three areas: 1) to provide fast-disbursing support during crises to help finance critical fiscal needs; 2) in support of medium-term programmes to accelerate growth and bolster inclusion in low income and fragile countries; and 3) to significantly scale up support for the global commons in the face of mounting risks posed by global warming, virulent pandemics, and economic interdependencies. In each of these directions, success in spurring sustainable growth, improving public service delivery, and securing the global commons must fundamentally rely on dialogue, and on learning and sharing technology in the interest of advancing human well-being.

Data and Methods[1]

Data for estimating budget support contributions across partners was triangulated from multiple sources. For MDBs and the EU, data from their respective evaluation departments were accessed. When unavailable, these were supplemented with data from agency annual reports. For agencies not reporting 2021 or 2022 commitments, these were projected based on historical averages compounded with their five-year historical rate of growth. For bilateral partners data from the OECD DAC credit reporting system were used. Figures from the World Bank were drawn from the internal business intelligence system, which is consistent with lending estimates produced by its evaluation department. The complete budget support dataset constructed is available as Table A.1 and is reported in terms of current prices.

There were considerable inconsistencies across data sources for MDBs. Data from MDB evaluation departments were considered most credible as publication goes through a multistage vetting process. The consistency and quality of data presented in annual reports is variable, data were at times partial and internally inconsistent. Annual reports of the Caribbean Development Bank were presented cumulatively since 1970 for some years, making it difficult to use. Data from the OECD DAC credit reporting system for MDBs was considered generally inadequate, with large differences to annual reports and evaluation department reports issued by the MDBs. MDB budget support loans have largely been excluded from the OECD DAC ODA database as they were not considered to meet the requirement of a grant element of no less than 25 per cent. Budget support would fall under the OECD DAC category of official development finance (ODF), or other official flows (OOF) but data for these categories are reported inconsistently and only partially.

The OECD DAC credit reporting system was used to estimate budget support commitments from bilateral development partners. These data were more reliable, as bilateral support was generally in terms of grants and therefore reported on. However, some definitional issues remain. Importantly, it is unclear whether commitments under the OECD/DAC purpose code 'general budget support' or 'sector budget support' includes conditionality or an element of policy or institutional reform. The data suggests that there is no clear differentiation. The accompanying glossary considers general budget support–related aid as 'Unearmarked contributions to the government budget; support for the implementation of macroeconomic reforms (structural adjustment programs, poverty reduction strategies); general program assistance (when not allocable by sector)'. In 2006, the OECD defined direct budget support as 'Development agencies increasingly provide financial support to macro-level policies and to government budgets to assist the recipient through a program of policy and institutional reform and implementation that promote growth and achieve sustainable reductions in poverty. Direct budget support agreements are the formal DBS instruments negotiated between the development agency and recipient government. The support may include a mix of general budget support and policy and institutional actions (including economy-wide reforms such as tax reforms, privatization, decentralization and trade liberalization)' (OECD 2006).

---

[1] This appendix explains the data and methods used in Chapter 3 of this volume.

Data from OECD DAC does not seem to suggest that conditionality or policy and institutional reform are a requirement for coding. Some partners have reported debt relief for re-engagement as budget support without conditionality or accompanying policy and institutional reform actions. Other outliers include support for cash transfer payments by USAID, which would typically not be classified as budget support.

Table A.1 Overview of budget support by agency, in USD millions (current prices)

Type	Partner	2006	2007	2008	2009	2010	2011	2012	2013	2014	2015	2016	2017	2018	2019	2020	2021*	2022*
DAC Bilateral	Australia	0	2	26	27	226	197	219	162	162	107	62	43	50	35	37	59	58
DAC Bilateral	Austria	0	0	5	8	12	10	6	10	7	6	3	3	0	2	2	2	3
DAC Bilateral	Belgium	9	4	10	0	63	32	32	37	39	20	12	24	9	2	2	13	13
DAC Bilateral	Canada	41	50	25	256	258	241	195	161	109	134	79	80	93	63	61	97	102
DAC Bilateral	Czech Republic	0	0	0	0	0	0	0	0	0	0	0	0	3	1	0	1	2
DAC Bilateral	Denmark	48	56	64	66	99	104	68	75	62	36	27	28	21	0	23	26	25
DAC Bilateral	Finland	21	28	40	39	57	69	35	59	60	29	18	17	15	15	17	21	22
DAC Bilateral	France	272	300	702	260	430	563	369	299	286	260	302	1164	424	1280	817	1029	1217
DAC Bilateral	Germany	88	73	58	136	129	441	66	40	271	751	637	285	1384	739	2696	1482	1700
DAC Bilateral	Greece	3	0	0	3	4	4	4	0	0	0	0	0	0	0	0	0	0
DAC Bilateral	Hungary	0	0	0	0	0	0	0	0	0	0	0	0	0	0	0	0	0
DAC Bilateral	Iceland	0	0	0	0	0	0	0	0	0	0	0	0	12	2	9	6	7
DAC Bilateral	Ireland	21	29	36	33	87	65	63	44	12	16	0	0	0	0	0	0	0

Continued

Table A.1 *Continued*

Type	Partner	2006	2007	2008	2009	2010	2011	2012	2013	2014	2015	2016	2017	2018	2019	2020	2021*	2022*
DAC Bilateral	Italy	42	13	55	10	5	1	6	7	10	15	7	12	12	16	8	14	16
DAC Bilateral	Japan	122	443	255	1386	888	368	174	2733	819	751	1071	915	333	343	2709	1387	1469
DAC Bilateral	Korea	0	0	0	0	0	0	29	20	0	10	0	0	90	130	330	142	179
DAC Bilateral	Luxembourg	0	0	0	0	0	1	2	2	10	2	8	6	22	29	18	21	25
DAC Bilateral	Netherlands	229	358	272	209	243	177	69	24	7	6	6	6	0	0	0	3	2
DAC Bilateral	New Zealand	12	17	34	11	43	38	49	54	44	39	45	34	61	48	65	66	71
DAC Bilateral	Norway	90	141	204	175	125	93	92	54	51	38	13	12	9	12	12	29	19
DAC Bilateral	Poland	0	0	0	0	0	0	0	0	0	0	0	0	0	0	0	0	0
DAC Bilateral	Portugal	3	2	7	4	5	6	4	3	2	1	1	1	1	1	1	1	1
DAC Bilateral	Slovak Republic	0	0	0	0	0	0	0	0	0	0	0	0	0	0	0	0	0
DAC Bilateral	Slovenia	0	0	0	0	0	0	0	0	0	0	0	0	0	0	0	0	0
DAC Bilateral	Spain	11	29	25	40	86	75	11	33	14	7	6	5	2	2	1	4	4
DAC Bilateral	Sweden	117	143	154	141	138	154	127	113	55	76	0	25	0	0	15	10	13

		35	33	33	33	45	40	35	46	55	32	31	25	18	23	35	34	35
DAC Bilateral	Switzerland	35	33	33	33	45	40	35	46	55	32	31	25	18	23	35	34	35
DAC Bilateral	United Kingdom	691	690	746	541	974	887	687	924	771	208	189	84	50	39	22	99	76
DAC Bilateral	United States	377	275	506	1307	489	496	518	949	192	402	24	582	896	836	1066	879	1100
Non-DAC Bilateral	Azerbaijan	0	0	0	0	0	0	0	0	0	0	0	0	0	0	0	0	0
Non-DAC Bilateral	Bulgaria	0	0	0	0	0	0	0	0	0	0	0	0	0	0	0	0	0
Non-DAC Bilateral	Croatia	0	0	0	0	0	0	0	0	0	0	0	0	0	0	0	0	0
Non-DAC Bilateral	Cyprus	0	0	0	0	0	0	0	0	0	0	0	0	0	0	0	0	0
Non-DAC Bilateral	Estonia	0	0	0	0	0	0	0	0	0	0	0	0	0	0	0	0	0
Non-DAC Bilateral	Israel	0	0	0	0	0	0	0	0	0	0	0	0	0	0	0	0	0
Non-DAC Bilateral	Kazakhstan	0	0	0	0	0	0	0	0	1	0	0	0	0	0	0	0	0

Continued

Table A.1 *Continued*

Type	Partner	2006	2007	2008	2009	2010	2011	2012	2013	2014	2015	2016	2017	2018	2019	2020	2021*	2022*
Non-DAC Bilateral	Kuwait	0	0	0	0	0	0	0	0	0	0	0	0	0	0	0	0	0
Non-DAC Bilateral	Latvia	0	0	0	0	0	0	0	0	0	0	0	0	0	0	0	0	0
Non-DAC Bilateral	Liechtenstein	0	0	0	0	0	0	0	0	0	0	0	0	0	0	0	0	0
Non-DAC Bilateral	Lithuania	0	0	0	0	0	0	0	0	0	0	0	0	0	0	0	0	0
Non-DAC Bilateral	Malta	0	0	0	0	0	0	0	0	0	0	0	0	0	0	0	0	0
Non-DAC Bilateral	Qatar	0	0	0	0	0	0	0	0	0	0	0	0	0	250	0	49	58
Non-DAC Bilateral	Romania	0	0	0	0	0	0	0	0	4	0	0	0	0	0	0	0	0
Non-DAC Bilateral	Saudi Arabia	0	0	0	0	0	0	0	0	0	22	24	649	2538	373	127	721	856
Non-DAC Bilateral	Chinese Taipei	0	0	0	0	0	0	0	0	0	0	0	0	0	0	0	0	0

Non-DAC Bilateral	Thailand	0	0	0	0	0	0	0	0	0	0	0	0	0	0	0	0	0
Non-DAC Bilateral	Timor-Leste	0	0	0	0	0	0	0	0	0	0	0	0	0	0	0	0	0
Non-DAC Bilateral	Turkey	0	0	0	0	0	0	0	0	0	0	0	0	0	19	0	4	4
Non-DAC Bilateral	United Arab Emirates	0	0	0	0	88	200	154	4009	220	2313	2453	2267	2010	807	945	1648	1491
Regional DB	ADB	3205	2921	2631	6099	1590	791	2394	1186	2326	3810	3066	3173	2465	4748	14703	6272	7647
Regional DB	AfDB	1029	203	1109	3278	404	1510	1240	820	1407	1627	3484	1897	1780	1189	3301	2841	2684
Regional DB	EU	1651	2450	5677	3172	2430	1850	3110	3288	1907	2619	4108	1950	2309	2054	2005	3029	2766
Regional DB	IADB	1821	875	1547	2681	3648	1690	2259	4014	3208	3624	3260	3385	4553	4910	4956	5200	5609
Regional DB	CDB	54	0	145	78	117	0	12	0	85	65	60	0	134	125	70	95	103
World Bank	World Bank	7340	6280	6643	18455	22993	12041	12473	9276	10660	9845	15140	9584	7209	13824	17877	17829	16592

* For agencies not reporting 2021 or 2022 commitments, these were projected based on historical averages compounded with their five-year historical rate of growth. World Bank commitment data were available for all years.

Source: MDB evaluation reports; MDB annual reports; World Bank business intelligence; OECD DAC credit reporting system.

Additional Tables[1]

Table B.1 World Bank Policy-Based Guarantee operations, 1999–2020

Operation title	Size of guarantee (millions of dollars)	Financing mobilized (millions of dollars)	Approval date	Country typology
Competitiveness and Growth Policy-Based Guarantee, Pakistan	420.0	700.0	June 21, 2016	LMIC/HC
Macroeconomic Stability for Competitiveness and Growth Credit, Ghana	400.0	1,000.0	June 30, 2015	LMIC/LC
First Fiscal Management Development Policy-Based Guarantee, Angola	200.0	1,000.0 at appraisal but cancelled	June 30, 2015	UMIC/LC
Public Finance Policy-Based Guarantee, Albania	226.7	250.0	March 27 2015	UMIC/HC
Public Expenditure Policy-Based Guarantee, FYR Macedonia	201.5	325.0	January 8, 2013	UMIC/HC
Financial Sector Policy-Based Guarantee, Montenegro	79.2	132.0	June 28, 2012	UMIC/HC
Policy-Based Guarantee, FYR Macedonia	134.9	175.0	November 10, 2011	UMIC/HC

Continued

---

[1] Additional tables for Chapter 3.

Table B.1 *Continued*

Operation title	Size of guarantee (millions of dollars)	Financing mobilized (millions of dollars)	Approval date	Country typology
Private and Financial Sector Policy-Based Guarantee, Serbia	400.0	400.0	February 10, 2011	UMIC/HC
Policy-Based Guarantee, Columbia	220.3	1,000.0	March 8, 2001	UMIC/HC
Policy-Based Guarantee, Argentina	250.0	1,500.0	September 16, 1999	UMIC/HC

Source: OECD DAC and World Bank Business Warehouse/Intelligence.
Note: UMIC = upper-middle income country; HC = high capacity; LC = low capacity.

Policy Impact of Budget Support:
Econometric Specification

Budget support may improve the quality of government economic policy through the number of policy actions (prior actions) it supports. Labelling the number of policy actions taken in year t as A_t, a straightforward way of depicting the relationship with the quality of government policy, Q_t, is:

$$\Delta Q_t = \alpha A_t + \varepsilon_t, \tag{1}$$

With ε_t other observable and unobservable factors influencing policy change. Suppose the initial level of quality in year 0 is Q_0. Then, building up the data-generating process, we get

$$Q_1 = Q_0 + \Delta Q_1$$
$$= Q_0 + \alpha A_1 + \varepsilon_1$$
$$Q_2 = Q_1 + \Delta Q_2 + \varepsilon_2$$
$$= Q_0 + \alpha A_1 + \alpha A_2 + \varepsilon_1 + \varepsilon_2,$$

and so on, so that

$$Q_t = Q_0 + \alpha \sum_{i=1}^{t} A_i + \sum_{i=1}^{t} \varepsilon_i \tag{2}$$

The (marginal) policy impact of budget support is thus captured by α. An α of greater than zero would imply a positive impact of World Bank lending while an α of less than zero indicates a negative policy impact.

Furthermore, the impact of policy actions on the change in quality in a particular year might not be linear. A simple and flexible way of allowing for contemporaneous decreasing or increasing returns is to raise the number of policy actions to a power γ, which can be estimated, thus:

$$\Delta Q_t = \alpha A_t^{\gamma} \tag{3}$$

An estimated γ of 1 would indicate that policy actions continue to be effective, irrespective of their number. A γ less than one would give decreasing returns, and greater than one increasing returns. A γ of zero would mean that the number of policy actions does not really matter, but the *fact that there was at least one policy action* matters.

Building up the same data-generating process as above, the equivalent relationship stated in levels is

$$Q_t = Q_0 + \alpha \sum_{i=1}^{t} A_i^y + \sum_{i=1}^{t} \varepsilon_i \tag{4}$$

Alternatively, one could substitute A^y with A and its square, so that equation (1) becomes

$$\Delta Q_t = \alpha_1 A_t + \alpha_2 (A_t)^2 + \text{other variables} \tag{5}$$

Building up the data-generating process, this yields

$$Q_t = Q_0 + \alpha_1 \sum_{i=1}^{t} A_i + \alpha_2 \sum_{i=1}^{t} A_i^2 \tag{6}$$

Furthermore, the length of the policy engagement may matter. It could be that in the initial years of a policy engagement the impact of development policy lending is small, but that it tends to grow with time. On the other hand, it could be that the initial years of a policy engagement are the most productive (see Moll and Smets 2020 for more detail).

A simple way of depicting the differential impacts of long engagements is the following. Define I_t as an indicator of whether there is a policy action in year t, thus $I_t = 0$ if $A_t = 0$, and $I_t = 1$ if $A_t > 0$. Then define the length of the engagement as the number of years in the past in which there has been a policy action, viz. $\sum_1^t I_t$. The simplest assumption is that the length of the engagement has a linear impact on the change in the quality of policy, as represented by the coefficient β, thus:

$$\Delta Q_t = \beta \sum_{i=1}^{t} I_i \tag{7}$$

Long engagements whose productivity blossoms have $\beta > 0$, while long engagements whose impact declines have $\beta < 0$.

Then combining equations (3) and (7):

$$\Delta Q_t = \alpha A_t^y + \beta \sum_{i=1}^{t} I_i \tag{8}$$

Building up the data-generating process, we have

$$Q_t = Q_0 + \alpha \sum_{i=1}^{t} A_i^y + \beta \sum_{i=1}^{t} \sum_{j=1}^{i} I_j + \sum_{i=1}^{t} \varepsilon_i \tag{9}$$

Some observable factors that are expected to be related with the quality of government policy include: GDP per capita, aid over GDP, political rights, and a year trend. We add these variables to equation (9) and assume a vector of coefficients δ for these. As time-invariant country characteristics may also influence policy choice, we add country dummies (θ_k) to equation (9). Indexing countries by k, we get:

$$Q_{t,k} = Q_0 + \alpha \sum_{i=1}^{t} A_{i,k}^y + \beta \sum_{i=1}^{t} \sum_{j=1}^{i} I_{j,k} + X_{t,k}\delta + \theta_k + \sum_{i=1}^{t} \delta_{i,k} \tag{10}$$

Policy Impact of Budget Support: Data and Methodology

The main dependent variables for the regression analyses are the World Bank's CPIA ratings. The CPIA assessments are ratings of sixteen policy indicators, grouped into four 'clusters', updated annually by World Bank staff. Possible scores on each indicator range from one to six, including half-point increments (e.g. 3.5). Clusters A and B cover macroeconomic management and structural policies, CPIA cluster C provides policy ratings on human development and social and environmental policies, and cluster D on public sector governance and institutions. We test our model on the average of CPIA cluster A and B, on CPIA cluster C, and on CPIA cluster D.

The CPIA is arguably an appropriate policy measure because its content reflects the views of World Bank management and staff regarding what policies are most conducive to poverty reduction and the effective use of aid resources. They are correlated with conceptually related objective indicators, as well as with subjective indicators produced by other organizations. Nevertheless, when replacing CPIA ratings with other dependent variables, similar results were obtained. See Smets and Knack (2018) and Moll and Smets (2020) for more detail.

The key variable of interest is the number of World Bank policy actions a development policy financing operation supports. We count only those policy actions that are conceptually related to the corresponding CPIA cluster (e.g., only counting public sector governance policy actions when CPIA D is the dependent variable).

Data generally covers the period 2005–15, even though we start counting policy actions from 1980 onwards, the starting point of adjustment lending.

For economic policy lending (CPIA clusters A and B), test statistics indicated that the model with $\gamma = 0$ was the preferred specification. For CPIA clusters C and D, the quadratic model came out with the best fit. The models were estimated with least squares, clustering standard errors at the country level.

Policy Impact of Budget Support During Economic Crises:
Regression Results

Table E.1 Policy Impact of Budget Support during Economic Crises

y: CPIA A&B	Coefficient	Robust std. err.	t	P-value	[95% conf.	interval]
Policy engagement	0.225829	0.053863	4.19	0	0.118193	0.333465
Length of engagement	−0.0094373	0.003437	−2.75	0.008	−0.01631	−0.00257
GDP per capita	0.0000895	0.00001	2.21	0.031	0.00001	0.00017
Aid over GDP	0.8872679	0.663303	1.34	0.186	−0.43824	2.212774
Political rights	0.0387216	0.054094	0.72	0.477	−0.06938	0.146819
Year	−0.0277169	0.021619	−1.28	0.205	−0.07092	0.015486
Constant	57.39893	43.08719	1.33	0.188	−28.704	143.5018
Country fixed effects	yes					
R-squared	0.2535					
Observations	135					
Countries	64					

Policy Impact of Budget Support by Country Context: Regression Results

Table F.1 Policy Impact of Economic Policy Lending - full sample

y: CPIA A&B	Coefficient	Robust std. err.	t	P-value	[95% conf.	interval]
Policy engagement	0.078178	0.018757	4.17	0	0.041104	0.115252
Length of engagement	−0.0035	0.001252	−2.79	0.006	−0.00597	−0.00102
GDP per capita	0.00001	0.00001	3.54	0.001	0.00001	0.00001
Aid over GDP	0.564642	0.197651	2.86	0.005	0.173971	0.955314
Political rights	−0.00714	0.023799	−0.3	0.765	−0.05418	0.039899
Year	0.000371	0.006922	0.05	0.957	−0.01331	0.014054
Constant	2.491121	13.81579	0.18	0.857	−24.8168	29.79908
Country fixed effects	yes					
R-squared	0.1657					
Observations	2280					
Countries	145					

Table F.2 Policy Impact of Economic Policy Lending - low-income countries

y: CPIA A&B	Coefficient	Robust std. err.	t	P-value	[95% conf.	interval]
Policy engagement	0.0544484	0.0210366	2.59	0.012	0.012532	0.096365
Length of engagement	−0.0030904	0.0014606	−2.12	0.038	−0.006	−0.00018
GDP per capita	−0.0000425	0.0000416	−1.02	0.31	−0.00013	4.03E−05
Aid over GDP	0.5318199	0.2159071	2.46	0.016	0.101616	0.962024
Political rights	−0.0173692	0.0246889	−0.7	0.484	−0.06656	0.031825
Year	0.013542	0.0103237	1.31	0.194	−0.00703	0.034112
Constant	−23.75201	20.5979	−1.15	0.253	−64.7942	17.2902
Country fixed effects	yes					
R-squared	0.0817					
Observations	1256					
Countries	75					

Table F.3 Policy Impact of Economic Policy Lending - Fragile and Conflict-affected States

y: CPIA A&B	Coefficient	Robust std. err.	t	P-value	[95% conf.	interval]
Policy engagement	0.0225496	0.026586	0.85	0.401	−0.03107	0.076166
Length of engagement	−0.000402	0.002435	−0.17	0.87	−0.00531	0.004508
GDP per capita	0.0001881	0.00001	3.67	0.001	0.00001	0.000292
Aid over GDP	−0.2352992	0.097124	−2.42	0.02	−0.43117	−0.03943
Political rights	−0.0439428	0.019727	−2.23	0.031	−0.08373	−0.00416
Year	−0.0013946	0.012057	−0.12	0.908	−0.02571	0.022921
Constant	5.63853	24.13302	0.23	0.816	−43.0304	54.30741
Country fixed effects	yes					
R-squared	0.3507					
Observations	228					
Countries	44					

Table F.4 Policy Impact of Social Policy Lending - full sample

y: CPIA C	Coefficient	Robust std. err.	t	P-value	[95% conf.	interval]
Policy actions, cumulated	0.004125	0.004433	0.93	0.355	−0.00469	0.012941
Squared policy actions, cumulated	−0.00033	0.000272	−1.2	0.232	−0.00087	0.000214
Length of engagement	−0.00072	0.001203	−0.6	0.549	−0.00312	0.001669
GDP per capita	−0.00001	0.000023	−0.57	0.569	−0.00001	0.00001
Aid over GDP	−0.15247	0.111325	−1.37	0.175	−0.37389	0.068956
Political rights	−0.05092	0.021323	−2.39	0.019	−0.09333	−0.00851
Year	0.015752	0.007237	2.18	0.032	0.001358	0.030145
Constant	−28.0338	14.4354	−1.94	0.056	−56.7452	0.677631
Country fixed-effects	yes					
R-squared	0.1217					
Observations	830					
Countries	84					

Table F.5 Policy Impact of Social Policy Lending - low-income countries

y: CPIA C	Coefficient	Robust std. err.	t	P-value	[95% conf.	interval]
Policy actions, cumulated	0.0051195	0.00462	1.11	0.271	−0.00409	0.014324
Squared policy actions, cumulated	−0.0004038	0.000283	−1.43	0.158	−0.00097	0.00016
Length of engagement	−0.0007469	0.001221	−0.61	0.543	−0.00318	0.001686
GDP per capita	−0.0000312	0.00001	−1.1	0.276	−0.00001	0.00001
Aid over GDP	−0.1699372	0.11334	−1.5	0.138	−0.39577	0.055898
Political rights	−0.0558395	0.021454	−2.6	0.011	−0.09859	−0.01309
Year	0.018081	0.007778	2.32	0.023	0.002583	0.033579
Constant	−32.65857	15.51236	−2.11	0.039	−63.5676	−1.74952
Country fixed-effects	yes					
R-squared	0.1339					
Observations	771					
Countries	75					

Table F.6 Policy Impact of Social Policy Lending - Fragile and Conflict-affected States

y: CPIA C	Coefficient	Robust std. err.	t	P-value	[95% conf.	interval]
Policy actions, cumulated	0.0814348	0.023561	3.46	0.001	0.033919	0.12895
Squared policy actions, cumulated	−0.0196044	0.004161	−4.71	0	−0.028	−0.01121
Length of engagement	0.004158	0.003114	1.34	0.189	−0.00212	0.010438
GDP per capita	0.0001622	0.00001	4.45	0	0.00001	0.000236
Aid over GDP	−0.2369316	0.095263	−2.49	0.017	−0.42905	−0.04482
Political rights	−0.0237707	0.029394	−0.81	0.423	−0.08305	0.035509
Year	−0.0154214	0.009629	−1.6	0.117	−0.03484	0.003997
Constant	36.39402	19.47363	1.87	0.068	−2.87831	75.66634
Country fixed effects	yes					
R-squared	0.4271					
Observations	226					
Countries	44					

Table F.7 Policy Impact of Public Sector Governance Lending - full sample

y: CPIA D	Coefficient	Robust std. err.	t	P-value	[95% conf.	interval]
Policy actions, cumulated	0.0101602	0.003348	3.03	0.003	0.003502	0.016818
Squared policy actions, cumulated	−0.0005145	0.000227	−2.27	0.026	−0.00096	−0.00001
Length of engagement	−0.0032215	0.000895	−3.6	0.001	−0.005	−0.00144
GDP per capita	−0.00001	0.00001	−0.38	0.702	−0.00001	0.00001
Aid over GDP	0.1453514	0.095268	1.53	0.131	−0.0441	0.334803
Political rights	−0.0648848	0.018577	−3.49	0.001	−0.10183	−0.02794
Year	0.0137771	0.006876	2	0.048	0.00001	0.02745
Constant	−24.20911	13.73359	−1.76	0.082	−51.5199	3.101639
Country fixed effects	yes					
R-squared	0.1775					
Observations	835					
Countries	85					

Table F.8 Policy Impact of Public Sector Governance Lending - low-income countries

y: CPIA D	Coefficient	Robust std. err.	t	P-value	[95% conf.	interval]
Policy actions, cumulated	0.0110293	0.004426	2.49	0.015	0.002211	0.019847
Squared policy actions, cumulated	−0.0006759	0.000379	−1.78	0.079	−0.00143	0.00008
Length of engagement	−0.0032465	0.000904	−3.59	0.001	−0.00505	−0.00145
GDP per capita	−0.00001	0.00001	−0.37	0.712	0.00001	−0.00001
Aid over GDP	0.1484305	0.098123	1.51	0.135	−0.04708	0.343945
Political rights	−0.0658336	0.018821	−3.5	0.001	−0.10333	−0.02833
Year	0.0148483	0.007433	2	0.049	0.00001	0.029658
Constant	−26.2954	14.85087	−1.77	0.081	−55.8864	3.295608
Country fixed effects	yes					
R-squared	0.1775					
Observations	774					
Countries	75					

Table F.9 Policy Impact of Public Sector Governance Lending - Fragile and Conflict-affected States

y: CPIA D	Coefficient	Robust std. err.	t	P-value	[95% conf.	interval]
Policy actions, cumulated	0.003633	0.00724	0.5	0.618	−0.01097	0.018234
Squared policy actions, cumulated	−0.00001	0.000716	−0.05	0.961	−0.00148	0.001408
Length of engagement	0.00276	0.001712	1.61	0.114	−0.00069	0.006211
GDP per capita	0.000104	0.00001	2.31	0.026	0.00001	0.000194
Aid over GDP	−0.06225	0.104844	−0.59	0.556	−0.27369	0.14919
Political rights	−0.06938	0.020117	−3.45	0.001	−0.10994	−0.02881
Year	−0.0172	0.010233	−1.68	0.1	−0.03784	0.003435
Constant	37.07231	20.44329	1.81	0.077	−4.15551	78.30012
Country fixed effects	yes					
R-squared	0.36					
Observations	226					
Countries	44					

Policy Impact of Budget Support and the Paris Declaration Principles: Regression Results

Table G.1 Economic Policy Lending and the Paris Declaration principles - ownership

y: CPIA A&B	Coefficient	Robust std. err.	t	P-value	[95% conf.	interval]
Policy engagement	0.042178	0.022547	1.87	0.069	−0.00336	0.087713
Length of engagement	−0.0036661	0.001342	−2.73	0.009	−0.00638	−0.00096
GDP per capita	−0.0000443	3.58E−05	−1.24	0.223	−0.00012	0.000028
Aid over GDP	0.8628716	0.502708	1.72	0.094	−0.15237	1.87811
Political rights	0.0012041	0.042269	0.03	0.977	−0.08416	0.086567
Year	0.0293584	0.012354	2.38	0.022	0.004408	0.054308
Constant	−55.07929	24.63301	−2.24	0.031	−104.827	−5.33193
Country fixed effects	yes					
R-squared	0.1045					
Observations	614					
Countries	42					

Table G.2 Economic Policy Lending and the Paris Declaration principles - no ownership

y: CPIA A&B	Coefficient	Robust std. err.	t	P-value	[95% conf.	interval]
Policy engagement	0.0764461	0.024658	3.1	0.003	0.026841	0.126051
Length of engagement	−0.0004533	0.001841	−0.25	0.807	−0.00416	0.00325
GDP per capita	0.0000198	0.00001	1.09	0.283	−0.00001	0.00001
Aid over GDP	0.17839	0.284745	0.63	0.534	−0.39444	0.751223
Political rights	−0.0240662	0.025483	−0.94	0.35	−0.07533	0.027199
Year	−0.0234311	0.01127	−2.08	0.043	−0.0461	−0.00076
Constant	50.14663	22.50028	2.23	0.031	4.881905	95.41136
Country fixed effects	yes					
R-squared	0.1437					
Observations	678					
Countries	48					

Table G.3 Social Policy Lending and the Paris Declaration principles - ownership

y: CPIA C	Coefficient	Robust std. err.	t	P-value	[95% conf.	interval]
Policy actions, cumulated	0.0076087	0.003766	2.02	0.053	−0.00011	0.015322
Squared policy actions, cumulated	−0.0003735	0.000226	−1.65	0.11	−0.00084	0.00001
Length of engagement	−0.0022768	0.001186	−1.92	0.065	−0.00471	0.000152
GDP per capita	−0.0000541	0.00001	−1.06	0.299	−0.00016	0.00001
Aid over GDP	0.1968201	0.240849	0.82	0.421	−0.29654	0.690178
Political rights	−0.0117764	0.026695	−0.44	0.662	−0.06646	0.042905
Year	0.031347	0.010185	3.08	0.005	0.010485	0.052209
Constant	−59.26673	20.33714	−2.91	0.007	−100.926	−17.608
Country fixed effects	yes					
R-squared	0.2655					
Observations	305					
Countries	29					

Table G.4 Social Policy Lending and the Paris principles - no ownership

y: CPIA C	Coefficient	Robust std. err.	t	P-value	[95% conf.	interval]
Policy actions, cumulated	−0.0022978	0.008656	−0.27	0.792	−0.01979	0.015197
Squared policy actions, cumulated	−0.0010078	0.000449	−2.25	0.03	−0.00191	−0.0001
Length of engagement	0.001438	0.002794	0.51	0.61	−0.00421	0.007084
GDP per capita	0.0000111	0.00001	0.49	0.626	−0.00001	0.00001
Aid over GDP	−0.2074947	0.167259	−1.24	0.222	−0.54554	0.130548
Political rights	−0.0487152	0.021946	−2.22	0.032	−0.09307	−0.00436
Year	0.0046007	0.008294	0.55	0.582	−0.01216	0.021364
Constant	−5.695822	16.6007	−0.34	0.733	−39.2471	27.85545
Country fixed effects	yes					
R-squared	0.1227					
Observations	414					
Countries	41					

Table G.5 Public Sector Governance Lending and the Paris Declaration principles - ownership

y: CPIA D	Coefficient	Robust std. err.	t	P-value	[95% conf.	interval]
Policy actions, cumulated	0.0081565	0.004266	1.91	0.066	−0.00057	0.016882
Squared policy actions, cumulated	−0.0004133	0.000339	−1.22	0.232	−0.00111	0.00028
Length of engagement	−0.0041625	0.000814	−5.12	0	−0.00583	−0.0025
GDP per capita	−0.000052	3.62E−05	−1.44	0.162	−0.00013	0.00001
Aid over GDP	0.078179	0.282975	0.28	0.784	−0.50057	0.656928
Political Rights	0.0011891	0.021625	0.05	0.957	−0.04304	0.045417
Year	0.0360924	0.007118	5.07	0	0.021535	0.050649
Constant	−68.81973	14.27136	−4.82	0	−98.0079	−39.6315
Country fixed effects	yes					
R-squared	0.2767					
Observations	310					
Countries	30					

Table G.6 Public Sector Governance Lending and the Paris Declaration principles - no ownership

y: CPIA D	Coefficient	Robust std. err.	t	P-value	[95% conf.	interval]
Policy actions, cumulated	0.0166356	0.009885	1.68	0.1	−0.00334	0.036615
Squared policy actions, cumulated	−0.0011127	0.000954	−1.17	0.25	−0.00304	0.000815
Length of engagement	−0.0026045	0.002786	−0.93	0.355	−0.00824	0.003027
GDP per capita	0.0000112	0.00001	0.64	0.526	−0.00001	0.00001
Aid over GDP	0.1226474	0.16982	0.72	0.474	−0.22057	0.465867
Political rights	−0.087929	0.020552	−4.28	0	−0.12947	−0.04639
Year	−0.0011541	0.009812	−0.12	0.907	−0.02099	0.018677
Constant	5.706914	19.57692	0.29	0.772	−33.8595	45.27335
Country fixed effects	yes					
R-squared	0.2775					
Observations	414					
Countries	41					

Bibliography

Acemoglu, Daron and James A. Robinson (2019) *The Narrow Corridor: States. Society, and the Fate of Liberty*. Penguin Random House.

Acharya, Arnab, Ana Teresa Fuzzo de Lima, and Mick Moore (2006) 'Proliferation and Fragmentation: Transactions Costs and the Value of Aid', *Journal of Development Studies* 42(1): 1–21. DOI: 10.1080/00220380500356225

AfDB, ADB, EBRD, EIB, IADB, IMF; WBG (2015) 'From billions to trillions: transforming development finance'. World Bank, Washington, DC. http://pubdocs.worldbank.org/en/622841485963735448/DC2015-0002-E-FinancingforDevelopment.pdf

Ahluwalia, Montek, Lawrence Summers, and Andrés Velasco et al. (2016) *Multilateral Development Banking for This Century's Development Challenges—Five Recommendations to Shareholders of the Old and New Multilateral Development Banks, High Level Panel on the Future of Multilateral Development Banking*. The Center for Global Development, Washington, DC.

Aldashev, Gani and Vincenzo Verardi. (2012) 'Is Aid Volatility Harmful?' *Mimeo*. https://www.tcd.ie/Economics/assets/pdf/AID_VOLATILITY_Draft_Jan8_2012_FULL.pdf

Alesina, Alberto, Silvia Ardagna, and Francesco Trebbi (2006) 'Who Adjusts and When? On the Political Economy of Reforms', NBER Working Paper No. 12049. National Bureau of Economic Research, Cambridge, MA.

Alesina, Alberto and Allan Drazen (1991) 'Why Are Stabilizations Delayed?' *The American Economic Review* 81(5): 1170–1188.

Alesina, Alberto and David Dollar (2000) 'Who Gives Foreign Aid to Whom and Why?' *Journal of Economic Growth* 5(1); 33–63.

Alesina, Alberto and Beatrice Weder (2002) 'Do Corrupt Governments Receive Less Foreign Aid?', *American Economic Review* 92(4): 1126–1137.

Andersen, Jorgen Juel, Niels Johannesen, and Bob Rijkers (2019) 'Elite Capture of Foreign Aid: Evidence from Offshore Bank Accounts', World Bank Working Paper, 13 December.

Andrews, Matt (2009) 'Isomorphism and the Limits to African Public Financial Management Reform', Harvard Kennedy School of Government Working Paper Series RWP09–012.

Andrews, Matt, Lant Pritchett, and Michael Woolcock (2013) 'Escaping Capability Traps Through Problem Driven Iterative Adaptation (PDIA)', *World Development* 51 (November): 234–244.

Andrews, Matt, Lant Pritchett, and Michael Woolcock (2017) *Building State Capacity: Evidence, Analysis, Action*. Oxford: Oxford University Press.

Andrews, Matt (2021) *Getting Real about Unknowns in Complex Policy Work*, RISE Working Paper 21/083, December, https://doi.org/10.35489/BSG-RISE-WP_2021/083

Arndt, Channing, Sam Jones and Finn Tarp (2016) 'What is the Aggregate Economic Rate of Return to Foreign Aid?' *The World Bank Economic Review* 30 (3) (October 2016): 446–474.

Asian Development Bank (ADB) (2017) 'Boosting ADB's Mobilization Capacity: The Role of Credit Enhancement Products'. Independent Evaluation Department. Manila. (Redacted)

Asian Development Bank (ADB) (2018a) 'Policy-based Lending 2008–2017: Performance, Results and Issues of Design'. Independent Evaluation, SES: REG 2018–06, CS-11, Manila.

Asian Development Bank (ADB) (2018b) 'Proposal for ADB's New Products and Modalities'. Policy Paper, June, Manila.

Asian Development Bank (ADB) (2020) '2020 Annual Evaluation Review: ADB's Project Level Self-Evaluation System'. Independent Evaluation Department (IED). Manila.

Asian Development Bank (ADB) (2021) 'Review of ADB's Comprehensive Response to COVID-19 Pandemic Policy (2020)'. June, Manila https://www.adb.org/sites/default/files/institutional-document/719971/review-adb-comprehensive-response-covid-19-pandemic-policy-2020-redacted-version.pdf

Asquith, Joanne, Shahrokh Fardoust, and Mark Sundberg (2023) *Policy Based Finance of Multilateral Development Banks: Lessons from Independent Evaluation the Asian Development Bank*. Manila, Philippines.

Attridge, Samantha and Lars Engen (2019) 'Blended finance in the poorest countries: The need for a better approach', Overseas Development Institute Report. London, April.

Azam, Jean-Paul and Jean-Jacques Laffont (2003) 'Contracting for Aid'. *Journal of Development Economics* 70 (1) (February 2003): 25–58.

Backus, Matthew and Andrew Little (2020) 'I Don't Know', *American Political Science Review* 114 (3) (August 2022): 724–743.

Badre, Bertrand (2018) *Can Finance Save the World? —Regaining Power over Money to Serve the Common Good*. Oakland, CA: Berrett-Koehler Publishers.

Bahl, Roy and Richard M. Bird (2018) *Fiscal Decentralization and Local Finance in Developing Countries: Development from Below*, Studies in Fiscal Federalism and State-local Finance series. Elgar-Online, March. https://www.elgaronline.com/view/9781786435293/9781786435293.xml

Baliamoune-Lutz, Mina L. and George Mavrotas (2009) 'Aid Effectiveness: Looking at the Aid-Social Capital-Growth Nexus', *Review of Development Economics* 13 (August): 510–525.

Banerjee, Abhijit and Ester Duflo (2011) *Poor Economics: A Radical Rethinking of the Way to Fight Global Poverty*. New York: Public Affairs.

Banuri, S. S. Dercon and V. Gauri (2015) 'The Biases of Development Professionals'. In *World Development Report 2015: Mind, Society and Behavior*. World Bank. 1790191.

Bazzi, Samuel and Michael Clemens (2013) 'Blunt Instruments: Avoiding Common Pitfalls in Identifying the Causes of Economic Growth', *American Economic Journal* 5 (2): 152–186.

Bénabou, R., and J. Tirole (2016) 'Mindful Economics: The Production, Consumption, and Value of Beliefs', *Journal of Economic Perspectives* 30 (3): 141–164.

Ben-Artzi, R. (2016) 'Origins, Politics, and Structure of Regional Development Banks', in *Regional Development Banks in Comparison*. Cambridge: Cambridge University Press. http://dx.doi.org/10.1017/cbo9781316681398.005

Benfield, Andrew and Nevila Como (2019) *Effectiveness to Impact: Study on the Application of the Effectiveness Principles*, AECOM International Development Europe SL. European Commission, Brussels.

Benn, Julia, Cécile Sangaré, and Tomáš Hos (2017) "Amounts Mobilized from the Private sector by Official Development Finance Interventions, Final Report, OECD, Paris.

Besherati, Naissan and Steve MacFeely (2019) *Defining and Quantifying South-South Cooperation*, Research Paper No. 30, March. UNCTAD, Geneva.

Besley, Tim and Torsten Persson (2011) *Pillars of Prosperity: The Political Economics of Development Clusters*. Princeton University Press.

Bhattacharya, Amar et al. (2018) 'The new global agenda and the future of the multilateral development bank system', Economics Discussion Papers. Kiel Institute for the World Economy No 2018–26. https://www.brookings.edu/wp-content/uploads/2018/02/epg_paper_on_future_of_mdb_system_jan301.pdf

Birdsall, Nancy and Scott Morris (2016) *Multilateral Development Banking for This Century's Development Challenges: Five Recommendations to Shareholders of the Old and New Multilateral Development Banks*. Center for Global Development, Washington, DC.

Bogetic, Zeljko, and Lodewijk Smets (2017). 'Association of World Bank Policy Lending with Social Development Policies and Institutions'. World Bank Policy Research Working Paper No. 8263. World Bank, Washington, DC.

Booth, David (2011) 'Aid Effectiveness; bringing country ownership (and politics) back in', Working Paper 336. Overseas Development Institute, August.

Boone, Peter (1996) 'Politics and the Effectiveness of Foreign Aid', *European Economic Review* 40 (2) (February 1996): 289–329.

Bourguignon, Francois and Mark Sundberg (2007) 'Aid Effectiveness: Opening the Black Box', *American Economic Review* 97(2) (May): 316–321.

Bricker, Darrell (2019) 'World Affairs: Citizens in 24 countries assess engagement in international affairs for a global perspective', Ipsos. https://www.ipsos.com/sites/default/files/ct/news/documents/2019-11/future-of-the-world-order-2019.pdf

Briggs, Ryan C. (2020) 'Results from Single-donor Analyses of Project Aid Success Seem to Generalize Pretty Well across Donors', *The Review of International Organizations* 15: 947–963.

Broccolini, Chiara, Giulia Lotti, Alessandro Maffioli, F. Andrea Presbitero, and Rodolfo Stucchi (2019) 'Mobilization Effects of Multilateral Development Banks'. *World Bank Economic Review*.

Browne, Stephen (2017) 'Vertical Funds: New Forms of Multilateralism?' *Global Policy* 8 (Supplement 5, August).

Bruce, Golda Lee (2019) *What is the Contingent Credit Facility?* Interamerican Development Bank. Washington, DC. https://blogs.iadb.org/caribbean-dev-trends/en/what-is-the-contingent-credit-facility/

Buchanan, James M. (1975) 'The Samaritan's Dilemma'. In Altruism, *Morality and Economic Theory*, edited by E.S. Phelps. New York: Russell Sage Foundation.

Bulman, David, Walter Kolkma and Aart Kraay (2017) 'Good Countries or Good Projects? Comparing Macro and Micro Correlates of World Bank and Asian Development Bank project performance', *The Review of International Organizations* 12 (3): 335–363.

Burnside, Craig and Dollar, David (2000) 'Aid, Policies and Growth', *American Economic Review* 90(4): 847–868.

Canavire-Bacazerra, Gustavo Javier, Eric Neumayer, andPeter Nunnenkamp (2015) 'Why Aid is Unpredictable: An Empiral Analysis of the Gap between Actual and Planned Aid Flows', *Journal of International Development* 27(4): 440–463, ISSN 09541748.

Canuto, Otaviano (2018) 'The World Bank as hummingbird: Leveraging knowledge for development finance', World Bank Blog. https://blogs.worldbank.org/eastasiapacific/world-bank-hummingbird-leveraging-knowledge-development-finance

Cardenas, Juan Camilo, and Jeffrey Carpenter (2008) 'Behavioural Development Economics: Lessons from Field Labs in the Developing World', *Journal of Development Studies* 44 (3): 311–338.

Chandy, Laurence, A. Hosono, H. Kharas, and J. Linn (2013) *Getting to Scale: How to Bring Development Solutions to Millions of People*. Washington, DC: Brookings Institute.

Chauvet, Lisa, Paul Collier, and Andreas Fuster, A. (2015) *Supervision and Project Performance: A Principal-Agent Approach*. Paris: DIAL.

Chenery, Hollys B. and Strout, Alan M. (1966) 'Foreign Assistance and Economic Development, *American Economic Review* 56: 679–733.

Chin, G. (2019) 'The Asian Infrastructure Investment Bank—New Multilateralism: Early Development, Innovation, and Future Agendas', *Global Policy* 10(4): 569–581. http://dx.doi.org/10.1111/1758-5899.12767

CICID (2007) *Doctrine d'Emploi des Aides Budgetaires Globales dans Les Etats Etrangers*. Paris: Comité Interministeriel de la Cooperation International et du Développement.

Clemens, Michael, Seven Radelet, Rikhil Bhavani and Samuel Bazzi (2012) 'Counting Chickens when they Hatch: Timing and the Effects of Aid on Growth', *The Economic Journal* 122 (561): 590–617.

Clemens, Michael, and M. Kremer (2016) 'The New Role for the World Bank', *Journal of Economic Perspectives* 30 (1): 53–76.

Clist, Paul (2016)'Payment by Results in Development Aid: All That Glitters Is Not Gold', *The World Bank Research Observer* 31 (2): 290–319.

Coady, David, Ian Perry, Nghia-Piotr Le, and Baoping Shang (2019) 'Global Fossil Fuel Subsidies Remain Large: An Update Based on Country-Level Estimates', *IMF Working Paper*, Fiscal Affairs Dept, May.

Collier, Paul (undated) 'Should Budget Support be Discontinued?', *mimeo*, International Monetary Fund Blog. https://blog-pfm.imf.org/files/op-ed.pdf

Collier, P., P. Guillaumont, S. Guillaumont, and J.W. Gunning, (1997) 'Redesigning conditionality', *World Development* 25(9), 1399–1407.

Commission on Growth and Development (2008) *The Growth Report: Strategies for Sustained Growth and Inclusive Development.*

Cornia, Giovanni, R. Jolly and F. Stewart (1987) *Adjustment with a Human Face.* UNICEF. Oxford: Clarendon Press.

Dag Hammarskjöld Foundation and UN Multi-Partner Trust Fund Office (2021) 'Financing the UN Development System: Time to Meet the Moment'. New York, NY. https://www.daghammarskjold.se/wp-content/uploads/2021/08/dhf-financial-report-time-to-meet-the-moment-2021-web-final.pdf

Deininger, K., L. Squire, and S. Basu (1998) 'Does Economic Analysis Improve the Quality of Foreign Assistance?' *World Bank Economic Review* 12(3): 385–418.

Denizer, Cevdet, Daniel Kaufmann, and Aart Kraay (2013) 'Good Countries or Good Projects? Macro and Micro Correlates of World Bank Project Performance', *Journal of Development Economics* 105: 288–302.

Department for International Development (DFID) (2004) 'Poverty Reduction Budget Support', *DFID Policy Paper.* London: DFID.

Department for International Development (DFID) (2015) 'UK AID: Tackling Global Challenges in the National Interest', November. Cm9163. London: HM Treasury and DFID.

Dercon, Stefan (2022) *Gambling on Development Why Some Countries Win and Others Lose.* London: Hurst Publishers.

DEval (2015) 'Accompanying measures to general budget support in Sub-Saharan Africa'. German Institute for Development Evaluation, Bonn.

DEval (2017) 'What we know about the effectiveness of budget support: Evaluation synthesis'. German Institute for Development Evaluation, Bonn.

Devarajan, Shanta, D. Dollar, and T. Holmgren (2001) *Aid and Reform in Africa: Lessons from Ten Case Studies.* Washington, DC: World Bank.

Dijkstra, Geske (2018) 'Budget Support, Poverty and Corruption: A Review of the Evidence', EBA Rapport 2018:04. Expert Group for Aid Studies, Sweden.

Djankov, Simeon, J.G. Montalvo and M. Reynal-Querol (2008) 'The Curse of Aid', *Journal of Economic Growth* 13(3): 169–194.

Dollar, David and Jakob Svensson (2000) 'What Explains the Success and Failure of Structural Adjustment Programmes?' *The Economic Journal* 110(466): 894–917.

Dollar, David and Aart Kraay (2002). 'Growth Is Good for the Poor', *Journal of Economic Growth* 7 (3): 195–225.

Dollar, David and Victoria Levin (2005) 'Sowing and reaping: institutional quality and project outcomes in developing countries', *Policy Research Working Paper Series* 3524. The World Bank.

Domar, Evsey D. (1947) 'Expansion and Employment', *American Economic Review* 37 (March): 34–55.

Doucouliagos, Hristos and Martin Paldam (2009) 'The Aid Effectiveness Literature: The Sad Results of 40 Years of Research', *Journal of Economic Surveys*, 10 June 2009, 23 (3): 433–461.

Dreher, A., Fuchs, A., Parks, B., Strange, A., and Tierney, M. (2022) *Banking on Beijing: The Aims and Impacts of China's Overseas Development Program*. Cambridge: Cambridge University Press. doi:10.1017/9781108564496

Duggan, Julian, Scott Morris, Justin Sandefur and George Yang (2020) 'Is the World Bank's COVOD Crisis Lending Big Enough, Fast Enough? New Evidence on Loan Disbursements', *Center for Global Development*, 12 October.

Easterly, William (1999) 'The Ghost of Financing Gap', *Journal of Development Economics* 60(2) (December): 423–438.

Easterly, William (2002) 'The Cartel of Good Intentions: The Problem of Bureaucracy in Foreign Aid', *The Journal of Policy Reform* 5 (4), 223–250.

Easterly, William (2003) 'IMF and World Bank Structural Adjustment Programs and Poverty', in Michael P. Dooley and Jeffrey A. Frankel (eds). *Managing Currency Crises in Emerging Markets*. University of Chicago Press.

Easterly, William (2005) 'What Did Structural Adjustment Adjust? The Association of Policies and Growth with Repeated IMF and World Bank Adjustment Loans', *Journal of Development Economics* 76: 1–22.

Easterly, William (2006) 'Planners vs. Searchers in Foreign Aid', *Asian Development Review* 23 (1): 1–35.

Easterly, William (ed.) (2008) *Reinventing Foreign Aid*. Cambridge, MA: MIT Press

Easterly, William (2015) *The Tyranny of Experts: Economists, Dictators and the Forgotten Rights of the Poor*. Basic Books

Easterly, William (2019) 'In Search of Reforms for Growth: New Stylized Facts on Policy and Growth Outcomes', Working Paper 26318, National Bureau of Economic Research, September 2019, DOI 10.3386/w26318

Edelman (2019) 'UN Youth Perception Survey'. https://www.edelman.com/news-awards/new-survey-reveals-strong-support-of-united-nations-from-millennials

Eichenauer, Vera and Bernhard Reinsberg (2017) 'What Determines Earmarked Funding to International Development Organizations? Evidence from the New Multi-Bi Aid Data', *The Review of International Organizations* 12(2): 171–197. http://dx.doi.org/10.1007/s11558-017-9267-2

Eifert, Benn, and Alan Gelb (2006) 'Improving the dynamics of Aid towards more predictable budget support'. In Budget Support as More Effective Aid? Recent Experiences and Emerging Lessons, edited by S. Koeberle, Z. Stavreski and J. Walliser. Washington, DC: World Bank.

Eifert, Benn and Alan Gelb (2008) 'Reforming Aid: Toward More Predictable, Performance-Based Financing for Development', *World Development* 36(10) (October): 2067–2081.

Engen, Lars and Annalisa Prizzon (2018) *A Guide to Multilateral Development Banks*. Overseas Development Institute, London. https://odi.org/en/publications/a-guide-to-multilateral-development-banks/

Erbeznik, Katherine (2011) 'Money Can't Buy You Law: The Effects of Foreign Aid on the Rule of Law in Developing Countries', *Indiana Journal of Global Legal Studies* (Summer).

European Bank for Reconstruction and Development (EBRD) (2020) 'EBRD Mobilization of Private Finance—A Special Study', EBRD Evaluation Department, London. https://www.ebrd.com/what-we-do/evaluation-latest-reports.html

European Commission (2005) *The European Consensus on Development*. Brussels: European Union.

European Commission (2017) *Joint Evaluation of Budget Support to Ghana (2005-2015)*. Brussels, Belgium: European Commission, World Bank's Independent Evaluation Group, and the Government of Ghana, Denmark, France, and Germany

European Commission (2018) *Budget Support Guidelines*, Directorate-General for International Cooperation and Development, Publications Office.

European Commission (2022) Commission disburses further €2 billion in exceptional macro-financial assistance to Ukraine. Press Release. Brussels. https://ec.europa.eu/commission/presscorner/detail/en/IP_22_6237

Evans, Alison (2010) *Aid Effectiveness Post-2010: A Think Piece on Ways Forward*. ODI, London.

Fardoust, Shahrokh and Ann Flannagan (2013) 'Quality of Knowledge and Quality Financial Assistance: A Quantitative Assessment in the Case of the World Bank', Washington, DC: Development Economics. *Mimeo*. Washington DC: World Bank.

Feldman, Jacob (2003) 'The simplicity principle in human concept learning', *Current Directions In Psychological Science*, 12(6): 227–232, Association for Psychological Science.

Fernandez, Raquel, and Dani Rodrik (1991) 'Resistance to Reform: Status Quo Bias in the Presence of Individual-Specific Uncertainty', *American Economic Review* 81(5): 1146–1155.

Fitch Ratings(2020) 'Sovereign Default History: Evidence of Supranationals' Preferred Creditor Status', March, Paris. https://www.fitchratings.com/research/sovereigns/sovereign-defaults-by-creditor-reflect-mdbs-preferred-creditor-status-16-03-2020

Financial Stability Board (2022) 'Global Monitoring Report on Non-Bank Financial Intermediation', 16 December, Basel.

Foster, Vivien and Anshul Rana (2020,) *Rethinking Power Sector Reform in the Developing World*. International Bank for Reconstruction and Development, Washington, DC.

Francisco, Manuela, Peter Moll, and Lodewijk Smets (2016) 'World Bank Development Policy Financing and the Improvement in Economic Policy'. *Mimeo* World Bank.

G20 (2015) Multilateral development banks: Action plan to optimize balance sheets, G20, http://www.g20.utoronto.ca/2015/Multilateral-Development-Banks-Action-Plan-to-Optimize-Balance-Sheets.pdf

G20 Eminent Persons Group (2018) 'Making the Global Financial System Work for All: Report of the G20 Eminent Persons Group on Global Financial Governance'. https://www.globalfinancialgovernance.org/assets/pdf/G20EPG-Full%20Report.pdf

Galiani, Sebastian, Stephen Knack, Lixin Xu, and Ben Zou (2017) 'The Effect of Aid on Growth: Evidence from a Quasi- Experiment', *Journal of Economic Growth*, 2017, 22: 1–33.

Gartner, David and Homi Kharas (2013) 'Scaling Up Impact: Vertical Funds and Innovative Governance', in Chandy et al. https://www.brookings.edu/wp-content/uploads/2014/11/getting-to-scale-chapter-4.pdf

Gehring, Kai, Katharina Michaelowa, Axel Dreher and Franziska Spörri (2017) 'Aid Fragmentation and Effectiveness: What Do We Really Know?' *World Development* 99(C): 320–334.

Gelb, Alan, and Nabil Hashmi (2014) 'The anatomy of program-for-results: An approach to results-based aid', *Center for Global Development Working Paper* 374 (2014). https://papers.ssrn.com/sol3/papers.cfm?abstract_id=2466657

General Accounting Office (2001) 'Multilateral Development Banks—Profiles of Selected Multilateral Development Banks', Report to the United States Congress, May. http://www.gao.gov/new.items/d01665.pdf

Gibson, Clark C., Krister Andersson, Elinor Ostrom, and Sujai Shivakumar (2005) *The Samaritan's Dilemma: The Political Economy of Development Aid*. Oxford: Oxford University Press.

Giordano, R. and P. Pagano (2017) 'Does the World Bank Foster Business?' *World Bank Policy Research Working Paper* No. 8047. World Bank, Washington, DC.

Glennie, Jonathan (2021) *The Future of Aid: Global Public Investment*. New York: Routledge.

Global Environmental Facility (2018) 'GEF-7 Replenishment Resource Allocation Scenarios and Global Environmental Benefits Targets', 25 April, Stockholm, Sweden.

Global Environmental Facility (2022) 'Fourth Meeting for the Eighth Replenishment of Resources of the GEF Trust Fund', 7–8April, Summary of the Co-Chairs, virtual meeting summary. https://www.thegef.org/sites/default/files/documents/2022-05/GEF_R.08_Summary_04.pdf

Grawe, Roger (2010) Poverty Reduction Support Credits: Lao PDR Country Study. *IEG Working Paper* 2010/11. World Bank. Washington, DC. https://ieg.worldbankgroup.org/sites/default/files/Data/reports/prsc_lao_cs.pdf

Green Climate Fund (2022) 'GCF: Financing Climate Action.' Incheon, South Korea. https://www.greenclimate.fund/sites/default/files/document/20221026-financing-climate-action.pdf

Green Finance and Development Center (2020) 'China's Role in Public External Debt in DSSI Countries and the Belt and Road Initiative (BRI) in 2020 '– Green Finance & Development Center (greenfdc.org)

Gu, B. (2017) 'Chinese Multilateralism in the AIIB', *Journal of International Economic Law* 20(1): 137–158, http://dx.doi.org/10.1093/jiel/jgx006

Gueorguieva, Anna and Katherine Bolt (2003) 'A Critical Review of the Literature on Structural Adjustment and the Environment', *Environment Department working papers*; No. 90. Environmental Economics series. World Bank, Washington, DC. https://openknowledge.worldbank.org/handle/10986/18396License:CCBY3.0IGO

Gulrajani, Nilimina (2016) 'Bilateral versus multilateral channels: Strategic choices for donors'. Overseas Development Institute, London. https://odi.org/en/publications/bilateral-versus-multilateral-aid-channels-strategic-choices-for-donors/

Gurtner, Bruno and John Christensen (2008) 'The Race to the Bottom: Incentives for New Investment?', Tax Justice Network, Beyond Bretton Woods: The Transnational Economy in Search of New Institutions, October.

Hallward-Driemeier, Mary and Gaurav Nayyar (2018) *Trouble in the Making?: The Future of Manufacturing-Led Development*. The World Bank Group, Washington, DC.

Hansen, Henrik and Finn Tarp (2001) 'Aid and Growth Regression', *Journal of Development Economics* 64(2):547–570.

Harrod, Roy F. (1939) 'An Essay in Economic Dynamic Theory', *Economic Journal* (March). 49 (193): 14–33

Hart, Tom, Sierd Hadley, and Bryn Welham (2015) Use of country systems in fragile states. ODI Report.

Harun (2007) 'Obstacles to Public Sector Accounting Reform in Indonesia', *Bulletin of Indonesian Economic Studies* 43 (3): 365–376.

Hashim, Ali and Moritz Piatti-Fünfkirchen (2016) *Lessons from Reforming Financial Management Information Systems: A Review of the Evidence*, Independent Evaluation Group, World Bank.

Hashim, Ali and Moritz Piatti-Fünfkirchen (2018) 'Lessons from Reforming Financial Management Information Systems: A Review of the Evidence', Policy Research Working Paper; No. 8312. World Bank, Washington, DC. https://openknowledge.worldbank.org/handle/10986/29222

Henderson, Rebecca (2020) *Reimagining Capitalism in a World on Fire*. New York, NY: Hatchett Book Group.

Herrling, Sheila and Steve Radelet (2006) *Should the MCC Provide Financing through Recipient Country's Budgets? An Issues and Options Paper*, Center for Global Development, Washington, DC, July 25.

Hicks, Norman (2010) 'Poverty Reduction Support Credits: Armenia Country Study', *IEG Working Paper* 2010/6. World Bank. Washington, DC. https://openknowledge.worldbank.org/handle/10986/27865

Hirschman, Albert O. (1965) 'Obstacles to Development: A Classification and a Quasi-vanishing Act', *Economic Development and Cultural Change* 13 (4): 385.

Hjort, Jonas, Diana Moreira, Gautam Rao, and Juan Francisco Santini (2021) 'How Research Affects Policy: Experimental Evidence from 2,150 Brazilian Municipalities.' *American Economic Review* 111 (5): 1442–80.

Hudson, John and Mosley, Paul (2008) 'Aid Volatility, Policy and Development,' *World Development* 36(10), 2082–2102.

Humphrey, Chris (2017) 'Six proposals to strengthen the finances of multilateral development banks', *ODI Working Paper*. https://www.odi.org/publications/10780-six-proposals-strengthen-finances-multilateral-development-banks

Humphrey, Chris (2020) 'All hands on deck: how to scale up multilateral financing to face the Covid-19 crisis', *ODI Briefing Paper*. https://www.odi.org/publications/16832-all-hands-deck-how-scale-up-multilateral-financing-face-coronavirus-crisis

Humphrey, Chris and Annalisa Prizzon (2014) *Guarantees for Development: A Review of Multilateral Development Bank Operations*. London: Overseas Development Institute.

IFC. 2019. *Mobilization of Private Finance 2018*. August, Washington, DC. https://www.ifc.org/wps/wcm/connect/publications_ext_content/ifc_external_publication_site/publications_listing_page/mdb-joint-report-on-mobilization-2018

IMF and World Bank (2022) 'Making Debt Work for Development and Macroeconomic Stability', prepared for the April 22,2022 Development Committee Meeting.

Independent Development Evaluation (IDEV) (2018). 'Independent Evaluation of the AfDB's Program Based Operations (2012–2017)'. The African Development Bank, Abidjan.

Independent Evaluation Department (IED) (2018) 'Policy-Based Lending 2008–2017: Performance, Results, and Issues of Design'. Asian Development Bank, CS-11, SES: REG 2018–06, Manila.

Independent Evaluation Group (IEG) (2009) 'The World Bank Group Guarantee Instruments 1990–2007'. World Bank, Washington, DC.

Independent Evaluation Group (IEG) (2010a) *Poverty Reduction Support Credits: An Evaluation of World Bank Support*. IEG Fast Track Brief. Washington, DC.

Independent Evaluation Group (IEG) (2010b) *Armenia Case Study: Poverty Reduction Support Credits*.

Independent Evaluation Group (IEG) (2011) *World Bank Progress in Harmonization and Alignment in Low-Income Countries*. World Bank, Washington, DC.

Independent Evaluation Group (IEG) (2013a) *Project Performance Assessment Report Tanzania. Poverty Reduction Support Credits 1–8*, Report No.: 78188. Washington, DC.

Independent Evaluation Group (2013b), *World Bank Group Assistance to Low-Income Fragile and Conflict-Affected States*, World Bank, Washington DC, December.

Independent Evaluation Group (IEG) (2015) *Project Performance Assessment Report Vietnam. Poverty Reduction Support Credits 6–10, Program 135 Phase 2 Support Credits, Public Investment Reform 1–2*. Washington, DC, Report No.: 96203. https://documents1.worldbank.org/curated/en/721331467986245693/pdf/96203-PPAR-REVISED-PUBLIC-VIETNAM-PPAR-FINAL.pdf

Independent Evaluation Group (IEG) (2016a) 'The Role of Political Economy Analysis in Development Policy Operations', IEG Learning Product. World Bank, Washington, DC.

Independent Evaluation Group (IEG) (2016b) 'Findings from Evaluation of Policy Based Guarantees', IEG Learning Product. World Bank, Washington, DC. https://ieg. worldbankgroup.org/sites/default/files/Data/reports/lp_policy_based_guarantees_102116. pdf.

Independent Evaluation Group (IEG)(2016c) 'Project Performance Assessment Report Ghana. Economic Governance and Poverty Credit, and Seventh and Eighth Poverty Reduction Support Credits', Report No.: 106279. Washington, DC. https://ieg.worldbankgroup. org/sites/default/files/Data/reports/ppar_ghanaecon_0716.pdf

Independent Evaluation Group (IEG)(2016d) 'Project Performance Assessment Report. Former Yugoslav Republic of Macedonia. Public Expenditure Policy Based Guarantee', Report No 106281. Washington, DC. https://documents1.worldbank.org/curated/pt/ 540671469190196702/pdf/106281-PPAR-P133791-Box396280B-PUBLIC-disclosed-7-21-16-ppar-macedoniapublic-0716.pdf

Independent Evaluation Group (IEG) (2016e) Zambia Public Sector Management Program Support Project. Project Performance Assessment Report. Report No. 106280. World Bank. Washington, DC. https://documents1.worldbank.org/curated/en/799841469432589449/ pdf/106280-ppar-P082452-PUBLIC-IEG-zambia-0716.pdf

Independent Evaluation Group (IEG) (2016f) Program for Results. An Early-Stage Assessment of the Process and Effects of a New Lending Instrument. World Bank. Washington, DC. https://ieg.worldbankgroup.org/sites/default/files/Data/Evaluation/files/program-for-results-full.pdf

Independent Evaluation Group (IEG)(2017) Romania Development Policy Loan with a Deferred Drawdown Option. Report No. 112699. World Bank. Washington DC. https:// ieg.worldbankgroup.org/sites/default/files/Data/reports/ppar-romaniadpl-08082017.pdf

Independent Evaluation Group (IEG) (2019) 'Approach Paper: The World Bank Group's Approach to Mobilization of Private Capital: An IEG Evaluation', 25 March. World Bank Group, Washington, DC. http://ieg.worldbank.org/sites/default/files/Data/reports/ ap_privatecapital.pdf

Independent Evaluation Group (IEG) (2020) 'The World Bank Group's Approach to Mobilization of Private Capital for Development: An IEG Evaluation'. World Bank Group, Washington, DC.

Independent Evaluation Group (IEG) (2021) 'World Bank Group Approaches to Mobilize Private Capital for Development: An Independent Evaluation'. World Bank, Washington, DC. https://openknowledge.worldbank.org/handle/10986/35040

Independent Expert Panel (2022) *Boosting MDBs' investing capacity: An Independent Review of Multilateral Development Banks' Capital Adequacy Frameworks.*

Inter-agency Task Force on Financing for Development (2020) 'Financing for Sustainable Development Report 2020'. United Nations, New York. https://developmentfinance.un.org/ fsdr2020

Interamerican Development Bank (2015) Design and use of policy-based loans at the IDB. Technical Note. Interamerican Development Bank. Washington, DC. https://publications. iadb.org/publications/english/document/OVE-Annual-Report-2015-Technical-Note-Design-and-Use-of-Policy-Based-Loans-at-the-IDB.pdf

Interamerican Development Bank (2020) IDB expands coverage for COVID-19 and public health risks in contingent loans. News Release. Interamerican Development Bank. Washington, DC. https://www.iadb.org/en/news/idb-expands-coverage-covid-19-and-public-health-risks-contingent-loans

International Development Association (IDA) (2021) *Financial Statements and Management's Discussion and Analysis.* https://www.worldbank.org/en/news/press-release/2021/08/09/ world-bank-group-releases-fy21-audited-financial-statements#:~:text=IDA%20FY21

%20Financial%20Statements%20and%20Management%E2%80%99s%20Discussion%20 and%20Analysis

International Energy Agency (2022) 'World Energy Investments 2022'. Paris. https://iea.blob.core.windows.net/assets/b0beda65-8a1d-46ae-87a2-f95947ec2714/ WorldEnergyInvestment2022.pdf

International Finance Corporation (IFC) (2020) *Growing Impact: New Insights into the Practice of Impact Investing*. Washington, DC, June.

International Monetary Fund (2011) 'International Capital Flows: Reliable or Fickle?' in *World Economic Outlook*, April, Washington, DC.

International Monetary Fund (IMF) (2013) Greece 2013 Article IV consultation. Country Report No. 13/154, International Monetary Fund

International Monetary Fund (IMF) (2015) *From Billions to Trillions: Transforming Development Finance Post-2015 Financing for Development: Multilateral Development Finance*. Joint Ministerial Committee of the Board of Governors of the World Bank and IMF, Washington, DC, April.

International Monetary Fund (IMF) (2021) 'Response to COVID-19' https://www.imf.org/en/ About/FAQ/imf-response-to-covid-19

International Monetary Fund and World Bank (2021) 'Joint IMF-World Bank Staff Note on Fiscal Monetary Assessment'. https://www.imf.org/-/media/Files/Publications/PP/2021/ English/PPEA2021062.ashx

International Monetary Fund and World Bank (2022) 'Making Debt Work for Development and Macroeconomic Stability', prepared for the 22 April Development Committee Meeting. Washington, DC. https://www.imf.org/-/media/Files/Publications/PP/2022/English/ PPEA2022019.ashx.

International Monetary and Finance Committee (2022) 'Statement of Secretary of the Treasury Janet L. Yellen to the Forty-Sixth Meeting of the International Monetary and Financial Committee of the International Monetary Fund', 13–14 October.

International Monetary Fund (IMF) (2022a) *COVID-19 Financial Assistance and Debt Service Relief*. Washington, DC. https://www.imf.org/en/Topics/imf-and-covid19/COVID-Lending-Tracker

International Monetary Fund (IMF) (2022b) '2022 Review of Adequacy of Poverty Reduction and Growth Trust Finances', April, Washington, DC. https://www.imf.org/-/media/Files/ Publications/PP/2022/English/PPEA2022016.ashx

International Monetary Fund (IMF) (2022c.) Proposal to Establish a Resilience and Sustainability Trust. *IMF Policy Paper*, April. Washington, DC. https://www.imf.org/en/ Publications/Policy-Papers/Issues/2022/04/15/Proposal-To-Establish-A-Resilience-and-Sustainability-Trust-516692

Irvin, Douglas (2020) *The Washington Consensus stands test of time better than populist policies*, Peterson Institute for International Economics, 4 December 2020 (www.piie.com)

James, J. and E. Gutkind (1985) 'Attitude change revisited: Cognitive dissonance theory and development policy', *World Development* 13 (10-11): 1139–1149.

Kanbur, Ravi (2015) 'What is the World Bank Good For? Global Public Goods and Global Institutions', CEPR Discussion Paper No. DP12090. https://ssrn.com/abstract=2988848

Kaul, Inge et al. (2015) 'Policy Debate: Financing the SDGs: Global vs Local Public Goods', *Revue internationale de politique de développement* 6(2). https://doi.org/10.4000/poldev. 2068

Kaul, Inge (2017) Providing global public goods: What role for the multilateral development banks?, Research Reports and Studies. Overseas Development Institute, April. https://www.odi.org/publications/10784-providing-global-public-goods-what-role-multilateral-development-banks

Kharas, Homi (2016) 'Rethinking the roles of multilaterals in the global aid architecture'. Brookings Institute. https://www.brookings.edu/wp-content/uploads/2016/07/09_development_aid_kharas2.pdf

Kharas, Homi (2020) "Cross-border financing flows impacting the Sustainable Development Goals," in United Nations (2020), *Financing of the UN System*, New York.

Kharas, Homi, and Megan Dooley (2021) 'International Financing of the Sustainable Development Goals', in Dag Hammarskjöld Foundation et al. (2021).

Kharas, Homi and Charlotte Rivard (2022) "Financing for sustainable development is clogged: the message of the April 2022 Spring Meetings," Brookings Institution, May 11. https://www.brookings.edu/blog/future-development/2022/05/11/financing-for-sustainFinancing%20for%20sustainable%20development%20is%20clogged%20The%20message%20of%20the%20April%202022%20Spring%20Meetingsable-development-is-clogged/

Kilby, Christopher (2009) 'The political Economy of Conditionality: An Empirical Analysis of World Bank Loan Disbursements', *Journal of Development Economics* 2009, 89 (1): 51–61.

Klingebiel, Stephan, Timo Mahn, and Mario Negre (eds) (2016) *The Fragmentation of Aid: Concepts, Measurements and Implications for Development Cooperation*. Palgrave Macmillan.

Khemani, Stuti (2017) 'Political Economy of Reform', World Bank Policy Research Working Paper No. 8224. World Bank, Washington, DC.

Knack, Stephen and Aminur Rahman (2007) 'Donor fragmentation and bureaucratic quality in aid recipients', *Journal of Development Economics* 83(1): 176–197.

Killick, Tony (1997) 'Principles, Agents and the Failings of Conditionality'. *Journal of International Development* 9 (4): 483–495.

Killick, Tony, Ramani Gunatilaka, and Ana Marr (1998) *Aid and the Political Economy of Policy Change*. London: Routledge.

Klitgaard, Robert (1990) *Tropical Gangsters*. New York: Basic Books.

Knack, Stephen, (2013) 'Aid and Donor Trust in Recipient Country Systems', *Journal of Development Economics* 101: 316–329.

Knack, Stephen and Nicholas Eubank (2009) 'Aid and Trust in Country Systems', World Bank Development Research Group, Policy Research Working Paper 5005, July.

Knack, Stephen (2000) *Aid Dependence and the Quality of Governance: A Cross-Country Empirical Analysis*. World Bank.

Knack, Stephen, Bradley Parks, Ani Harutyunyan, and Matthew DiLorenzo (2020) 'How Does the World Bank Influence the Development Policy Priorities of Low-Income and Lower-Middle Income Countries ?' Policy Research Working Paper Series 9225, World Bank.

Koch, Svea, Stefan Leiderer, Joerg Faust, and Nadia Molenaers (2017) 'The Rise and Demise of European Budget Support: Political Economy of Collective European Union Donor Action', *Development Policy Review* 35(4): 455–473.

Koeberle, Stefan (2003) 'Should Policy- Based Lending Still Involve Conditionality?' *World Bank Research Observer* 18(2) (Fall): 249–273.

Koeberle, Stefan, Harold Bedoya, Peter Silarszky, and Gero Verheyen (2005) *Conditionality Revisited: Concepts, Experiences and Lessons*. World Bank.

Koeberle, Stefan, Zoran Stavreski, and Jan Walliser (2006) *Budget Support as More Effective Aid?* World Bank.

Kose, M. Ayhan, Eswar S. Prasad, Marco E. Terrones (2008) "Does financial globalization promote risk sharing?" Journal of Development Economics, 89, 258–270

Krueger, Anne O. (1993) *Political Economy of Policy Reform in Developing Countries*. Cambridge, MA and London: The MIT Press.

Landers, Clemence, Rakan Aboneaaj (2021) 'World Bank Budget Support in the Time of COVID: Crisis Finance… with Strings Attached', Center for Global Development, 8 July.

Lawson, Andrew (2014) *Synthesis of Budget Support Evaluations: Analysis of the Findings, Conclusions and Recommendations of Seven Country Evaluations of Budget Support.* Fiscus Public Finance, Analysis for Economic Decisions, Oxford.

Lawson, Andrew and David Booth (2004) *Evaluation Framework for General Budget Support: Report to management Group for the Joint Evaluation of General Budget Support.* Overseas Development Institute, London.

Lazarus, Joel (2008) 'Participation in Poverty Reduction Strategy Papers: Reviewing the Past, Assessing the Present and Predicting the Future', *Third World Quarterly* 29(6): 1205–1221. DOI: 10.1080/01436590802201188

Le Drian, Jean-Yves and Heiko Maas (2019) 'Who, if not us? *Süddeutsche Zeitung* Munich, 14 February 2019. https://onu.delegfrance.org/Who-if-not-us-An-alliance-for-multilateralism

Lee, Chris, Aron Betru, and Paul Harrocks (2018) 'Guaranteeing the Goals: Making Public Sector Guarantees to Unlock Blended Financing for the U.N. Sustainable Development Goals'. Milken Institute and OECD, April. https://milkeninstitute.org/sites/default/files/reports-pdf/Guaranteeing-the-Goals-FINAL-4.pdf

Lee, Nancy and Dan Preston (2019) *The Stretch Fund: Bridging the Gap in the Development Finance Architecture.* Center for Global Development, Washington, DC, December

Lee, Nancy and Mauricio Cardenas Gonzalez (2022) 'Stuck Near Ten Billion: Public-Private Infrastructure Finance in Sub-Saharan Africa', CGD Policy Paper 251, February, Washington, DC. https://www.cgdev.org/sites/default/files/stuck-near-ten-billion-public-private-infrastructure-finance-sub-saharan-africa.pdf

Lee, Nancy and Asad Sami (2018) 'Three Surprises about Private Capital Flows to Low-Income Countries', Center for Global Development blog post, Washington DC, 12 October.

Lee, Nancy and Asad Sami (2019) Trends in Private Capital Flows to Low-Income Countries: Good and Not-So-Good News, *Center for Global Development Policy Paper* 151, Washington DC, July 2019.

Lee, Nancy and Mauricio Cardenas Gonzalez (2022) Stuck Near Ten Billion: Public-Private Infrastructure Finance in Sub-Saharan Africa', CGD Policy Paper 251, Center for Global Development, February, Washington, DC. https://www.cgdev.org/sites/default/files/stuck-near-ten-billion-public-private-infrastructure-finance-sub-saharan-africa.pdf.

Leiderer, Stefan (2012) *Fungibility and the Choice of Aid Modalities*, UNU-WIDER, Helsinki, August 2012.

Levy, Brian (2014) *Working With the Grain: Integrating Governance and Growth in Development Strategies.* Oxford University Press.

Lichtenstein, Natalie (2019) 'AIIB at Three: A Comparative and Institutional Perspective', *Global Policy* 10(4): 582–586. https://doi.org/10.1111/1758-5899.12703

Limodio, Nicola (2019) 'Bureaucrat Allocation in the Public Sector: Evidence from the World Bank', Working Papers 655. IGIER (Innocenzo Gasparini Institute for Economic Research) Bocconi University.

Liaquat Ali Khan, Samia (2010) *Poverty Reduction Strategy Papers: failing minorities and indigenous peoples.* Minority Rights Group International.

Limodio, Nicola (2021) 'Bureaucrat Allocation in the Public Sector: Evidence from the World Bank', *The Economic Journal* 131(639): 3012–3040.

Lister, Stephen and Rebecca Carter (2006) *The Joint Evaluation of General Budget Support 1994–2004.* Glasgow: DFID.

Lynn, Matthew (2011) *Bust: Greece, the Euro and the Sovereign Debt Crisis.* New Jersey: John Wiley and Sons.

Mahler, Daniel Gerszon et al. (2022) 'Pandemic, poverty, and prices', World Bank.Washington, DC, 13 April. https://blogs.worldbank.org/opendata/pandemic-prices-and-poverty

Malesa, Thaddeus and Peter Silarszky (2005) 'Does World Bank Effort Matter for Success of Adjustment Operations?' in: Koeberle (2005) Conditionality Revisited: Concepts, Experiences, and Lessons. World Bank, Washington, DC, pp. 127–141.

Martens, Bertin (2005) 'Why Do Aid Agencies Exist?' *Development Policy Review*: 643–663. https://doi.org/10.1111/j.1467-7679.2005.00306.x

Mitsopoulos, M. and T. Pelagidis (2011) *Understanding the Crisis in Greece: From Boom to Bust.* New York: Palgrave Macmillan.

McDade, Kacy Kennedy, Kraus J, Petitjean H, Schrade C, Fewer S, Beyeler N, Yamey G. (2019) 'Aligning multilateral support for global public goods for health under the Global Action Plan', *Duke Global Working Paper Series*. https://doi.org/10.2139/ssrn.3448704

McKee, Caitlin, C. Blampied, I. Mitchell, and A. Rogerson (2020) 'Revisiting Aid Effectiveness: A New Framework and Set of Measures for Assessing Aid "Quality"', *Working Paper* 524. Center for Global Development, Washington DC.

Milner, H. and D. Tingley (2013) 'The Choice for Multilateralism: Foreign Aid and American Foreign Policy', *Review of International Organizations* 8(3): 313–341. http://dx.doi.org/10.1007/s11558-012-9153-x

Molenaers, N., A. Gagiano, L. Smets, and S. Dellepiane (2015) 'What Determines the Suspension of Budget Support?' *World Development* 75: 62–73.

Moll, Peter, P. Geli and P. Saveedra (2015) 'Correlates of Success in World Bank Development Policy Lending', *Policy Research Paper* 7181. World Bank Group.

Moll, Peter and Lodewijk Smets (2018) 'Is It the Journey That Matters? A Fresh Look at the Impact of World Bank Policy Lending', *World Bank Policy Research Working Paper* No. 8645. World Bank, Washington, DC.

Moll, Peter and Lodewijk Smets (2020) 'Is It the Journey That Matters? A Fresh Look at the Impact of World Bank Policy Lending', *Journal of International Development* 32 (7): 1194–1228.

Monterrey Consensus on Financing for Development (2002) 'United Nations, International Conference on Financing for Development', Monterrey, Mexico, 18–22 March 2002.

Mosley, Paul, John Hudson, and Arjan Verschoor (2004) 'Aid, Poverty Reduction and "New Conditionality"', *The Economic Journal* 114 (June): F217–F243.

Mosley, P. J. Harrigan and J. Toye (1991) *Aid and Power: The World Bank and Policy-Based Lending.*London, Routledge.

Netherlands Ministry of Foreign Affairs (2012) *Budget Support: Conditional Evaluations.* Policy and Operations Evaluation Department (IOB) The Hague.

Nielson, D. (2017) 'International Organizations and Development Finance: Introduction to the Special Issue', *The Review of International Organizations* 12: 157–169. https://doi.org/10.1007/s11558-017-9270-7

Nishio, Akihiko and Gaiv Tata (2021) 'How the structure of global aid and development finance is changing. Future Development,' Brookings Institution, November. https://www.brookings.edu/blog/future-development/2021/11/03/how-the-structure-of-global-aid-and-development-finance-is-changing/

Nordhaus, William (2013) *The Climate Casino: Risk, Uncertainty, and Economics for a Warming World*. New Haven, CT: Yale University Press.

Obstfeld, Maurice. (2022) 'The International Financial System After COVID-19'. Working Paper 22-2, February, Peterson Institute. Washington, DC. https://www.piie.com/publications/working-papers/international-financial-system-after-covid-19

Overseas Development Institute (ODI). 2019. *Blended finance in the poorest countries: the need for a better approach.* London. https://odi.org/documents/5946/12666.pdf

OECD (1996) *Shaping the 21st Century: The Contribution of Development Co-operation*. Paris: OECD/DAC.

OECD (2005) *Paris Declaration on Aid Effectiveness: Ownership, Harmonisation, Alignment, Results and Mutual Accountability,* High Level Forum, Vol. 28, Paris.

OECD (2006) *Harmonizing Donor Practices for Effective Aid Delivery.* DAC guidelines and reference series, Vol. 2: Budget Support, Sector-Wide Approaches and Capacity Development in Public Financial Management. Paris: OECD/DAC.

OECD (2008) *2008 Survey on Monitoring the Paris Declaration: Making Aid More Effective by 2010, Better Aid.* Paris: OECD Publishing.

OECD (2011a) *Multilateral Aid 2010.* Paris: OECD Publishing. https://dx.doi.org/10.1787/9789264046993-en

OECD (2011b) 'The OECD at 50: Development co-operation past, present and future', in *Development Cooperation Report 2011: 50th Anniversary Edition.* Paris: OECD Publishing. 28–37.

OECD (2011c) *Aid Effectiveness 2011: Progress in Implementing the Paris Declaration,* Better Aid. Paris: OCED.

OECD (2017) *Measuring the Impact of Business on Well-being and Sustainability.* Paris. https://www.oecd.org/statistics/Measuring-impacts-of-business-on-well-being.pdf

OECD (2018a) *Multilateral Development Finance: Towards a New Pact on Multilateralism to Achieve the 2030 Agenda Together.* Paris: OECD Publishing. https://doi.org/10.1787/9789264308831-en

OECD(2018b) *The Global Outlook on Financing for Sustainable Development 2019.* Paris. https://www.mzv.cz/public/2b/4f/e/3101343_2044487_Global_Outlook.pdf

OECD(2018c) *Multilateral Development Finance.* Paris. https://www.oecd.org/dac/financing-sustainable-development/development-finance-topics/multilateralaid.htm

OECD (2019) 'European Union institutions', in *Development Co-operation Profiles.* Paris: OECD Publishing. https://dx.doi.org/10.1787/c0ad1f0d-en

OECD (2019) *SDG Financing Lab.* https://sdg-financing-lab.oecd.org/

OECD (2020a) *Global Outlook on Financing for Sustainable Development 2021.* Paris.

OECD (2020b) *The Impact of the Coronavirus (COVID-19) Crisis on Development Finance.* Paris.

OECD (2020c) 'Policy Responses to Coronavirus (COVID-19)', 24 June, Paris.

OECD (2020d) 'Blended Finance Principals Guidance'. September, Paris. http://www.oecd.org/officialdocuments/publicdisplaydocumentpdf/?cote=DCD/DAC(2020)42/FINAL&docLanguage=En

OECD (2020e) *Annex 2: List of ODA-eligible international organisations.* https://www.oecd.org/dac/financing-sustainable-development/development-finance-standards/annex2.htm

OECD (2020f) *COVID-19 Survey: Main Findings, DAC Working Party on Development Finance Statistics.* https://one.oecd.org/document/DCD/DAC/STAT(2020)35/en/pdf

OECD (2020g) Creditor Reporting System (database). Paris: OECD. https://stats.oecd.org/Index.aspx?DataSetCode=crs1

OECD (2020h) 'Survey on DAC providers' policies and practices vis-a-vis the multilateral development system', unpublished. Paris: OECD.

OECD (2020i) *The impact of the coronavirus (COVID-19) crisis on development finance, OECD Policy Responses to Coronavirus (COVID-19).* Paris: OECD. http://www.oecd.org/coronavirus/policy-responses/the-impact-of-the-coronavirus-covid-19-crisis-on-development-finance-9de00b3b/

OECD (2021a) 'COVID-19 spending helped to lift foreign aid to an all-time high in 2020', Detailed Note, 13 April. Paris: OECD.

OECD (2021b) "Closing the SDG Financing Gap in the COVID-19 era." A scoping note for the G20 Development Working Group, Paris. https://www.oecd.org/dev/OECD-UNDP-Scoping-Note-Closing-SDG-Financing-Gap-COVID-19-era.pdf.

OECD (2021c) Development Assistance Committee (DAC). https://www.oecd.org/dac/development-assistance-committee/

OECD (2021d) 'Amounts Mobilised by Official Development Finance Interventions, 2018–2019: Highlights' (https://www.oecd.org/dac/financing-sustainable-development/development-finance-standards/mobilisation.htm).

OECD (2022) 'Global Outlook on Financing for Development 2023.' November, Paris. https://www.oecd-ilibrary.org/finance-and-investment/global-outlook-on-financing-for-sustainable-development-2023_fcbe6ce9-en

OECD-DAC (2020) 'Amounts mobilised from the private sector for development'. Paris. https://www.oecd.org/dac/financing-sustainable-development/development-financestandards/mobilisation.htm

OECD-DAC (2022) ODA Levels in 2021. Detailed Summary Note—Preliminary data for 2021. April, Paris. https://www.oecd.org/dac/financing-sustainable-development/development-finance-standards/ODA-2021-summary.pdf

Orth, Magdalena, Johannes Schmitt, Franziska Kirsch, and Stefan Oltsch (2017) *What We Know About the Effectiveness of Budget Support: Evaluation Synthesis*. DEval, The German Institute for Development Evaluation.

Oxfam (2022) "Donors throw out the aid rule book - Oxfam reaction to OECD preliminary stats", April. https://www.oxfam.org/en/press-releases/donors-throw-out-aid-rule-book-oxfam-reaction-oecd-preliminary-stats

Paul, Elisabeth, Lucien Albert, B. N. Bisala et al. (2018) 'Performance-based financing in low-income and middle-income countries: Isn't it time for a rethink?' *BMJ Global Health*. 2018;3:e000664. doi:10.1136/ bmjgh-2017-000664 (https://gh.bmj.com/content/bmjgh/3/1/e000664.full.pdf)

Paul, E., O. Bodson, and V. Ridde (2021) 'What theories underpin performance-based financing? A scoping review', *Journal of Health Organization and Management*. DOI:10.1108/JHOM-04-2020-0161. (https://www.researchgate.net/publication/348621372_What_theories_underpin_performance-based_financing_A_scoping_review)

Peters, R. Kyle (2006) *Reform and Growth: Evaluating the World Bank Experience*. Routledge. https://www.routledge.com/Reform-and-Growth-Evaluating-the-World-Bank-Experience/Peters/p/book/9781412805230

Pew Research Center (2019) 'Spring 2019 Global Attitudes Survey'. https://www.pewresearch.org/wp-content/uploads/2019/09/FT_19.09.23_ViewsOfUN_PewResearchCenter_UNGA_TOPLINE_FOR_RELEASE_Sept_23_2019.pdf

Piatti-Fünfkirchen, Moritz, A. Hashim, S. Alkenbrack, and S. Gurazada (2021) *Following the Government Playbook? Channeling Development Assistance for Health through Country Systems*. World Bank. https://openknowledge.worldbank.org/handle/10986/36525

Presidential Memorandum on Restoring Trust in Government Through Scientific Integrity and Evidence-Based Policymaking, signed by President Biden, 27 January 2021, White House, Washington, DC https://www.whitehouse.gov/briefing-room/presidential-actions/2021/01/27/memorandum-on-restoring-trust-in-government-through-scientific-integrity-and-evidence-based-policymaking/

Pritchett, Lant, and F. de Weijer (2010) 'Fragile States: Stuck in a Capability Trap?' Background Paper for the 2011 World Development Report, World Bank, Washington, DC.

Pritchett Lant, Salimah Samji, and Jeffrey Hammer (2013) 'It's All About MeE: Using Structured Experiential Learning ('e') to Crawl the Design Space', CGD Working Paper 322. Washington, DC: Center for Global Development. http://www.cgdev.org/publication/its-all-about-mee

Pritchett, L., M. Woolcock, and M. Andrews (2013) 'Looking Like a State: Techniques of Persistent Failure in State Capability for Implementation', *Journal of Development Studies*;49 (1): 1–18.

Ranis, Gustav (2012) 'Another Look at Foreign Aid', *Discussion Paper* No. 1015. Yale University, Economic Growth Center, August.

Rajan, Raghuram and Arvind Subramanian (2008) 'Aid and Growth: What does the Cross-Country Evidence Really Show?' *Review of Economics and Statistics*, February 2008, 90(4): 1–33, 643–665.

Reisen, H., M. Soto, and T. Weithöner (2004) 'Financing Global and Regional Public Goods through ODA: Analysis and Evidence from the OECD Creditor Reporting System', Working Paper No. 232. OECD Development Centre, Paris, https://www.oecd.org/development/pgd/24482500.pdf

Rodrik, Dani (2014) 'When Ideas Trump Interests: Preferences, Worldviews, and Policy Innovations', *Journal of Economic Perspectives* 28 (1): 189–208.

Rodrik, Dani (2015) *Premature Deindustrialization*. Cambridge, MA: John F. Kennedy School of Government, Harvard University.

Rodrik, Dani (2022) 'A Better Globalization Might Rise from Hyper-Globalization's Ashes', *Project Syndicate*, 9 May.

Rome Declaration on Harmonization (2003) in OECD (2003) 'Harmonizing Donor Practices for Effective Aid Delivery: Good Practice Papers' [DCD/DAC/TFDP(2002)12/REV].

Rudolph, A. (2017) 'The Concept of SDG-Sensitive Development Co-operation: Implications for OECD-DAC Members'. German Development Institute. https://www.die-gdi.de/uploads/media/DP_1.2017.pdf

Sachs, Jeffrey, John W. McArthur, Guido Schmidt-Traub, Margeret Kruk, Chandrika Bahadur, Michael Faye, and Gordon McCord (2004) 'Ending Africa's Poverty Trap', *Brookings Papers on Economic Activity*, Issue 1.

SAPRIN (2002) 'The Policy Roots of Economic Crisis and Poverty: A Multi-Country Participatory Assessment of Structural Adjustment', Structural Adjustment Participatory Review International Network, Washington DC. April 2002, (www.saprin.org)

Schick, Alan (2011) 'Repairing the Budget Contract between Citizens and the State', *OECD Journal on Budgeting Volume* 3. Organization for Economic Cooperation and Development.

Selbervik, Hilde (1999) 'Aid and Conditionality: The role of the bilateral donor: A case study of Norwegian–Tanzanian aid relationship'. A Report submitted to the Norwegian Ministry of Foreign Affairs by Chr. Michelsen Institute, July 1999.

Seymour, Frances and Navroz Dubash (2000) 'The Right Conditions: The World Bank, Structural Adjustment, and Forest Policy Reform'. World Resources Institute, Washington, DC.

Shand, David (2006) 'Managing Fiduciary Issues in Budget Support Operations', in Koeberle et al. (2006), pp. 27–47.

Sharot, Tali (2011) *The Optimism Bias: A Tour of the Irrationally Positive Brain*. Pantheon Books.

Skovgaard, Jakob and Harro van Asselt (2018) *The Politics of Fossil Fuel Subsidies and Their Reform*. Cambridge University Press (open access online).

Smets, Lodewijk (2020) 'Supporting Policy Reform from the Outside', *World Bank Research Observer* 35(1): pp. 19–43.

Smets Lodewijk, and Stephen Knack (2016) 'World Bank Lending and the Quality of Economic Policy', *Journal of Development Studies* 52(1): 72–91.

Smets, Lodewijk and Stephen Knack (2018) 'World Bank Policy Lending and the Quality of Public Sector Governance', *Economic Development and Cultural Change* 67(1): 29–54.

Smets, Lodewijk, Stephen Knack, and Nadia Molenaers, N. (2013) 'Political Ideology, Quality at Entry and the Success of Economic Reform Programs', *Review of International Organizations* 8(4): 447–476.

Smets, Lodewijk and Richard Record (2022) 'The Pandemic's Extensive Reform Agenda: How can the Development Community Contribute?' *World Bank Group Research and Policy Briefs*, Malaysia Hub, No. 54, 15 February.

Steffen, Will, Katherine Richardson, Johan Rockstrom, Sarah Cornell, Ingo Fetzer, Elena Bennet, Reinette Biggs, Stephen R. Carpenter, Wim de Vries, Cynthia A. de Wit, Carl Folke, Dieter Gerten, Jens Heinke, Georgina M. Mace, Linn M. Persson, Veerabhadran Ramanathan, Belinda Reyers, and Sverker Sörlin (2015) 'Planetary Boundaries: Guiding Human Development on a Changing Planet', *Science* Volume 347(Issue 6223) (15 January). DOI: 10.1126/science.12598. https://www.science.org/doi/10.1126/science.1259855

Stern, Nicholas (2022) 'A Time for Action on Climate Change and a Time for Change in Economics', *The Economic Journal* 132: 1259–1289, May.

Stiglitz, Joseph (2008) 'Is there a Post-Washington Consensus?' In Narcis Serra and Joseph Stiglitz (eds). *The Washington Consensus Reconsidered.* Oxford University Press.

Subacchi, Paola (2015) 'The AIIB is a Threat to Global Economic Governance', *Foreign Policy*. https://foreignpolicy.com/2015/03/31/the-aiib-is-a-threat-to-global-economic-governance-china/

Svensson, Jakob (2003) 'Why Conditional Aid Does Not Work and What Can Be Done about It?' *Journal of Development Economics* 70(2): 381–402.

Svensson, Jakob (2000) 'Foreign Aid and Rent-Seeking', *Journal of International Economics* 51: 437–461.

Svensson, Jakob (2006) 'The Institutional Economics of Foreign Aid', *Swedish Economic Policy Review,* 13 (2006): 115–137.

Tax Justice Network (2012) 'Tax competition in East Africa: A Race to the Bottom?' Tax Justice Network Africa, Kenya and Action Aid International, South Africa, April.

Temple, Jonathan and Nicolas Van de Sijpe (2017) 'Foreign Aid and Domestic Absorption', *Journal of International Economics* 108: 431–443.

Thomas, Vinod (2023) 'Risk and Resilience in the Era of Climate Change', forthcoming.

Thomas, Vinod and John Nash (1991) 'Reform of Trade Policy: Recent Evidence from Theory and Practice', *World Bank Research Observer* 6 (2): 219–240.

Thomas, Vinod, Mansoor Dailami, Ashok Dhareshwar, Daniel Kaufmann, Nalin Kishor, Ramon Lopez, and Yan Wang (2000) *The Quality of Growth.* Oxford University Press for the World Bank, 1 September.

UN (2020a) 'A UN framework for the immediate socio-economic response to COVID-19', United Nations, New York. https://unsdg.un.org/resources/un-framework-immediate-socio-economic-response-covid-19

UN (2020b) 'Shared responsibility, global solidarity: responding to the socio-economic impacts of Covid-19', United Nations, New York. https://unsdg.un.org/sites/default/files/2020-03/SG-Report-Socio-Economic-Impact-of-Covid19.pdf

United Nations (2022) 'Financing for Sustainable Development Report 2022: Inter-agency Task Force on Financing Development'. April, New York. https://developmentfinance.un.org/fsdr2022

UNCTAD (2014) *World Investment Report 2014: Investing in the SDGs—An Action Plan,* United National Conference on Trade and Development, New York and Geneva. https://unctad.org/en/PublicationsLibrary/wir2014_en.pdf

UNCTAD (2020) 'Impact of the Pandemic on Trade and Development—Transitioning to a New Normal'. Geneva.

UNCTAD (2022a) 'Investments Trend Monitor'. January, Geneva. https://unctad.org/system/files/official-document/diaeiainf2021d3_en.pdf

UNCTAD (2022b). World Investment Report 2022, Geneva, Switzerland. https://unctad.org/system/files/official-document/wir2022_en.pdf

US Treasury (2022) 'Transcript of Press Conference from Secretary of the Treasury Janet L. Yellen as Part of 2022 IMF-World Bank Spring Meetings, G7 and G20 Finance Ministers and Central Bank Governors Meetings', 21 April.

Vivalt, Eva and Aidan Coville (2022) How do Policy-Makers Update their Beliefs? *mimeo*

Vorisek, Dana and Shu Yu (2020) 'Understanding the Cost of Achieving the Sustainable Development Goals', Policy Research Working Paper 9146. The World Bank Group, February.

Wane, Waly (2004) 'The Quality of Foreign Aid: Country Selectivity or Donors Incentives?' Policy Research Working Paper No.3325. World Bank, Washington, D.C.

Wang, H. (2019) 'The New Development Bank and the Asian Infrastructure Investment Bank: China's Ambiguous Approach to Global Financial Governance', *Development and Change* 50(1): 221–244. http://dx.doi.org/10.1111/dech.12473

Williamson, John (2009) 'A Short History of the Washington Consensus, Law and Business', *Review of the Americas* 15 (7).

Williamson, Oliver E. (2000) 'The New Institutional Economics: Taking Stock, Looking Ahead', *Journal of Economic Literature* XXXVIII (September): 595–613.

Wilson, Gavin ER. (2015) Billions to Trillions: Financing the Global Goals. The World Bank. Washington DC. https://blogs.worldbank.org/voices/billions-to-trillions-financing-the-global-goals#:~:text=Together%20with%20the%20IMF%20and,where%20we%20need%20to%20improve.

World Bank (1981) 'Accelerated Development in Sub-Saharan Africa: A Plan for Action', ('Berg Report'). Washington, DC.

World Bank (1988) 'Adjustment Lending: An Evaluation of Ten Years of Experience', *Policy and Research Series Paper* No. 1. Washington, DC: World Bank (RAL-I).

World Bank (1990) 'Adjustment Lending Policies for Sustainable Growth', *Policy and Research Series Paper* 14. Washington, DC: World Bank (RAL-II).

World Bank (1992) 'Adjustment Lending and Mobilization of Private and Public Resources for Growth', *Policy and Research Series Paper* 22. Washington, DC: World Bank (RAL-III).

World Bank (1994) 'Adjustment in Africa: Reforms, Results, and the Road Ahead'. Washington, DC: World Bank.

World Bank (1998) *Assessing Aid: What Works, What Doesn't, and Why*. Washington, DC: Oxford University Press.

World Bank (1999). 'President of the International Bank for Reconstruction and Development to the Executive Directors on a Proposed Policy Based Guarantees Operation in the Amount of US$ 250 Million to the Republic of Argentina,' September 10, 1999. https://documents1.worldbank.org/curated/en/114681468209354918/pdf/358950AR0P0688450rev0PBG1Note01PUBLIC1.pdf

World Bank (2000) *World Development Report 2000/2001: Attacking Poverty*. Washington, DC: Oxford University Press.

World Bank (2001a) *Adjustment from Within: Lessons from the Structural Adjustment Participatory Review Initiative*. Washington, DC.

World Bank (2001b) *Adjustment Lending Retrospective*. Washington, DC.

World Bank Group (2002) *From Adjustment Lending to Development Policy Support*. Washington, DC.

World Bank (2005a) *Review of World Bank Conditionality*, Operations Policy and Country Services, World Bank, Washington DC, September 2005.

World Bank (2005b) *Poverty Reduction Support Credits: A Stocktaking*. Washington, DC: Operations Policy and Country Services, World Bank, Washington DC.

World Bank Group (2005c) *Economic Growth in the 1990s: Learning from a Decade of Reform*. Washington, DC.

World Bank Group (2015) *Development Policy Financing Retrospective: Results and Sustainability*. Washington, DC.

World Bank Group (2016a) *Climate Change Action Plan 2016–2020*. Washington, DC.

World Bank Group (2016b) 'Statement by Multilateral Development Banks: Delivering on the 2030 Agenda', World Bank Group, Washington DC. https://www.worldbank.org/en/news/press-release/2016/10/09/delivering-on-the-2030-agenda-statement

World Bank Group (2016c) 'World Bank Group Guarantee Products Guidance Note', April, Washington, DC.

World Bank (2018a) 'Forward Look—A Vision for the World Bank Group for 2030', March. Washington, DC. https://olc.worldbank.org/system/files/Forward_Look___A_Vision_for_the_World_Bank_Group_in_2030_Pg_3.pdf

World Bank Group (2018b) 'Maximizing the Impact of Development Policy Financing in IDA Countries: A Stocktaking of Success Factors and Risks', Independent Evaluation Group Meso Evaluation, 23 May.

World Bank (2018c) 'MDBs" Methodology for Private Investment Mobilization – Reference Guide', June, Washington, DC. (http://documents.worldbank.org/curated/en/495061492543870701/pdf/114403-REVISED-DocumentsPrivInvestMob-Draft-Ref-Guide-Master-June2018-v3.pdf

World Bank Group (2020a) 'Saving Lives, Scaling-Up Impact and Getting Back on Track: World Bank Group Covid-19 Crisis Response Approach Paper', World Bank Group, Washington DC, http://documents1.worldbank.org/curated/en/136631594937150795/pdf/World-Bank-Group-COVID-19-Crisis-Response-Approach-Paper-Saving-Lives-Scaling-up-Impact-and-Getting-Back-on-Track.pdf

World Bank (2020b) 'Supporting Africa's Recovery and Transformation: Regional integration and Cooperation Assistance Strategy Update for FY 21-FY23, IBRD, IDA, IFC and MIGA', 7 December.

World Bank (2020c) 'Madagascar Program Document for Investing in Human Capital Development Policy Financing'. https://documents1.worldbank.org/curated/en/515991583511474198/pdf/Madagascar-Investing-in-Human-Capital-Development-Policy-Financing-Program.pdf

World Bank (2020d) 'Rwanda First Programmatic Human Capital for Inclusive Growth DPF'. https://projects.worldbank.org/en/projects-operations/document-detail/P171554?type=projects

World Bank (2021) 'Project Appraisal Document Zambia Emergency Health Service Delivery Project'. https://documents.worldbank.org/en/publication/documents-reports/documentdetail/853711639155092912/zambia-emergency-health-service-delivery-project

World Bank (2022a) '2021 Development Policy Financing Retrospective: Facing Crisis, Fostering Recovery'. Committee on Development Effectiveness, Washington, DC, CODE2021–0073.

World Bank (2022b) International Debt Report 2022 : Updated International Debt Statistics. Washington, DC; World Bank. https://openknowledge.worldbank.org/handle/10986/38045 License: CC BY 3.0 IGO. http://hdl.handle.net/10986/38045

World Bank (2022c) 'World Development Indicators'. Washington, DC. https://data.worldbank.org/products/wdi

World Bank (2022d) 'Poverty and Shared Prosperity 2022: Correcting Course.' Washington, DC. https://openknowledge.worldbank.org/bitstream/handle/10986/37739/9781464818936.pdf?sequence=73&isAllowed=y

World Bank (2022e) 'Private Participation in Infrastructure (PPI): Half Year (H1) Report 2022'. Washington, DC. https://openknowledge.worldbank.org/bitstream/handle/10986/37739/9781464818936.pdf?sequence=73&isAllowed=y

Yellen, Janet L. (2022) 'Statement by Janet L. Yellen Secretary United States Department of the Treasury before the Committee on Financial Services U.S. House of Representatives', 6 April, Washington, DC. https://docs.house.gov/meetings/BA/BA00/20220406/114626/HHRG-117-BA00-Wstate-YellenJ-20220406.pdf

Zhengrong Lu, Jason, Jenny Jing Chao, and James Robert Sheppard (2019) 'Government Guarantees for Mobilizing Private Investment in Infrastructure'. World Bank, PPIAF, Washington, DC. https://ppiaf.org/documents/5798/download

Zmigrod, Leor, and Manos Tsakiris (2021) 'Computational and neurocognitive approaches to the political brain: Key insights and future avenues for political neuroscience'. *Philosophical Transactions of the Royal Society B* 376: 20200130.

Endorsements for "Retooling Development Aid in the 21st Century: The Importance of Budget Support"

'Development strategy and practice in the 21st century must change in the face of continuing poverty, destruction of the natural environment, and global crises. Rich countries have both a moral obligation and self-interest in supporting sustainable development and resolving crises, but must learn from past failures and successes. This valuable and thoughtful book, from experienced practitioners and academics, carries lessons of great importance, particularly around the role of budget support. It is full of insight for all who take development seriously.'

Nicholas Stern, Lord Stern of Brentford, IG Patel Professor of Economics and Government, Chairman of the Grantham Research Institute on Climate Change and the Environment at the London School of Economics

'This book is an excellent and timely review of our experience with budget support. It is a reminder that budget support is not an instrument of the past, discarded as failure, but should be one for the present and future. Budget support has to be the tool of choice for financial cooperation with developing countries genuinely committed to inclusive and resilient growth. As the book shows, it is essential for genuine ownership of context-relevant development strategies, and central to meaningful donor coordination.'

Stefan Dercon, Professor of Economic Policy at the Blavatnik School of Government and the Economics Department, and a Fellow of Jesus College, University of Oxford

'Budget support is a 21st century adaptation of the much-bedeviled structural adjustment loans of last century, but different in two respects. First, the authors argue that donors should provide money directly to developing country budgets, not to "buy" market reforms but to strengthen pillars of long-term development such as public financial management and tax systems. The focus is on better government. Second, they emphasize leveraging private finance through support for these basic government functions. The argument is well-researched, careful, and constitutes a quiet revolution in the way to deliver development aid.'

Nancy Birdsall, the founding president of the Center for Global Development, and former executive vice president of the Inter-American Development Bank

'Budget support was once thought to be the most effective way of delivering aid. This book is a fascinating tale of how this simple idea became bureaucratized and inefficient. But the authors, all highly experienced and knowledgeable aid practitioners, provide a wealth of evidence for how to fix the problem. I hope that donors will listen.'

Homi Kharas, Senior Fellow, the Brookings Institution

'This volume provides a very coherent and well evidenced statement of the case for aid in the form of budget support. The discussion of how to respond to sceptics among the bilateral aid agencies, how to handle the diversity of recipient-country types and what to do about volatile country politics, is intelligent and followed up with clear recommendations. There is no doubt this will be the go-to volume on its subject for the next decade.'

David Booth, Senior Research Associate, Overseas Development Institute (ODI)

Index

For the benefit of digital users, indexed terms that span two pages (e.g., 52–53) may, on occasion, appear on only one of those pages. Italicized *f, t, n* and *b* following page numbers refer to figure, table, footnotes and box references respectively.